About This Book

Why is this topic important?

In these challenging and fast-moving times, organizations of all kinds are focusing increased attention on workforce performance and strategically important organizational results. Top managers want to know the payoff in performance and results for all performance-related interventions. They have recognized the very common lack of achievement of desired levels of performance following typical training activities and other performance interventions. Measures of success in desired performance improvement and organizational results are now commonplace requirements by managers. This leads managers, human resource professionals, performance consultants, and other organizational change agents to look for proven ways to increase levels of performance following interventions.

What can the reader achieve with this book?

This book provides foundation blocks and tools to help these key players in organizations to gain the workforce performance and organizational results they want. The foundation blocks—the organization's complex internal and external system, major stakeholders in the system, and the role and expertise of the performance consultant—lay the groundwork for performance consultants, managers, and other stakeholders to improve performance in the system. The tools—effective stakeholder strategies and new evaluation approaches that support performance, and a partnering process for managers and performance consultants—link all stakeholders in collaborating to achieve improved performance. Finally, two case studies on learning and organizational change interventions in complex systems, and an analysis of performance issues related to e-learning, give practitioners detailed examples of applications to achieve desired performance in widely differing settings.

How is the book organized?

In Part 1, the first three chapters establish the foundation for performance improvement. They guide readers through analyses of the complex organizational systems they serve, identification of key stakeholders with a wide range of functions throughout the system, and definition of the emerging role of the performance consultant who helps the organization reach desired performance outcomes.

In Part 2, the next three chapters focus on tools for stakeholders to use in performance improvement interventions. These include research-based strategies for stakeholders as tools to support effective performance, and advances in evaluation methods as tools to encourage and measure performance. The third chapter in Part 2 presents a step-by-step process tool for performance consultants and managers to collaborate, analyze a performance problem, recruit stakeholders to provide support, develop and implement a performance improvement intervention, and evaluate outcomes.

Part 3 presents applications to real-world challenges. In Chapters 7 and 8, two detailed case studies show how different complex systems have turned low-performance patterns into successful workplace performance and desired organizational results, through involving stakeholders to strengthen support for full performance. The final chapter shows how advances in e-learning can improve performance, factors that enable and disable e-learning as a strategy, and case studies and examples that illustrate key issues.

About Pfeiffer

Pfeiffer serves the professional development and hands-on resource needs of training and human resource practitioners and gives them products to do their jobs better. We deliver proven ideas and solutions from experts in HR development and HR management, and we offer effective and customizable tools to improve workplace performance. From novice to seasoned professional, Pfeiffer is the source you can trust to make yourself and your organization more successful.

Essential Knowledge Pfeiffer produces insightful, practical, and comprehensive materials on topics that matter the most to training and HR professionals. Our Essential Knowledge resources translate the expertise of seasoned professionals into practical, how-to guidance on critical workplace issues and problems. These resources are supported by case studies, worksheets, and job aids and are frequently supplemented with CD-ROMs, Web sites, and other means of making the content easier to read, understand, and use.

Essential Tools Pfeiffer's Essential Tools resources save time and expense by offering proven, ready-to-use materials—including exercises, activities, games, instruments, and assessments—for use during a training or team-learning event. These resources are frequently offered in looseleaf or CD-ROM format to facilitate copying and customization of the material.

Pfeiffer also recognizes the remarkable power of new technologies in expanding the reach and effectiveness of training. While e-hype has often created whizbang solutions in search of a problem, we are dedicated to bringing convenience and enhancements to proven training solutions. All our e-tools comply with rigorous functionality standards. The most appropriate technology wrapped around essential content yields the perfect solution for today's on-the-go trainers and human resource professionals.

Pfeiffer
www.pfeiffer.com

Essential resources for training and HR professionals

 # About ISPI

The International Society for Performance Improvement (ISPI) *is dedicated to improving individual, organizational, and societal performance.* Founded in 1962, ISPI is the leading international association dedicated to improving productivity and performance in the workplace. ISPI represents more than 10,000 international and chapter members throughout the United States, Canada, and 40 other counties.

ISPI's mission is to develop and recognize the proficiency of our members and advocate the use of Human Performance Technology. This systematic approach to improving productivity and competence uses a set of methods and procedures and a strategy for solving problems for realizing opportunities related to the performance of people. It is a systematic combination of performance analysis, cause analysis, intervention design and development, implementation, and evaluation that can be applied to individuals, small groups, and large organizations.

Website: www.ispi.org
Mail: International Society for Performance Improvement
1400 Spring Street, Suite 260
Silver Spring, Maryland 20910 USA
Phone: 1.301.587.8570
Fax: 1.301.587.8573
E-mail: info@ispi.org

This book is dedicated to my husband, **STU**, and to my children: **DICK**, **CATHY**, **TOM**, **MARTHA**, and **BOB**.

We have all learned about human performance together!

Beyond

Transfer of Training: Engaging Systems to Improve Performance

Mary L. Broad

Pfeiffer

A Wiley Imprint
www.pfeiffer.com

Published by Pfeiffer
An Imprint of Wiley
989 Market Street, San Francisco, CA 94103-1741
www.pfeiffer.com

Library of Congress Cataloging-in-Publication Data

Broad, Mary L.
Beyond transfer of training: engaging systems to improve performance / Mary L. Broad.
    p. cm.
  Includes bibliographical references and index.
  ISBN: 978-0-7879-7748-1 (alk. paper)
  ISBN: 978-0-470-44818-2 (paperback)
  1. Performance technology. 2. Transfer of training. 3. Employees—Training of. 4. Organizational
effectiveness. I. Title.
  HF5549.5.P37B73 2005
  658.3'14—dc22

                                                                                    2005005160

Acquiring Editor: Matthew Davis   Editor: Rebecca Taff
Director of Development: Kathleen Dolan Davies   Manufacturing Supervisor: Becky Carreño
Production Editor: Dawn Kilgore

Printing 10 9 8 7 6 5 4 3 2 1

CONTENTS

9. e-Learning and Support for Performance 207

Kenneth W. Finley, Jr.

LIST OF FIGURES, EXHIBITS, AND TABLES

PREFACE

The primary purpose of this book is to address the daunting challenge of how to help people perform effectively on their jobs. It is nearing twenty years since John Newstrom and I found a common goal—to help people in the "training" business find ways to make sure that their learners were able to, and did, apply their learning in their work. He and I wrote a book called *Transfer of Training* (1992). In the ensuing years, we have been very pleased with that book's reception, and we still receive enthusiastic nods of recognition when we mention its authorship.

This new book is not a second edition of that groundbreaking volume. This book brings together, in a very personal way, many of the ideas, research findings, and best practices that have emerged in recent years on how to support desired performance. The new developments and outlooks presented are based on my own experiences and the endlessly valuable contributions of colleagues. These developments have intrigued and excited me in my professional activities over the last decade, and I hope they will prove meaningful and useful to you, the reader. The way the ideas in this book are organized is provided in detail in the Introduction.

However, there is another underlying purpose for this book. I realized, years ago, how I personally was—and many of my colleagues in the training business were as well—*part of the problem* of the lack of effective work performance. I want to pay my dues and continue to be *part of the solution,* and hope I can help readers avoid the backtracking I had to do to turn my professional activities around.

How was I—were we—part of the problem? Years ago, as part of an early cohort of newly minted professionals with graduate degrees in the emerging discipline called "human resource development" (HRD), I was eager to make a difference in the ways that people were prepared for the work that organizations needed to have done. I was quite sure that training was usually the solution to performance problems and that I, as a "training expert," knew what it took to train very well. We were developing expertise in training needs analysis and in instructional design and delivery methods and materials, and felt we had all the skills necessary to do great training. I, among many others, took pains to convince managers that they could leave the worries about training to us training experts, and that we would produce the learning they required to get work done well.

Wrong! It took several years and many informative experiences before I realized that my skills and expertise were far from enough. As the push for evaluation grew, we discovered that the training we produced so expertly was not producing the desired improvements in performance that we had expected. It became obvious to many of us that training expertise was not the single answer to improved performance and that we really needed the efforts and support of those managers (and other stakeholders) whom we had encouraged to sit on the sidelines while we did our expert magic.

I lucked into a training course in the late 1970s with the incomparable Joe Harless and was delighted to learn about "front-end analysis" and alternative interventions, which often were much more helpful than training in producing improved performance. These experiences launched my long journey toward human performance technology (HPT) and the systems view that

I now see as essential in shaping effective performance. This book describes and illustrates the important concepts (a systems view of organizations, stakeholder involvement, and the performance consulting role) that form the foundation for the performance improvement enterprise to produce desired organizational results.

With this solid foundation in place, we can figure out just what the performance problems are and what solutions will be most helpful. We can build partnerships with managers and other important stakeholders—within and outside the organizational system—who care about improved performance, and together we can provide the support for the desired performance that eluded us before we learned that we had to work together.

I hope that this book provides useful ideas, models, and examples that you, the reader, find useful. I have done my best to give recognition to those practitioners from whom I have learned so much. I also applaud the organizations that provide examples in these chapters for allowing us all to profit from the resource investments they have made in gaining higher levels of performance.

Acknowledgments

Many people have contributed significantly to my personal development in this most fascinating enterprise, supporting effective human performance. Of the many luminaries from whom I learned so much, I will name here only those with whom I had direct personal contact. In somewhat consecutive order, they are

Dr. Leonard Nadler, my major professor at the George Washington University for both master's and doctoral degrees, who suggested *transfer of training* issues as my dissertation topic and thus opened wonderful new vistas to explore.

Joe H. Harless, a contributor to the foundations of human performance technology, who opened my eyes to other (and often better) ways to support effective performance besides training (and kept us laughing as we learned).

Dr. Gabriel D. Ofiesh, one of the founders of the professional association now called the International Society for Performance Improvement, then head of the Educational Technology Department at Catholic University, who guided my exploration of instructional systems and performance outcomes as I worked on a supporting field for my doctorate at GW.

Dr. John W. Newstrom, esteemed colleague with a similar passion for transfer of learning, my co-author for *Transfer of Training* (1992), and creator of our eye-catching subtitle for that book, *Action-Packed Strategies to Ensure High Payoff from Training Investments.*

Members of the Washington, D.C., Human Resource Development Consortium (WHRDC), a group of colleagues *(you know who you are!)* with varied interests and expertise who have met regularly over twenty years to explore and share new insights and solutions to professional challenges and to nourish friendships that are beyond price.

Three highly valued colleagues are also contributors to this book:

- Kenneth W. Finley, Jr. (Ken), an early and creative user and expander of transfer concepts, who has provided a chapter on transfer issues in e-learning;

- Julie S. Hile, a farsighted colleague (and much loved daughter-in-law), who has taken transfer concepts to new heights in her applications for the transportation industry's safety concerns; and

- Dr. Richard L. Sullivan (Rick), whose experience in managing learning projects and applying transfer concepts in very challenging international systems has shown the value of those concepts in a wide range of organizational, political, and social settings.

I also want to recognize the contributions of others who helped organize and implement cases that illustrate transfer concepts in the first two chapters. In the sequence in which they appear:

- Chapter 1: Julie Hile (MA), principal of the Hile Group (and author of Chapter 7), worked with a complex railroad system that preferred to remain anonymous. Stakeholders were primarily the organizational entities within the "ABC" Railroad system, plus the Federal Railway Administration as regulators in the federal government, and families of ABC employees. Her efforts in that complex system—and in many other systems in the transportation industry—have contributed to significantly improved organizational safety records and safer lives for many who work in those organizations.

- Chapter 1: Jeanette Edwards Lewis (MA, LPC) arranged my involvement in the highly complex system through which the Georgia State Division of Mental Health, Mental Retardation, and Substance Abuse hoped to develop and deliver improved mental health services throughout the state. With the approval and support of her boss, Thomas W. Hester, M.D., she conceptualized, designed, and developed an innovative multifaceted program involving many important stakeholder organizations representing federal and state government, professional groups, hospitals, community mental health centers, public and private providers, mental health advocates, consumers, and families.

- Also Chapter 1: Diane Harris (RN, MSc HRD, CPT) was a leader in planning and developing the Long Term Care Innovation and Leadership Institute of Southwestern Ontario, a highly complex system focusing on delivering best practices to clients of long-term care, for which I provided training and consultation. With many contributing partners, she pulled together stakeholder organizations representing provincial government, university researchers, professional groups, unions, hospitals, physicians, public and private long-term care facilities, clients, and families. She has also been an important partner in the development of an offshoot of the original project, the Ontario Knowledge Exchange in Community and Long Term Care.

- Chapter 2: Bradford N. Grant (MS) of the Warning Decisions Training Branch in the National Weather Service, part of the National Oceanic and Atmospheric Administration, contacted me originally for help with developing Level 3 instruments for their new online interactive Advanced Weather Operations Course (AWOC). Eventually, they decided to focus also on identifying and bringing multiple organizational stakeholders into the training delivery and evaluation process, to support high levels of learning and performance by forecasters during and after their involvement in AWOC.

I also want to thank Roger Chevalier (Ph.D., CPT), Director of Information for the International Society for Performance Improvement, who gave me invaluable suggestions on my book proposal and publication arrangements with Pfeiffer.

I believe this book is much the richer due to these contributions, and I thank those responsible very much. Of course, they are in no way responsible for any errors or muddy thinking in the chapters that I have written myself.

Mary L. Broad
Chevy Chase, Maryland
June 2005

Beyond Transfer of Training: Engaging Systems to Improve Performance

PART 1

Establishing the Foundation for Performance Improvement in Complex Systems

Organizations need help in improving the outcomes and results that follow performance improvement interventions. Measures of performance following many training and other interventions have shown very low levels of payoff, only 10 to 30 percent of desired performance levels, according to several experts. Yet there is substantial research and best practice experience that shows how to raise performance outcomes significantly. This can happen when organizations are viewed as complex systems with important stakeholders who can make or break the desired outcomes. Readers will find insights, evidence, and tools that help build a network of collaborating stakeholders who act to support an intervention for which they recognize value and feel ownership.

This book is designed for performance consultants, managers, and other change agents who help organizational systems achieve their desired performance goals. These practitioners operate in many settings in the public or private sectors, in organizations and communities of small, large, and enormously complex dimensions. They can be highly experienced internal or external consultants or managers—or relative newcomers—who share responsibilities for sponsoring, analyzing, and defining performance requirements and for approving, designing, delivering, or evaluating outcomes of interventions to meet those requirements. Those who have experienced the typical frustrations of finding performance outcomes far below what had been hoped are most likely to see the value in new perspectives on organizational systems, key stakeholders, and effective research-based strategies.

The first three chapters lay the foundation blocks for improving performance in today's world. Chapter 1 looks at complex organizational systems and their components and stakeholders. Some of these complex systems have a single organization as their primary component. Others include several organizations that interact toward a common goal. The challenges of improving human performance in these complex systems are daunting, and the value of conceptualizing and diagramming the systems is illustrated in several case examples.

Chapter 2 more closely examines key stakeholders in these complex systems. Some stakeholders are usually closely involved in performance improvement interventions—managers, performers, and change agents of various kinds. Other stakeholders may play roles as well, such as co-workers, subject-matter experts, and evaluators. Important factors in the workplace that support performance are the responsibility of certain stakeholders—who often are unaware of these responsibilities or how to meet them.

Chapter 3 defines three important areas of expertise for the emerging role of performance consultant: human performance technology (HPT), organizations as complex systems, and partnering and consulting with managers and other stakeholders to improve performance. Suggestions are given on how to prepare for these areas of expertise, and how to provide what other stakeholders (managers, performers, and others) need to know about the performance consulting role in order to collaborate effectively. Together, the three chapters in Part 1 build the conceptual foundations for improving performance in complex systems. They equip the reader to proceed to Part 2, which describes some important tools that performance consultants, managers, and other stakeholders can use as they work to improve performance.

1

Organizations as Complex Systems

THIS CHAPTER FOCUSES ON complex organizational systems, one of the three foundation blocks for our examination of improving performance in today's complex systems. We discuss the groups and entities that make up the range of systems in which we function and why it is important for us—and our clients—to view them as interactive systems. We look at what constitutes moderately or highly complex systems, consider examples of each of these, and discuss the value of developing visual diagrams of the systems. The major topics for this chapter are

- Living and working in complex systems
- Moderately complex systems
- Highly complex systems
- Diagramming the system

Living and Working in Complex Systems

As we begin to address the challenges of improving performance in organizations, we must first explore complex work settings and their internal and external environments. The individuals, groups, and organizations that make up any work setting interact in a variety of ways that must be examined before performance improvement projects are defined and undertaken.

Over many thousands of years, human societies have organized themselves in collaborative, interactive, and sometimes ferociously antagonistic groups to achieve their goals. We need to understand the basics of how these groups or systems function in today's organizations in order to help people in various systems to become more productive and satisfied with their contributions to the system and its goals. In this chapter we introduce some basic concepts and definitions related to complex organizational systems, as a foundation for exploration of improving performance in those systems.

Complexity

The organizations, groups, and communities in which we work, live, and function are astonishingly more complex than those typical of decades or hundreds of years ago. The early environmentalist John Muir (founder and first president of the Sierra Club in 1892) recognized the underlying complexity of our world almost a hundred years ago: "When we try to pick out anything by itself, we find it hitched to everything else in the Universe" (Muir, 1911, p. 110).

Considering worldwide complexity, journalist Thomas Friedman—three-time Pulitzer-Prize-winning foreign-affairs correspondent for the *New York Times*—addressed the almost unbelievable speed with which today's economic, political, and social systems interact: "What is new today is the degree and intensity with which the world is being tied together into a single globalized marketplace. What is also new is the sheer number of people and countries able to partake of this process and be affected by it" (Friedman, 1999, p. xv).

Systems

Over a decade ago, Peter Senge brought systems thinking (his "fifth discipline") to our attention, as an important approach for making sense of information overload and rapid change: "Today, systems thinking is needed more than ever because we are becoming overwhelmed by complexity. Perhaps for the first time in history, humankind has the capacity to create far more information than anyone can absorb, to foster far greater interdependency than anyone can imagine, and to accelerate change far faster than anyone's ability to keep pace" (Senge, 1990, p. 69).

Organizations are *systems* with interrelated components that take in resources (inputs), apply some work (process), turn out products and services (outputs), and respond to internal or external factors by changing those inputs, processes, or outputs. Any given complex organizational system (such as the local pharmacy in a neighborhood) is part of some larger system (such as a nationwide pharmaceutical chain or the ad hoc pharmaceutical retail system) and also has subsystems as its components (its departments, salesforce, accountants, suppliers, and others).

As another example, the U.S. *healthcare system* is part of the nation's *economic system.* It includes physicians, pharmacies, hospitals, pharmaceutical companies, insurance companies, government regulators, and many other related groups. Each of these systems functions as a subsystem of the healthcare system and contributes in some way to providing the healthcare services we want and need.

All of these organizational systems are *adaptive* in responding to events and forces from the external and internal environments. In the complex *healthcare system,* events and forces may include government legislation, research on new medications, advertising of new methods and medicines, and unanticipated situations such as the sudden drastic cut in flu vaccine supply in the United States in 2004.

Multiple Systems

Each of us is involved in several systems, although we may not recognize them. Our *family system* is one, with both previous and subsequent generations adding to the complexity. As we grow, we become involved in various levels of the *school system,* with its facilities, curricula, administrators and staff, teachers, parent groups, sports teams, and many other subsystems. The communities we live in include cities and towns, within counties and states and nations, with *government systems* related to transportation, politics, finance, and healthcare that affect our lives on a daily basis.

It can be useful—and occasionally vitally important—to explore some of those systems, to learn how they interact in our lives and how to take advantage of their benefits, as well as protect ourselves from possible adversities. For example, current efforts to educate people on the dangers of *identity theft* involve information on our *banking* and *credit systems* and how to keep personal information private and secure. In general, information areas to explore to learn about a complex system include its mission, vision, goals, operations, products and services, competitors, and so on.

Stakeholders in Organizational Systems

Organizations are made up of people who contribute in various ways to the organization's functions. A *stakeholder* in an organizational system is an individual, group, organizational component, or organization with a share or interest—a *stake*—in the goals or operations of an activity, process, project, organization, or intervention in a complex system. These stakeholders may be internal or external to the organization. Stakeholders are extremely important contributors to improving performance; they will be addressed in detail in later chapters. In this chapter we will refer to stakeholders and their roles briefly.

No "Simple" Systems

Complex adaptive systems vary in degrees of complexity, but a "simple" organizational system is an oxymoron in today's world! A simple organizational system would be one that functions primarily internally to one organization, with minimal input or output relationships with others. However, even the "mom and pop" convenience store in the next block and the street corner vendor selling jewelry out of a pushcart are complex systems with many stakeholders. They have *input* relationships with suppliers of goods and services and with local government regulators setting and monitoring zoning, sanitation, and other standards. They apply some sort of *processing* or *work* to their inputs, resulting in their products and services. They also have *output* relationships with customers, neighborhood residents, and perhaps with the local police officer patrolling her beat. So our focus here will be on *moderately* and *highly* complex systems.

Moderately Complex Systems

A moderately complex system can be defined by its characteristics. It has

- A single organization as its major component;

- Often (but not always) a traditional hierarchical structure within the major organization, with lines of *authority* from the executive level through successive levels of the organization's internal stakeholder components (chain of command); and

- Other groups or organizational components outside the boundaries of the organization that also are stakeholders with an interest in the organization's goals and operations, and which are linked with the major organization by lines of *influence* (not authority).

Diagram of a Moderately Complex System

Figure 1.1 shows a simplified diagram of a moderately complex and traditionally hierarchical organization. It has important internal stakeholder components (small rectangles within the larger rectangle of the organization) and several external stakeholder components (in rounded boxes) that may have an interest in the organization's goals and/or operations.

Consider, as an example, how you might use Figure 1.1 as a model to sketch a moderately complex system familiar to you, such as your local pharmacy, the board of directors of your condominium, or your child's soccer team. What

Figure 1.1. Moderately Complex Organizational System with Important Internal and External Components

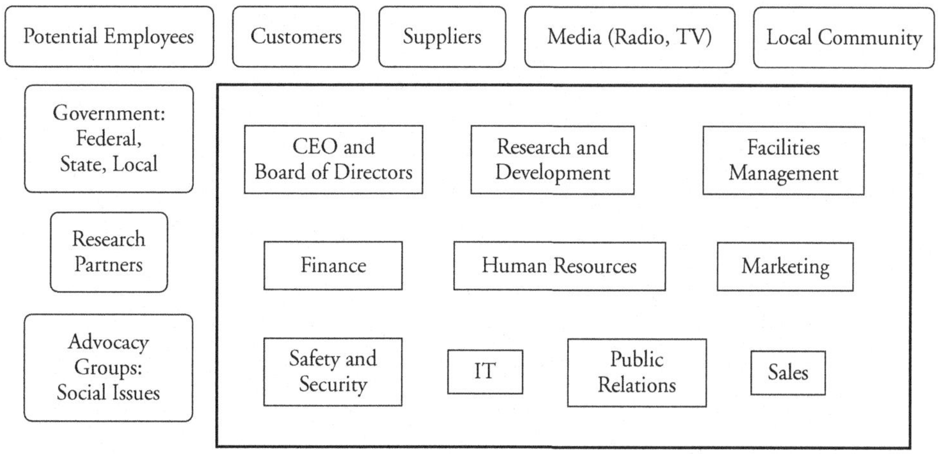

[*Note:* Rectangular boxes denote system components within the organization. Rounded boxes denote system components outside the organization.]

are the inputs, processes, and outputs of that system? Who or what group is in charge as "CEO" or "top dogs"? What are the internal components (employees and suppliers, project groups, coaches, and others)? What are groups or organizations external to that system that have an interest in how the system functions (such as the State Zoning Office, the condominium's insurance company, or the local soccer league)? What is an important performance-related goal (such as increased sales, agreement on raising condominium fees, or winning more soccer games)?

The simple diagram in Figure 1.1 can be used to illustrate system concepts for new clients or other interested parties to help them identify important stakeholder components in their own systems. However, specific authority or influence relationships (often shown as arrows between components) are not indicated in Figure 1.1. Those relationships depend on the specific performance challenges that the client or stakeholder focuses on.

For example, if a local school system is being studied and diagrammed, the components and authority/influence arrows would be different for different performance challenges. The system focusing on children's safety issues would involve stakeholders, including the principal, teachers, front office staff, parents, children, school bus drivers, crossing guards, traffic specialists, and others. The system focusing on curriculum design would include some of the same stakeholders (principal, teachers, parents), but also would probably include state education officials, university researchers, publishers of educational materials, and others. So the system should be explored according to the performance issue being addressed (such as product design, marketing, or ethical behaviors) in order to identify and organize the important stakeholders.

If the system does not involve a traditional hierarchical organization, it might be sketched very differently from Figure 1.1. For example, an early version of the organization chart for Saturn Corporation, a subsidiary of General Motors (GM) showed the teams that construct cars at the center of a series of concentric circles, with the executive and management team on the outside circle. Current diagrams of Saturn's structure ("decision rings," all based on circles) are featured in a student guide on the Saturn website. The diagrams illustrate the nontraditional collaborative nature of decision making throughout the organization and the close working relationship of Saturn management with the United Auto Workers union (Saturn Corporation, 2005).

The traditional hierarchical chain of command is alive and well in many organizations, with recognized leaders (such as director, CEO, and/or board of directors). The leader's directions about what is to be done are relayed through the organization in successive levels of authority.

"ABC" Railroad: A Moderately Complex System

Figure 1.2 shows an example of a traditional organizational structure. Consultants with the Hile Group, working with "ABC" Railroad (a U.S. railroad that prefers to remain anonymous), diagrammed the major components of that system as they affected the issue of safety rules and compliance prior to an intervention. Note that they identified only one major external stakeholder

Figure 1.2. Safety Relationships at "ABC" Railroad Before Intervention

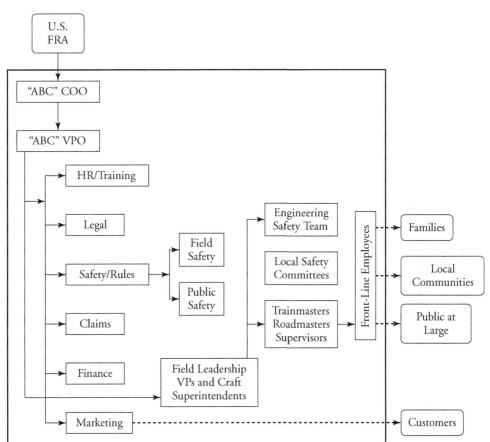

providing *input* to the system, the Federal Railway Administration (U.S. FRA in the rounded box at the top left of the diagram), the source of many railroad rules and regulations. The solid lines show lines of authority from the FRA to the organization's Chief Operating Officer (COO) and Vice President of Operations (VPO), and then through several internal organizational components.

On the right side of Figure 1.2, dashed lines (for influence without authority) go from Front Line Employees (inside the organization in a rectangular box) to important stakeholders outside the organization (in rounded boxes). These stakeholders (families, local communities, and the public at large) are affected by the safety-related *outputs* of the system. (There is also a dashed line for non-safety-related outputs, from marketing to customers.) Note that, in this "before" diagram of the system, it became clear that Local Safety Committees had no formal or significant input or output.

SIDEBAR: DIAGRAMMING THE SYSTEM

A diagram of a complex system can be a very useful tool for several purposes:

- To create an initial sketch of the system and its stakeholder components;
- To illustrate the system to interested parties inside and outside the system, with a focus on the relationship of system components for a particular performance challenge; and
- To update and revise the system diagram as new information and stakeholder viewpoints become available.

To my knowledge, there are no widely accepted standards for how such a system diagram should be constructed. I have chosen the following guidelines for myself:

- Follow an "input → process → output" sequence, from left to right, to place components and show directions of authority and influence among components. However, this must often be modified by complex space and time considerations.

- Use arrows from one component to another to show directions of authority (solid line arrows) or influence (dashed or dotted line arrows).
- For a moderately complex system where the focus is on a single organization with internal and external system components, show essential within-the-organization components in rectangles (as in the familiar organization chart) and show external system stakeholder components in rounded boxes or ovals or other matching shapes.
- For a highly complex system where the focus is on the interaction of several organizations, show similar key organizations (such as government agencies) in rectangular boxes, with other stakeholder organizations (such as private sector enterprises) in rounded boxes or ovals or other matching shapes.

I try not to let graphic artists shape the diagram, at least at first. They are likely to make it neat and symmetrical, while the reality (as best as it is known) is usually *messy* and *chaotic*. I find it easier for those inside and outside the system to grasp—and suggest revisions for greater accuracy to—a realistically messy and chaotic diagram than an unrealistic neat and symmetrical one. What Wheatley and Kellner-Rogers say about the biological world is often true in complex organizational systems: "Networks, patterns, and structures emerge without external imposition or direction. . ." in ". . .a world that makes it up as it goes along" (1996, pp. 3, 11).

The "ABC" Railroad system diagram is significantly different following the intervention (Figure 1.3). Here we see several entities that were added to the moderately complex system to support both process and performance improvement efforts: the Hile Group, performance consultants who left the system after the interventions were completed; the new Senior Safety Leadership Council, a permanent group of top managers who focus on safety issues across the organization; and two groups of performers, Special Safety Project Teams who address specific safety projects and Safety Audit Process Teams who measure outcomes and progress.

Figure 1.3. Safety Relationships at "ABC" Railroad After Intervention

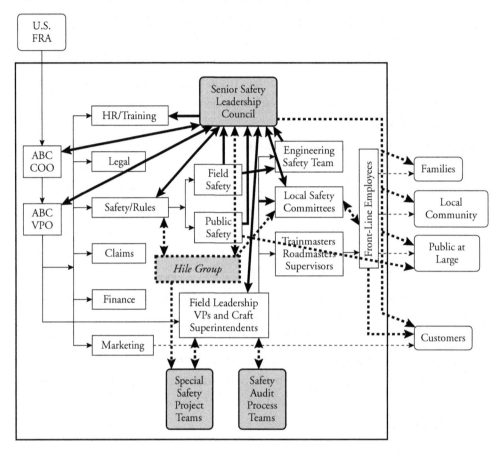

Figure 1.3 also shows new solid lines of authority that now connect the Senior Safety Leadership Council with parts of the organization, show interaction between the two new teams and the field, and show input to and output from the Local Safety Committees. Dotted lines of influence also connect the Senior Safety Leadership Council and frontline employees with customers, to show the railroad's new efforts to communicate with customers on safety issues.

Diagrams such as these can be extremely useful in helping stakeholders understand the system in which they function and track the arrows of authority and influence related to specific issues. Even if the diagram is not completely accurate—and it is difficult to attain or maintain accuracy as complex situations continually change—a diagram can help clarify the goals of an intervention and identify revisions that are necessary for greater accuracy.

Highly Complex Systems

A highly complex system can also be defined by its characteristics. It has

- Several relatively independent organizations as primary components, with other groups or organizations as supportive or opposing components;

- A common goal shared by the primary components, toward which they work interdependently; and

- Some component organizations linked by fully accepted lines of *authority* and other components linked by lines of *influence* (not authority); however, there is no fully accepted chain of command throughout the system.

Examples of highly complex systems include relatively decentralized organizational structures (such as large multinational corporations) in which there may be no clear lines of authority all the way from top decision-makers to every front-line performer within system components. Intermediate decision-makers may have very significant authority of their own.

Other highly complex systems are comprised of groups of relatively independent stakeholder organizations. These component organizations have common goals and are somewhat interdependent (formally or informally), but have no clearly acknowledged lines of power or authority; they depend on voluntary collaboration. The project described below is an example of such a highly complex organizational system without a solid chain of command across all components.

The Georgia Mental Health Training Project

The Georgia State Division of Mental Health, Mental Retardation, and Substance Abuse (MHMRSA as it was then titled) began planning a project in 1999 to support widespread application of the best practices in mental health services that had been identified in the U.S. Surgeon General's Report on Mental Health, published earlier that year.

Previously, the Division had funded annual state-wide best practices conferences, which had not resulted in significant change in mental health practices in the state. To improve the odds of clinical training resulting in best practice service delivery to consumers (as clients are called) and families, the Division's Medical Director, Thomas W. Hester, M.D., assisted by Jeanette Edwards Lewis (MA, LPC), developed a transfer of learning plan. The key components of the plan within the highly complex system are shown in Figure 1.4.

Figure 1.4. Georgia State Mental Health Services Delivery System, 1999-2001

Diagram by Mary L. Broad (Ed.D.) and Jeanette Edwards Lewis (MA, LPC).

Note: This is an informal diagram to illustrate the complexity of the system; it does not presume to reflect formal, legal, or contractual linkages. Shaded boxes are primary components of the project sponsored by the Georgia State Division of Mental Health, Mental Retardation, and Substance Abuse, 1999-2001, to encourage wider application of mental health best practices in the state. The Division provided funding to regional boards, which then supported programs provided by community mental health centers (CMHCs) and other providers to assist clients and consumers in the regions. Other organizations and groups were also stakeholders, to some extent, in this project. Solid arrows reflect authority; dashed arrows reflect influence without authority.

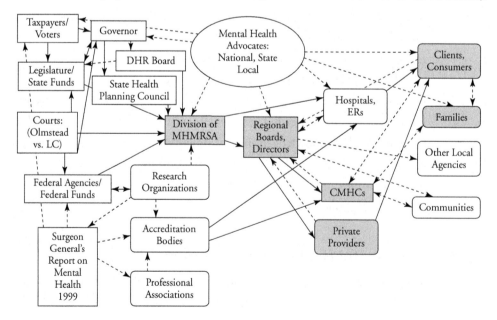

In lieu of the annual best practices conference, MHMRSA provided training funds and some guidance, but not full direction, to Regional Mental Health Boards to support training in—and delivery of—new best practices as described in the Surgeon General's report. Training was offered to key provider groups (physicians, nurses, emergency room personnel, and others) in the boards' regions. In turn, the regional boards contracted with Community Mental Health Centers (CMHCs) and other providers to receive free training in exchange for demonstrable implementation of one new best practice. Shaded boxes in Figure 1.4 indicate key organizations and groups in the system. Advocates, families, consumers, and other non-provider stakeholders offered varying degrees of encouragement and involvement in the training-to-service-delivery sequence.

Figure 1.4 is definitely messy and chaotic! But its lack of neatness and symmetry was an advantage in helping stakeholders and others identify additional system components and define more accurately their complicated interactions in moving toward a common goal.

However, the MHMRSA project illustrates the vulnerability to change of such highly complex systems without clear and authoritative chains of command. With changes in higher level state leadership, Dr. Hester's move to a "dream" job in Hawaii in 2001, and Ms. Lewis's retirement, the resources directed to this project were diluted and the project lost steam.

The Ontario Long Term Care Institute

A somewhat longer-lasting effort is illustrated by another highly complex organizational system, shown in Figure 1.5. A group of senior leaders from the community care and long term care health sector in southwestern Ontario initiated planning in 1999 for the Long Term Care Innovation and Leadership Institute of Southwestern Ontario, a complex system focusing on delivering best practices to clients of long term care (LTC) providers.

This diagram, by one of the Institute's leaders, is oval-shaped, with the clients—LTC recipients—at the center. With the assistance of Diane Harris (RN, MSc HRD, CPT), the leaders' group brought together administrators

**Figure 1.5. Long Term Care Innovation and Leadership Institute,
Southwest Ontario, 2000**

Diagram by Diane Harris (RN, MSc HRD, CPT)

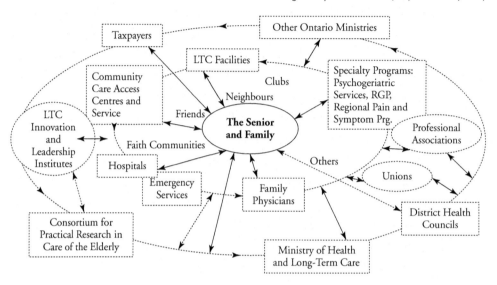

of both public and private LTC facilities in the area, as well as other interested stakeholders: university researchers, the Ministry of Health, and other organizations and groups interested in improving services to LTC clients. They presented a series of meetings and workshops, and developed an online newsletter and website (http://ltc-innovation.medix.ca).

In early 2000, the LTC Institute's Interim Steering Committee produced a set of operating assumptions for the emerging system. These are shown in Exhibit 1.1. These assumptions might be a useful resource for other complex systems as they get under way. Written in a nonbureaucratic style, they capture the spirit and commitment among stakeholders that seems essential for such a highly complex system to start up and flourish, at least for a time (Long Term Care Innovation and Leadership Institute, 2000).

Exhibit 1.1. Operating Assumptions

Draft Operation Plan, March 2000

Assumption 1   The Long Term Care Innovation and Leadership Institute is dealing with changing consumer expectations and is committed to improving care while facing fiscal restraints.

Assumption 2   The area of primary concern to administrators relates to maximizing resident satisfaction, improving the quality of service and quality of life for residents through effective management of HR, finances, information systems, etc.

Assumption 3   Administrators have developed some solutions to commonly experienced problems and would like access to their colleagues to share their innovations.

Assumption 4   Working collaboratively is key to identifying processes/changes that will offer the most to improving resident care.

Assumption 5   Those who attend the February workshop are willing to contribute to the development and implementation of an Action Plan for the Institute and gather feedback from those not in attendance to strengthen the plan.

Assumption 6   Members are prepared to think big, be bold, act fast, and have fun as they build the Institute and are prepared to leave workplace constraints at home and devote their attention to the ideals of the Institute.

Assumption 7   Members wish to communicate their work with other health care providers as well as the community to increase recognition of the people requiring LTC services, and respect and value for the people caring for them. Interacting with a broad range of community groups is seen as a priority.

Assumption 8   Members support increased research into understanding the aging process and the maintenance of quality of life. The priority support for research has practical applications to improving the quality of life for LTC customers.

Assumption 9   Members recognize there will always be political agendas that present barriers and opportunities and their challenge is to creatively manage these agendas in a way that removes many of the barriers and maximizes the opportunities.

Assumption 10   Members are committed to common goals driven by our shared values, which lead to innovations, which make a difference in performance.

From Diane Harris (R.N., MSc, HRD, CPT) for LTC Innovation and Leadership Institute, Southwestern Ontario.

By early 2005, almost five years after its beginning, the Institute has lost its original momentum. Annual events through 2003 had been well attended, and some "communities of interest" had been successful in linking people together. But its initial resources, finances, and leadership did not continue. The newsletter and workshops, which worked effectively for a while to identify and share best practices in long term care in the region, now seem dormant.

However, as an evolutionary outcome, the Institute's experience has contributed to the framework for a recently proposed online community of practice, the Ontario Knowledge Exchange in Community and Long Term Care (OKE). A community of practice is a network of individuals and groups with common interests and expertise that share information, ideas, and assistance (Wenger, McDermott, & Snyder, 2002). One component of the OKE, the Alzheimer Knowledge Exchange, has been funded. The goals of these knowledge exchanges are very parallel and consistent with those of the Institute. (Because it is still in early stages of formation, the OKE does not have an official website as this book goes to press.)

Further research is necessary to identify the factors that support or undermine the success of these highly complex systems. Shifts in top leadership and resources, and lack of processes to develop successive committed leaders and continued financial support from component organizations, seem important factors that affected the LTC Institute. Also, it may be that the Institute had met some important initial goals and that further progress in community and long-term care will be well-supported by the new knowledge exchanges.

Other Highly Complex Systems

Throughout recent history, there have been many highly complex systems of individuals and groups that organized themselves to take actions related to particular issues or events. Some of these systems have evolved and lasted, and others have disbanded when their work was done. Only a few of many examples, small and large, are included here.

In 1862 during the American Civil War, Clara Barton organized battlefield nursing and relief efforts that eventually led to the organization of the American Red Cross in 1881. This system began in response to a wartime emergency, and since then has evolved into a major highly complex system that is part of an even more complex worldwide system, the International Federation of Red Cross and Red Crescent Societies.

Author and organizational expert Peter Senge and others created the Society for Organizational Learning (SoL) in 1997. This is a decentralized global network of corporations and other organizations, groups, and individuals who address worldwide issues (health, poverty, destruction of ecosystems, and global warming, among others) that can't be solved by any single organization or nation (Senge, 2003).

In early 2001, a group of Washington, D.C., residents organized to prevent the destruction of the local Avalon Theater. They developed a network of collaborating organizations, maneuvered through city bureaucracies, wrote grant proposals, orchestrated community support, and eventually financed the theater's rehabilitation and successful 2003 reopening under local control (Avalon Theater, 2003).

In response to the September 11, 2001, attacks on the World Trade Center in New York City, informal leadership and decision-makers (fire fighters and police, obscure city officials, unionized construction workers, contractors, barge owners, and many others) collaborated quickly, creatively, and around the clock to address the horrors and urgencies of the disaster. This highly complex system emerged—totally apart from existing organizational structures and procedures—to deal with an enormous tragedy. It evolved into an unorthodox, sometimes internally combative, and amazingly effective effort to clear Ground Zero, and then dissolved when its work was finished about eight months later (Langewiesche, 2002).

Each of these complex systems has emerged to address a problem or opportunity important to its stakeholders. In each case, the stakeholders involved had to think in terms of the entire system (even, in some cases, without having a clear concept of systems) in order to make headway toward their goals.

Summary of This Chapter

It is essential for managers, learning specialists, other stakeholders, and organizational change agents of all kinds to consider each organization and its components in their system context as they begin to analyze performance challenges. Moderately and highly complex organizational systems can have many components that contribute, positively or negatively, to organizational change efforts.

The more that stakeholders in a change effort know about the complex system they hope to affect, the better they will be able to communicate their goals and objectives, gain supporters, and achieve their goals. They should first define the organizational system that is the setting for a specific performance challenge, such as providing good customer service, working effectively as a team, or giving helpful feedback to subordinates. They should identify the primary organizations that are involved in that performance challenge and the types and locations of the performers whose behaviors and accomplishments are to be improved.

The next step is to identify the system's important stakeholder components, both internal to key organizations and external. The stakeholders may include customers and suppliers, successive links in the chain of command, regulatory agencies, co-workers, funding sources, professional associations, special interest groups, evaluators, local communities, and others.

Finally, stakeholders need to describe the sources, directions, and recipients of both authority and influence related to the performance challenge among the stakeholder components. This may be complicated and take some time, but the effort pays off in a clearer picture of the complex system.

When this system information is clarified and agreed on (and diagrammed if possible), major stakeholders are in a position to continue the exploration to reach performance improvement goals. We address the roles of major stakeholders in the next chapter.

Suggestions for Further Reading

Listed below, with brief comments, are several books that were particularly helpful in this author's exploration of complex organizational systems. They are listed alphabetically by authors' last names, but readers might benefit by reading them somewhat in order of their publication dates.

Senge, Peter M. (1990). *The fifth discipline: The art & practice of the learning organization.* New York: Doubleday/Currency. Systems thinking is Senge's fifth discipline, which integrates the other four key disciplines (personal mastery, mental models, building shared vision, and team learning) that lead to the learning organization.

Senge, Peter M., Kleiner, Art, Roberts, Charlotte, Ross, Richard B., & Smith, Bryan J. (1994). *The fifth discipline fieldbook: Strategies and tools for building a learning organization.* New York: Doubleday Currency. The section on systems thinking has several notes, reflections, and exercises to help understand systems concepts and apply them in complex organizational systems.

Waldrop, M. Mitchell. (1992). *Complexity: The emerging science at the edge of order and chaos.* New York: Simon & Schuster. Waldrop describes studies of the emerging science of complexity at the Santa Fe Institute, exploring how elements of biological and commercial worlds have spontaneously organized into highly complex ecosystems and economies.

Wheatley, Margaret. (2001). *Leadership and the new science: Discovering order in a chaotic world* (rev. ed.). San Francisco: Berrett-Koehler. Wheatley explores breakthroughs in biology, quantum theory, and chaos theory in the physical world, showing that life seems to seek order but uses chaotic means to reach it. She finds thought-provoking relevance to relationships and collaborations in human organizations.

2

Stakeholders and Support for Performance

IN THIS CHAPTER we focus on *stakeholders* and their responsibilities in supporting effective performance, another foundation block for improving performance in today's complex organizational systems. Before we discuss stakeholders themselves, we must first set the context for effective performance. Next, we examine the primary stakeholders who are involved in most efforts to improve performance, as well as other stakeholders who may play a role, depending on the organizational setting and the particular performance involved. Then we consider the important factors that affect performance in organizations and the stakeholders who can provide those factors.

The major topics for this chapter are

- Performance and performers
- Stakeholders in performance
- Organizational factors that support performance

Performance and Performers

Stakeholders are the important individuals, groups, units, and organizations that make up complex systems. Before discussing stakeholders and their support for performance, we must be clear on what we mean by *performance* and *performers*. The mission and goals of any complex organizational system are accomplished by the performance of the people who do the work.

Our focus in this book is primarily on the activities and interactions at the *job/performer level* where the work is done, as described by Rummler and Brache (1995). We do not focus in the same detail at the higher *process level*, how work is organized, or the even higher *organizational level*, the way the business is set up and managed. (However, many of the principles of stakeholder support apply at those levels as well.) Our attention is on the way that the organization's work is done and on the people who do that work.

Performance

Effective performance is the goal of every organizational system. Thomas Gilbert's *Human Competence: Engineering Worthy Performance* (1978) is credited by many with laying the groundwork for the critically essential analysis that underlies support for improvement of individual and organizational performance (Chevalier, 2003).

Performance is a combination of *behaviors* by individuals, groups, and teams and the *accomplishments* (products and services) that they produce (adapted from Dean, 1999, p. 6, & Gilbert, 1978, p. 17.). Thus, performance is a combination of the behaviors (decisions and actions) of those who do the work and the products and services that result from those decisions and actions.

For a successful restaurant, one very important performance consists of the decisions and actions by the chef and the food that the chef produces for the customers. Other examples of important performances (behaviors plus accomplishments) for that restaurant are managers' purchases of supplies and the wait staff's services to customers.

Performers

The term *performer* refers to the individual—working alone or in groups and teams—who performs some work. This allows us to consider, as performers, those who work as volunteers or other contributors to an activity, as well as those who are more formally employed. In this book, the term *performers* is used to refer specifically to those whose performance is the focus of an intervention. At the restaurant, performers who are the focus of an intervention might include managers, the chef, all who assist her in the kitchen, the wait staff, the cleaning crew, and others.

Stakeholders in Performance

A *stakeholder* is an individual, group, organizational component, or organization with a share or interest—a "stake"—in the goals or outcomes of an activity, process, project, organization, or intervention in a complex system. Stakeholders provide the information, work, requirements, support, encouragement, oversight, and all the other resources that help shape the survival and success of organizations and communities in today's complex world.

All major stakeholders must recognize—and look for constructive ways to intervene in—our complex systems to provide useful support and encouragement for improved performance throughout the systems. The goal at the job/performer level is to make sure that *performers,* individuals as well as groups and teams, can perform effectively.

Individual stakeholders have many different roles in supporting performance—as managers at several levels, performers (employees and other community and group members), organizational change agents (such as learning specialists and quality control professionals), internal and external suppliers and customers, regulators, experts, and others. Units of an organization may be stakeholders in a moderately complex system that has a single organization as its major component. In highly complex systems made up of several organizations, more than one organization may be a major stakeholder. We must understand—and help individuals, groups, and organizations understand—who they are as stakeholders and what they can do to support and improve performance in these complex systems.

Stakeholders Who Support Performance

No matter how timely, ingenious, or creative the strategic goals of any organization or community may be, those goals can only be met through the competent, committed, and often collaborative performance of the people who do the work. Stakeholders, as individuals, groups, and organizations, can provide ongoing support for that performance in several ways: encouragement, recognition, resources, and so on. In this chapter, we concentrate on identifying key stakeholders and the important factors in the work environment that they can provide. Later, in Chapter 4, we explore specific strategies and best practices by stakeholders to support performance.

Stakeholder support clearly becomes very important when an intervention is planned or under way to develop or improve performance to reach a recognized goal. These interventions may be *instructional* (such as training, coaching, or e-learning) to improve or develop new knowledge and skills that performers then transfer to performance on the job. Interventions often are *noninstructional* (such as process improvement, organizational restructuring, changes in compensation, or performance management) that enhance the work environment to support improved performance. Interventions may be combinations of both instructional and noninstructional efforts; they are discussed in more detail in Chapter 3.

Stakeholder support for performance can be applied in both work and nonwork settings, such as civic groups and communities, voluntary creative activities, and performance challenges and opportunities of all kinds. Stakeholders in nonwork situations might not fit easily into some of the typical organizational categories described below, but they can still be identified as having a "stake" in the performance outcomes.

Table 2.1 shows typical stakeholders to support performance, their roles, and when they should be involved in planning or implementation of a performance improvement intervention. Research and best practices in interventions (addressed in Chapter 4) show that visible and demonstrable stakeholder support is essential to achieve full desired performance.

Table 2.1. Typical Stakeholders in Performance Improvement Interventions

Stakeholders	Description of Role	When Involvement Is Important
Executives and Managers of Performers (I)	Executives and managers who are involved in decisions about performance interventions for high-priority strategic outcomes (such as setting priorities, funding, selecting consultants, choosing type of intervention, approving evaluation metrics)	As primary stakeholders when intervention focuses on strategic goals
Supervisors, Team Leaders (I)	Supervisors, team leaders, and other job titles for those who are responsible for and oversee the work of performers who are the focus of the intervention; may have formal or informal authority	
Performers (I)	Employees or other workers of all sorts at various levels whose performance is the focus of the intervention	As primary stakeholders in all interventions
Performance Consultants (I/E)	Professionals who contribute to analysis, design, development, implementation, and/or evaluation of the intervention and may have many job titles: • For instructional interventions: trainer, instructional designer, facilitator, instructor, and others • For non-instructional interventions: organizational development specialist, change agent, performance analyst, human resource specialist, and others	
Evaluators (I/E)	Professionals focusing on intervention assessments that are • Formative: design, methods, materials • Summative: reaction, learning, performance, results Note: performance consultants or others may serve as evaluators in some situations (see Chapter 5)	Early in planning and implementation when evaluation is important

Note: Stakeholders may be internal (I), external (E), or either (I/E) to key organizations in the organizational system.)

(Continued)

Table 2.1. Typical Stakeholders in Performance Improvement Interventions, Cont'd

Stakeholders	Description of Role	When Involvement Is Important
Performance Partners (I/E)	Experts in special aspects of performance, such as information technology, physical and information security, health and safety, customer relations, marketing, and quality	
Co-workers (I/E)	Organizational system members whose work is involved with that of performers, but who are not the focus of the intervention	
Subject Matter Experts (SMEs) (I/E)	Content experts who contribute information and review methods and materials for accuracy and completeness	
Clients, Customers, and Users (I/E)	Those who make use of products or services that are developed by the performers who are the focus of the intervention	
Suppliers (I/E)	Those who supply the physical or intangible resources from which performers develop products and services	Early in planning and development when the stakeholder has the power to support or undermine the intervention
Regulators (E)	Monitors from local, state, national, or international governments who oversee or enforce compliance with rules, laws, and treaties	
Union Representatives (I/E)	Those representing local or international unions with contractual relationships with one or more organizations in the system	
Special Interest Group Representatives (I/E)	Advocates for certain issues (such as environment, mental health, civil rights) with strong concerns related to an organization's operations, products, and services	
Community Residents (I/E)	Residents of an area near an organization in the system, or near an area affected by system operations, products, or services	
Mentors, Sponsors, Funders (I/E)	Those who provide support to performers or other stakeholders; foundations that provide funding for nonprofits	

Note: Stakeholders may be internal (I), external (E), or either (I/E) to key organizations in the organizational system.)

Primary Stakeholders Supporting Performance

Primary stakeholders are very important and must always be involved in an intervention to achieve full performance. As Table 2.1 indicates, primary stakeholders for any intervention may include *executives* and *higher level managers of performers* if the performance improvement intervention is focused on reaching strategic organizational goals (affecting the organization's attainment of its vision and mission). In all interventions, strategic or tactical (affecting operational effectiveness), *supervisors* and *team leaders, performers,* and—with increasing frequency—*performance consultants* (who often use other job titles, discussed below) are primary stakeholders.

Executives and Managers of Performers. When a performance intervention focuses on *strategic* organizational goals, executives and managers of performers make key decisions related to the intervention. They help determine the strategic goals, approve funding, often select consultants, help shape the intervention, approve evaluation metrics, and review progress and outcomes. They often make decisions that affect the work environment and how work is done. They should be involved as primary stakeholders for all strategically related interventions to improve performance that affects the organization's vision, mission, and goals. (Managers of other functions in an organizational system, not in the management chain for the performance improvement intervention itself, may fit in other stakeholder roles such as customer or supplier.)

Supervisors, Team Leaders. These primary stakeholders have responsibility for and oversee the performance that is the focus of the intervention. (Supervisors and team leaders of other workers who are not the focus of the intervention may fit in another stakeholder category, such as co-worker or subject matter expert.) For interventions affecting management performance, higher level managers function as supervisors. For front line employees and those in the organization who directly support them (finance, human resources, safety, and other functions), *supervisors* and *team leaders* are typical titles in the traditional chain of command; there may be other titles in nontraditional settings.

Often there are several levels in the management chain (executives, managers, supervisors) who serve as primary stakeholders for performance support for strategic interventions. They usually are formally in charge, although in unusual circumstances they may exercise informal authority. In the excavation and clearing of the World Trade Center site in 2001–2002, many people became accepted as supervisors and managers—through expertise or take-charge talents—who had no formal authority in the horrific and incredibly challenging days and months after September 11 (Langewiesche, 2002).

Performers. Those who perform the work that is the focus of the intervention are essential primary stakeholders. Their performance is the target for change or improvement through participation in an instructional intervention that results in enhanced job performance, some noninstructional intervention, or a combination of both. These are the individuals and groups (such as miners, physicians, teachers, managers, salespeople, brokers, and police officials) who produce or oversee the production of the accomplishments (products and services) that organizations provide to the community and society.

Performers also help provide and maintain the work environment that supports producers; examples are specialists in finance, safety, human resources, building maintenance, and information technology. Performers' accomplishments include an uncountable number of products and services from for-profit, not-for-profit, and government organizations and from other groups and individuals. The levels of motivation, commitment, and competence of all these performers make very significant differences in the value of the products and services to their ultimate users in the larger system.

There may be subsets of performers in some situations. For example, there may be several cohorts of performers: those who are currently involved in the intervention, those who have previously completed the intervention's activities, and those who have not yet become involved in the intervention. Frontline as well as higher level performers may be primary stakeholders. All performers may not share all characteristics, such as job titles, projects, or location in the organizational structure. What all performers do share is the task of enhancing their performance through involvement in the intervention.

Performance Consultants. The primary stakeholder group to which many readers of this book may belong is termed "performance consultants" here. Our working definition of a *performance consultant* (adapted from Robinson & Robinson, 1995, p. 10) is a professional who focuses on what people *do* (their performance) and then considers what it takes (in skills, knowledge, and a range of workplace resources) to do that well. (The performance consultant role is discussed in more detail in Chapters 3, 4, and 6.)

The performance consultant role is a quantum leap forward from the role of the traditional trainer. The trainer is engaged in developing and delivering learning experiences that result in new knowledge and skills for the participant. The performance consultant may well contribute to those learning experiences, but is ultimately focused on the effective application of new knowledge and skills to job performance. Thus, the performance consultant's attention is on the intervention, instructional or noninstructional, as well as on the workplace where the application of new learning to performance takes place.

For an instructional intervention to improve knowledge and skills that are then applied to job performance, actual job titles of performance consultants might include trainer, facilitator, instructional designer, or learning specialist. For noninstructional interventions to improve work processes or other work environment characteristics that support improved performance, their titles might include organizational development specialist, performance analyst, human resource specialist, or quality control expert. Managers of some of these specialists may be directly involved. As performance consultants, all of these professionals focus on helping performers—whatever their functions in the complex organizational system—to develop, improve, or maintain desired performance so that the organization's desired results are achieved effectively and efficiently.

Performance consultants have extremely important roles in the design and delivery of both instructional and noninstructional interventions. They contribute to the analysis that determines a performance gap, the content and approach of the intervention, its implementation, and the evaluation that measures impact on performance and results. An essential tool for the performance consultant is the practice of human performance technology (HPT), a systematic and systemic approach to attaining desired performance. (The HPT process is described at greater length in Chapter 3.)

Of course, many interventions are decided on and implemented by managers without direct involvement of other primary stakeholders, such as the performers who do the work or any of the specialists who are considered performance consultants here. An underlying theme of this book is to show the benefits, in terms of improved performance and organizational results, from involving performers and performance consultants as primary stakeholders in planning, implementing, and evaluating interventions to ensure that all available expertise contributes to important decisions.

Other Stakeholders Supporting Performance

Other stakeholders also may be important in supporting performance in many interventions. They can include individuals, groups, or communities of people at local, regional, national, or international levels who have concerns related to the complex system. Wise primary stakeholders (managers, performers, and performance consultants) should scrutinize the complex system's diagram and speak with other stakeholders to identify all the stakeholders who should be involved. It is not necessary to involve every possible stakeholder, but those who can significantly support or undermine the intervention should be included. Here, and in Table 2.1, are some of the "usual suspects" who may contribute as stakeholders. Also, primary stakeholders should always check for other important stakeholders in their interventions that are not listed here.

Evaluators. There has been a recent and rapid increase in management requests for evaluations of the outcomes of strategically important interventions (Phillips & Stone, 2002). Evaluators are important stakeholders (internal or external to an organizational system) who should be involved from the beginning of an intervention project whenever evaluation is planned. They can assist with selection of metrics and the design, implementation, and reporting of these assessments. Besides their basic measurement functions, evaluators can also develop assessment information that directly supports full performance following an intervention. (Chapter 5 gives a brief overview of recently developed evaluation approaches that directly support performance.) Occasionally, performance consultants and others take on the role of evaluators.

Performance Partners. Primary stakeholders should consider other functions in the organizational system as potential *performance partners* to support an intervention. These include people with expertise in special areas such as information technology, physical and information security, quality, marketing, customer relations, ethics, and environmental safety and health. They have particular interests in performance that may dovetail or overlap in certain situations with the concerns of the primary stakeholders and may provide significant additional leverage for an intervention. These performance partners may be internal or external to organizational components in the complex system. (Chapter 7 gives a case study involving close collaboration between performance consultants and one set of performance partners.)

Co-Workers. There are others in the organizational or community setting whose work is involved in some way with the work of performers, but whose own performance is not the focus of the particular performance improvement intervention. These *co-workers* may be internal or external customers or suppliers, may provide other kinds of encouragement or support for performers, or may potentially undermine the performance improvement effort. In any case, they should be involved as stakeholders if they can have a significant effect, positive or negative, on the intervention's outcomes. (Chapter 6 discusses ways to involve these stakeholders.)

Subject Matter Experts. Those with content expertise in areas that are involved in a performance improvement intervention are referred to as *subject matter experts* (SMEs). They often contribute to development of content and review the intervention's methods and materials for accuracy and completeness.

Clients, Customers, and Users. Those who use the products and services of others, internally to an organization or externally by purchase or other means, are very important stakeholders in many complex organizational systems. These stakeholders often (although not always) can choose the products or services they use and have varying degrees of satisfaction with them.

Suppliers. Those who provide the resources, internally or externally to the organizational system, from which products and services are developed are another important stakeholder group. These suppliers may provide physical resources (such as materials or equipment) or more intangible resources (such as information or expertise). They definitely have an interest as stakeholders in how effectively the organizational system, their customer, produces its results.

Regulators. Officials from some governmental entity—local, state, national, or international organization—may be important stakeholders for an intervention. They oversee or enforce compliance with laws and regulations such as local building codes, city or state zoning requirements, civil rights or other national legislation, or international commitments and treaties.

Union Representatives. Officials of local or international unions may inspect or intervene on behalf of some union members and other workers in the complex system. They may have a significant contractual impact on policies, procedures, and activities.

Special Interest Group Representatives. Issue-related advocates may campaign, lobby, or otherwise exert influence on components of the complex system to help the viewpoints of their members or constituents be considered. They may be internal or external to key organizations in the system. For example, members of the Georgia chapter of the Mental Health Association (MHA) served on advisory committees for some of the regional boards and community mental health centers for the Georgia State Mental Health Delivery System (Chapter 1).

Community Residents. Those who reside geographically near an organization's site or near an area affected by the complex system's goals or operations may have strong concerns relating to environmental, political, social, economic, or other issues. For example, many residents of urban neighborhoods become closely engaged with local governing bodies on issues such as housing and commercial development, street repairs, and police protection and insist on involvement as stakeholders.

Mentors, Sponsors, Funders. Those who provide personal guidance as mentors or provide financial or other support to individuals or groups (performers or other stakeholders) in a complex system may intervene to influence the system on behalf of those persons. For example, various groups and individuals sponsor college scholarships for inner city youth who successfully graduate from high school; these sponsors often serve as advocates for school system improvements. For nonprofit organizations, foundations that provide funds may be important stakeholders.

Supporting and Opposing Stakeholders

Usually, stakeholders—wherever they are in the complex system—are considered to be interested in *supporting* or *encouraging* the activity to achieve a common goal. Key supporting stakeholders for any moderately complex organizational system would include the organization's primary stakeholders: top executives and managers, who define the organization's mission, vision, goals, and success indicators; employees of the organization, who perform many different types of work; and performance consultants, internal or external to the organization, who work with other stakeholders to identify and address needs for improved performance.

Depending on specific performance improvement needs, other supporting stakeholders for a moderately complex system might include suppliers of the many resources used in accomplishing the organization's goals, customers who purchase or obtain the organization's products and services, stockholders who have invested in the organization, government regulators, and nongovernmental organizations (NGOs) such as community residents and special interest advocacy groups.

Occasionally there are stakeholders whose concern about the activity or goal is in opposition to its accomplishment and who can interfere to suppress or undermine the activity. These stakeholders must always be considered in order to address the reasons for their opposition. When possible, supporters may lessen or neutralize opposition by negotiating acceptable changes to goals and activities with the opposing stakeholders and by strengthening the backing of supportive stakeholders for those goals and activities.

An example of the impact that opposing stakeholders may have is the grounding of nearly four hundred flights of financially troubled US Airways over the 2004 Christmas weekend. The airline attributed the scratched flights—and ensuing chaos for passengers—to receiving "an unusually high number of sick calls from flight attendants and baggage handlers," although there was no sign of a job action. Struggling to reduce labor costs, the airline's management had negotiated significant pay cuts with reservations and gate agents, but had not yet reached new agreements with flight attendants and baggage handlers (Rein & de Tantillo, 2004).

There occasionally are some very "strange bedfellows," stakeholder organizations at opposite sides of issues that may join together on an ad hoc basis to achieve a common goal. An example was the joint 2004 effort by the Sierra Club and Judicial Watch—with very different political perspectives—to challenge the withholding of information on membership and deliberations of the National Energy Policy Development Group, established by Vice President Cheney. The challenge was eventually denied by the U.S. Supreme Court (Sierra Club, 2004). Such ad hoc relationships are usually relatively short-term with rather limited performance impacts.

Examples of Stakeholders in Moderately Complex Systems

National Weather Service

The National Weather Service (NWS), part of the National Oceanic and Atmospheric Administration (NOAA) in the Department of Commerce, is a moderately complex system with a single organization as its main component. (NWS is, of course, a subsystem of NOAA.) NWS develops weather-related forecasts and warnings for all U.S. states and territories. A new online synchronous and asynchronous training system for forecasters (Advanced Warning Operations Course or AWOC) was launched in 2004. The NWS Warning Decision Training Branch (WDTB) identified the following stakeholders to provide various types of support—before, during, and after forecasters complete AWOC—for full application of the training by forecasters in their work.

Managers at several levels in the organization are among the primary stakeholders for the AWOC intervention. They include the NWS Director and six regional directors; the Director, Office of Climate, Water, and Weather Services; Meteorologists in Charge (MICs), managers of 124 Weather Forecast Offices in all states and territories; and Hydrologists in Charge (HICs), managers of thirteen River Forecast Centers in North America.

Performers who are primary stakeholders are the forecasters, approximately 1,600 professionals who monitor weather conditions around the clock in all

U.S. states and territories. They determine when to issue warnings on potentially destructive weather conditions (such as floods, thunderstorms, tornadoes, hurricanes, blizzards, and high winds).

Performance consultants, also primary stakeholders, provide internal management and assistance for the intervention at several levels. These include the managers of AWOC and its component programs: the NWS Training Division Director, the Chief of the Warning Decision Training Branch (WDTB), and instructors in WDTB who manage key AWOC programs (AWOC for forecasters, facilitator training for onsite AWOC facilitators, and evaluation processes for both AWOC and facilitator training). Also serving as internal performance consultants are facilitators who support AWOC at local sites: the National Science and Operations Officers (SOO) Program Coordinator, and individual SOOs who facilitate AWOC at each Weather Forecast Office; and the Development and Operations Hydrologist (DOH) Representative for Training at the National Center's Field Requirements Group, and individual DOHs who facilitate AWOC at each River Forecast Center.

An external performance consultant, the author, assisted WDTB with identifying major AWOC stakeholders, building stakeholder support, developing Level 3 evaluation instruments for measuring performance on the job, and suggesting possible future Level 4 measures of organizational results.

An additional potential internal stakeholder was a representative of the National Weather Service Employees Organization (NWSEO). Other potential stakeholders external to NWS—who may be considered for future roles to support AWOC during and after its rollout—include private sector organizations (consultants, media, and information service companies) that make NWS information widely available and provide specialized services to organizations and the public outside the NWS mission.

Canadian National Railway, U.S. Operation

Another example of stakeholders in a moderately complex system, the U.S. Operations of the Canadian National Railway, is provided in Chapter 7. Detailed descriptions of the interventions, key stakeholder groups, and their strategies to support performance are provided.

Examples of Stakeholders in Highly Complex Systems

Highly complex systems typically include several moderately complex organizations that work interactively toward a common goal. They may cross regional, state, or national boundaries and include a very wide range of potential stakeholders. Two examples (each lasting only a few years) are briefly described in Chapter 1: the Georgia Mental Health Delivery System and the Long Term Care Innovation and Leadership Institute of Southwestern Ontario.

A highly complex system involving multiple moderately complex organizations, with a much longer successful track record (thirty years to date), is described in detail in Chapter 8. JHPIEGO Corporation is a nonprofit affiliate of Johns Hopkins University, based in Baltimore, Maryland. It provides advocacy, education, and performance improvement services in underdeveloped host countries in relation to family planning and maternal and neonatal care, through the U.S. Agency for International Development. JHPIEGO's long-term success in improving performance in health care, with low resources in very culturally challenging situations, is due in large part to continual efforts to develop productive partnerships with stakeholders of many kinds.

Organizational Factors That Support Performance in Complex Systems

In any complex system, what are the factors that make effective performance more likely? What factors distinguish the work settings in which performers generally meet or exceed expectations from the settings in which performers generally do not meet those expectations? Which stakeholders can provide these supportive factors in the work setting?

Two sets of factors are described below. One set supports performers in any typically supervised work setting (such as a moderately or highly complex organization, a community, or a family). The other set of factors provides additional support for performers who are relatively autonomous in choosing whether to adopt new knowledge or skills. For both sets, the stakeholders who can provide those factors are identified or suggested. Widespread recognition and use of these two sets of factors by all stakeholders can make performance improvement a collaborative priority across the organization.

Factors Supporting Performance That Is Supervised

Several levels of management and supervision typically oversee performance in both moderately and highly complex organizations. Following Gilbert's groundbreaking work (1978), various models have been derived that identify factors in these supervised work environments, at the job/performer level, that are necessary to support effective performance. One of these, widely used, is by Rummler and Brache (1995). An adapted version of their model is shown in Table 2.2.

Table 2.2. Factors That Support Performance in Complex Systems

Factor	Description	Responsible Stakeholders
1. Clear performance specifications	Outputs, standards, and results for performers to attain	Managers and Supervisors
2. Necessary resources and support	Signals to act, priorities, tools, information, responsibility, lack of task interference, practice opportunities, and other support	
3. Appropriate consequences	Recognition, rewards, incentives that are meaningful to performers	
4. Timely and relevant feedback	Timely, relevant, specific information on how well performance meets specifications	
5. Individual capability	The right person in the job: physical, mental, emotional abilities to perform	
6. Necessary skills and knowledge	Ability to perform effectively, based on experience, coaching, or learning	Managers and Supervisors, Performers, Performance Consultants

Adapted from Rummler and Brache (1995).

Factors Supporting Supervised Performers

The model in Table 2.2 for typically supervised performers has six factors. These factors are applicable in any organizational setting and have been very easy to explain and illustrate to stakeholders in many different types of organizations.

All six factors in Table 2.2 are necessary for supervised performers to be able to perform effectively:

- Without *clear performance specifications,* outputs and achievement of standards would be inconsistent.

- Without *necessary resources and support,* performance would be delayed, sporadic, and perhaps below standards.

- Without *appropriate consequences,* motivation and incentives for successful performance would be absent.

- Without *timely and relevant feedback,* performers wouldn't know whether they were performing well or poorly.

- Without *individual capability,* performers would not have the capacity for effective performance.

- Without *necessary skills and knowledge,* performers would not know how to perform.

The first five factors are the direct responsibility of top managers (for strategic interventions) and supervisors of performers (for all interventions). These stakeholders are responsible for defining the work, providing resources and support, establishing consequences, providing feedback, and selecting the right people for the job. Performance consultants do not have a direct role in the first five factors, but can be instrumental in coaching managers and supervisors on the factors and their management responsibilities.

Managers and supervisors also have responsibility for the sixth factor, because they must ensure that performers have the necessary skills and knowledge to perform the work. They share responsibility for this factor with performers, who must use the necessary skills and knowledge, and with performance consultants, who often must design and deliver or manage learning experiences to help performers gain new knowledge and skills.

Applying Factors for Supervised Performers

The six factors can be continually applied to supporting supervised performance. The first four factors provide a supportive work environment. The fifth factor places a capable person in the job. The sixth factor provides the training or other preparation for that person's effective performance. The more familiar all stakeholders—managers, performers, performance consultants, and others—are with these factors, the easier it is for them to communicate with each other about support for improved performance.

When there is a *deficiency* in *existing* performance, unfortunately, there is a well-known tendency for managers to assume that training is the obvious solution to improve performance. Rummler and Brache strongly disagree. They emphasize (1995, p. 73) that in their experience:

- About 80 percent of performance problems relate to the first four factors in the *work environment;*

- Only 15 to 20 percent of performance problems can be resolved through *training* to develop new skills or knowledge (sixth factor); and

- A mere 1 percent, or fewer, of performance problems relate to an *incapable person* in the job (fifth factor).

There is another good reason to avoid selecting training (sixth factor) as the solution without careful analysis of other factors. Instructional interventions are often significantly more expensive than other possible solutions. Performance consultants have an important role in coaching managers on the need to consider the first four factors in the work environment before considering training or replacing the performer as a way to resolve performance problems.

When *new* performance is necessary, an instructional solution to develop new knowledge or skills (sixth factor) may well be required. However, a noninstructional solution such as work process redesign may also be helpful. The first four work environment factors are always necessary for effective performance and should be addressed as part of the intervention package, even when instruction is determined necessary to address the sixth factor.

Factors Supporting Performance That Is Relatively Autonomous

Besides the Rummler and Brache factors, other factors also apply in some less-supervised work settings. A 2004 study by Yelon, Sheppard, Sleight, and Ford addressed factors affecting performers who are relatively autonomous in doing their work. By their definition, autonomous performers are those who:

- Are not required to follow set procedures;
- Are not closely supervised on performance;
- Decide for themselves *how* to operate for some or all tasks; and
- Decide *whether* and *when* to apply new knowledge and skills to their performance.

These autonomous performers may have some flexibility in the extent to which they require (or even desire) support from several of the Rummler and Brache factors in Table 2.2. They may establish their own *performance specifications.* They may develop their own *resources and support* (such as determining their own signals to act and finding the information and tools they need). They may set their own *consequences,* and may function well without *feedback* from supervisors. They may make judgments about their own *capabilities* for the work they do. Finally, they are quite likely to make their own determinations on the *skills and knowledge* they need to perform capably.

The performers in the Yelon, Sheppard, Sleight, and Ford study were physicians who were lecturers on the faculties of medical schools and who attended workshops on effective instruction; they are clearly an extreme example of autonomous performers. At a lesser extreme are the many situations in which employees are autonomous in some respects, such as being empowered to make certain individual decisions that the organization will uphold.

One example is the retail sales staff at Nordstrom stores, who have significant leeway to accompany customers to various parts of the store and provide very personalized sales service. Their sales policy manual for many years has consisted of a small card with a single sentence: *Use your own best judgment at all times* (Tyson, 2004).

The Yelon, Sheppard, Sleight, and Ford study found that autonomous performers usually decide, *during* or *after* a learning experience, whether and how to apply what they have learned to their performance. Three factors they use to make this decision are shown in Table 2.3.

Table 2.3. Factors Supporting Autonomous Performers in Applying New Knowledge and Skills

Factor	Description	Responsible Stakeholders
1. Credibility of new knowledge and skills	New knowledge and skills seem logical, examples are convincing, they are used by respected colleagues, and they seem effective.	Managers and Supervisors, Performers, Subject Matter Experts, Others
2. Practicality of new knowledge and skills	New approach seems clear, reasonably operational, and easy to apply to performance.	Managers and Supervisors, Performers, Others
3. Recognized need to improve own performance	New approach would help achieve a goal, solve a problem, or improve performance.	

Adapted from Yelon, Sheppard, Sleight, and Ford (2004).

Factors Supporting Autonomous Performers

For relatively autonomous performers, all three of the factors in Table 2.3 are important as they consider adopting new knowledge and skills:

- Without *credibility* for suggested new knowledge and skills, performers would lack confidence that their use would improve their own performance.

- Without *practicality* of easy application, performers would be unlikely to adopt new knowledge and skills.

- Without their own *recognized need* to improve their performance, performers would not be interested in learning new knowledge or skills.

Applying Factors Supporting Autonomous Performers

Because the Yelon, Sheppard, Sleight, and Ford research is very new (2004), there is no hard evidence on which stakeholders can best provide these factors in the work environment. All three factors are important when either *new* performance or *improvement* in existing performance is required for performers who are autonomous to some extent. In those situations, all primary stakeholders should be coached about these three factors, so they can provide the appropriate support for use of new skills and knowledge.

The *credibility* of new skills for improving performance, the first factor, could be addressed effectively by the management chain in the organization— to show the importance of the new skills and the value to the organization of their application in the work environment. Managers should identify and include other stakeholders, such as subject matter experts, who can vouch for the credibility of the new skills. Other performers may also contribute to supporting this factor.

The *practicality* of the new skills for application to performance, the second factor, could also be addressed by managers and supervisors. Performers themselves could contribute to determining the most effective application approaches. There may be other stakeholders who can support the practicality of the new skills.

The *need* for improving their performance using the new skills, the third factor, must be recognized and accepted by the relatively autonomous performers themselves. This factor can also be emphasized by the performers' managers and supervisors. Again, there may be other stakeholders who can support the need for improved performance.

Performance consultants may not have a direct role in providing these three factors, but they may be able to support the responsible stakeholders in several ways. They can emphasize the *credibility* and *practicality* of the new skills, as vouched for by others, and help performers recognize their own *need* for improved performance. They will also need to coach *all* responsible stakeholders, as well as other stakeholders who may be able to contribute, on the importance of emphasizing these three factors for relatively autonomous performers.

Summary of This Chapter

Success in complex organizations is based on the effective performance of the people who do the work. *Performance* (behaviors and accomplishments) and *performers* must be the focus of efforts to improve the organization's operations, products, and services.

There are many *stakeholders* in complex organizations who have strong interests in effective performance and who can provide necessary support for that performance. For all interventions to develop or improve performance, primary stakeholders include:

- Supervisors and team leaders, and—for strategically important interventions—top executives and managers;
- Performers whose work is the focus of the intervention; and
- Performance consultants who provide the expertise to analyze performance gaps, suggest appropriate interventions, and contribute to design and delivery of the interventions.

Often other important stakeholders also can contribute to the performance improvement process. Stakeholders provide information, suggestions, contacts, encouragement, and other resources that strengthen and support interventions.

Stakeholders are particularly important in providing key factors that support performance for both supervised and autonomous performers. Recognition and application of these factors by all stakeholders makes performance improvement an organization-wide collaborative enterprise with strong chances for success. In the next chapter, we address the role of a particularly important stakeholder, the performance consultant, in helping the complex organization achieve the performance it needs for success.

Suggestions for Further Reading

Stakeholders are frequently described as important players in both fact and fiction, although they may not have that label. Descriptions of the lives and careers of historic personages (for example, the first Queen Elizabeth, Benjamin Disraeli, and Franklin D. Roosevelt) identify contemporary stakeholders who affected their lives in significant ways. Many of Shakespeare's plays, notably *Othello, Hamlet,* and *Macbeth,* describe the interaction of key stakeholders in power relationships.

Readers may find the following nonfiction discussions of stakeholders of some interest. (There are, of course, many other descriptions of business and historical events involving stakeholders that could be explored.)

Bethune, Gordon. (1999). *From worst to first: Behind the scenes of Continental's remarkable comeback.* Hoboken, NJ: John Wiley & Sons. Bethune, CEO of Continental Airlines, describes the detailed interactions over several years with all employees, other internal stakeholders, and with external stakeholders, such as financiers, regulators, and others, that turned Continental into a profitable enterprise (at least for some time).

Block, Peter. (2000). *Flawless consulting: A guide to getting your expertise used* (2nd ed.) San Francisco: Pfeiffer. This updated classic describes how to develop the relationships between clients and consultants that are essential for effective organizational improvement.

Langdon, Danny. (1995). *The new language of work.* Amherst, MA: Human Resources Development Press. A common language of work for use by all stakeholders strengthens and simplifies the resolution of work-related issues.

Langewiesche, William. (2002). *American ground: Unbuilding the World Trade Center.* New York: North Point Press, a division of Farrar, Straus and Giroux. The author, the only reporter allowed total access to Ground Zero, spent nine months there capturing the gripping story of harrowing events and the amazingly resourceful stakeholders of all kinds who developed the relationships and processes that got an impossible job done.

3

The Performance Consultant

THIS CHAPTER presents our third foundation block for improving performance in complex systems, the role of the performance consultant. An essential characteristic of this role is commitment to the process of human performance technology (HPT), which has become a benchmark for developing and implementing effective performance improvement interventions in many organizations worldwide. Two other important areas of expertise for the performance consultant are organizations as complex systems and partnering and consulting with stakeholders. Together, these three areas are valuable resources for performance consultants as they work collaboratively with other stakeholders (including managers at all levels and performers) to reach organizational goals through performance improvement interventions.

Major topics for this chapter are

- The role of the performance consultant
- The human performance technology (HPT) process
- Organizations as complex systems
- Partnering and consulting with other stakeholders

The Role of the Performance Consultant

As background for our exploration of the performance consultant role, Exhibit 3.1 presents some key definitions from the previous chapters. Readers can review these to confirm their understanding of important concepts as we go forward.

Exhibit 3.1. Review of Definitions from Chapters 1 and 2

Review of these definitions (repeated or summarized from Chapters 1 and 2, in the order in which they were presented) will help confirm the reader's understanding of these concepts:

Stakeholder	(Chapters 1 and 2) An individual, group, organizational component, or organization with a share or interest—a "stake"—in the goals or outcomes of an activity, process, project, organization, or intervention in a complex system.
A moderately complex system	(Chapter 1) has: • A single organization as its major component; • Usually (but not always) a traditional hierarchical structure within the major organization, with lines of authority from the executive level through successive levels of the organization's internal stakeholder components (chain of command); and • Other groups or organizational components outside the boundaries of the organization that also are stakeholders with an interest in the organization's goals and operations and linked with the major organization by lines of influence (not authority).
A highly complex system	(Chapter 1) has: • Several relatively independent organizations as primary components, with other groups or organizations as supportive or opposing components; • A common goal shared by the primary components, toward which they work interdependently; and • Some component organizations linked by fully accepted lines of authority, and other components linked by lines

Exhibit 3.1. Review of Definitions from Chapters 1 and 2, Cont'd

	of influence (not authority); however, there is no fully accepted chain of command throughout the system.
Performance at the individual, group, and team performer levels	(Chapter 2) A combination of behaviors by individuals, groups, and teams, and the results or accomplishments that they produce (adapted from Dean, 1999, & Gilbert, 1978).
Performer	(Chapter 2) The individual, working alone or in groups and teams, who performs some work.
Primary stakeholders	(Chapter 2) For an intervention focused on reaching strategic organizational goals (affecting the organization's attainment of its vision and mission), executives and higher-level managers of performers are primary stakeholders. For all interventions, strategic or tactical (affecting operational effectiveness), supervisors and team leaders, performers, and frequently performance consultants are primary stakeholders.
Performance consultant	(Chapter 2) A change agent who focuses primarily on what people do, their performance, and then considers what it takes (in skills, knowledge, and a range of workplace resources) to do that well (adapted from Robinson & Robinson, 1995).
Factors that support effective performance	(Chapter 2, adapted from Rummler & Brache, 1995) • Clear performance specifications • Necessary resources and support • Appropriate consequences • Timely and relevant feedback • Individual capability • Necessary skills and knowledge
Factors that support use of new knowledge and skills by autonomous performers	(Chapter 2; from Yelon, Sheppard, Sleight, & Ford, 2004): • Credibility of new knowledge and skills • Practicality of application of new knowledge and skills • Recognized need to improve own performance

In Chapter 2, we briefly introduced the performance consultant as a primary stakeholder in performance improvement interventions (in collaboration with managers at appropriate levels and performers). Our definition there (and also in Exhibit 3.1) characterized the performance consultant as focusing on what people *do,* their performance, and then considering what it takes (in skills, knowledge, and other workplace resources) to do that well. We also defined performance as a combination of behaviors and accomplishments (Exhibit 3.1).

These definitions have important implications for performance consultants, who:

- Are oriented to the *workplace* where the behaviors occur and to the *business purposes* for the accomplishments (products and services);

- Consider the *complex system* in which the workplace exists and the major *stakeholders* who have *authority* or *influence* over *performers*;

- Are committed to analyze *performance* in terms of the *desired results* and to look for ways to support new or improved performance to accomplish those results; and

- Consider a range of possible ways to support new or improved performance and are not limited to a single approach (such as training, incentives, or leadership development) as a standard solution.

Some readers of this book have already established successful careers as performance consultants and have made valued contributions to the success of many groups, organizations, and communities. Other readers may be fairly new at the practice of performance consulting, with significant challenges and opportunities ahead in the complex systems they serve. Managers at all levels in organizations, also readers, need to understand the performance consultant's role and relationships with other stakeholders in a performance improvement intervention. This book does not attempt to give a comprehensive and detailed set of instructions to develop performance consulting skills, but gives suggestions on resources, topics, and actions that would be useful.

The Performance Consultant's Expertise

In their earlier work on performance consulting, Robinson and Robinson (1995) identified four sets of knowledge and skills for performance consultants to achieve successful performance improvement interventions: business knowledge, knowledge of human performance technology (HPT), partnering skill, and consulting skill. In subsequent years, the practice of performance consulting has grown and matured.

In this book, we address the performance consultant's knowledge and abilities in three areas:

- Knowledge of *human performance technology (HPT)* and abilities to identify and analyze performance problems and opportunities and to design, implement, and evaluate interventions to resolve them;

- Knowledge of organizations as *moderately or highly complex systems* (component groups and organizations, stakeholders, mission, goals, businesses, industries, operations, and other aspects) and ability to apply this knowledge effectively in many organizational settings;

- Knowledge of concepts of *partnering and consulting with stakeholders* and abilities to develop ongoing informed partnerships with business leaders on business strategies and issues, and to consult collaboratively with the client and other stakeholders throughout the intervention process.

In Table 3.1, developmental resources in all three areas of performance consulting expertise are shown in columns. In each area, selected *resources for reading* are identified to provide a range of expert sources. (Of course, these are by no means all the useful resources for reading that could be consulted; they are ones that the author has found particularly helpful.) The next row presents selected *knowledge topics* in each area; again, not all possible areas, but useful ones. Finally, *useful actions* are presented as ways to apply the area's knowledge and skills. All three columns and rows represent suggestions, not prescriptions, to show a variety of possibilities that will contribute to developing performance consulting expertise. In following sections of this chapter, we explore each of these three areas of expertise in more detail.

**Table 3.1. Selected Developmental Resources
and Actions for Performance Consultants**

	Human Performance Technology (HPT)	*Organizations as Complex Systems*	*Partnering and Consulting with Stakeholders*

Selected Resources for Reading	*Performance Improvement*
	Broad
	Broad & Newstrom
	Gilbert
	Hale
	Harless
	Hodges
	Langdon
	Mager
	Phillips
	Rossett
	Rummler
	Rummler & Brache
	Stolovitch & Keeps
	Van Tiem, Moseley, & Dessinger
		Wall Street Journal
		Nonprofit Quarterly
		Time, Newsweek (and others)
		Competitors' reports
		Conference Board reports
		Foundation grants
		Industry trade journals
		Organizational reports:
		  Annual report
		  Strategic plan
		  R&D reports
		  Financial reports
		  Customer service data
		Oshry
		Senge
		Wheatley
			Bellman
			Biech
			Block
			Brinkerhoff & Montesino
			Feldstein & Boothman
			Fuller
			Robinson & Robinson
			Senge
			Senge, Kleiner, Roberts, Ross, & Smith
			Svenson
			Ulrich
			Weisbord
			Weisbord & Janoff

Selected Knowledge Topics	Certified performance technologist standards e-Learning Evaluation and measurement Factors that support performance HPT process Instructional systems design Job aids Open systems Performance analysis Performance at organization, process, job/performer levels	Complex organizational systems Language of business and culture, including: Business and industry; competition; downsizing; mergers; mission, vision, goals; operating revenue; regulations; return on investment Stakeholders Strategic business and industry issues and trends Technologies	Authenticity Business of the business Complex adaptive systems Collaborative consulting relationships Contracting Identifying potential clients Interpersonal communications Learning organizations Networking Organizational culture Partnering relationships

Table 3.1. Selected Developmental Resources
and Actions for Performance Consultants, Cont'd

	Human Performance Technology (HPT)	Organizations as Complex Systems	Partnering and Consulting with Stakeholders
	Performance interventions: instructional and non-instructional		
Useful Actions	Analyze performance in unit Attend ASTD, ISPI, other professional conferences Complete HPT courses Offer performance analysis support to receptive manager Prepare for CPT certification Propose an HPT project for a performance problem Respond to training requests with performance questions Shadow an experienced performance consultant	Confer with stakeholder groups (such as quality, diversity) Diagram a complex system Interview key thinkers Organize systems task force Participate in task forces Propose an action learning project Research key issues and resources on the web Shadow a key manager Volunteer for special system assignments	Develop partnering relationship with key manager Look for formal or informal clients Partner with colleagues and stakeholders Provide consultation to receptive managers, employee groups Provide pro bono consultation for community groups

More formal ways to develop performance consulting skills are available. Several universities have graduate programs in areas suitable for performance consulting. Two major professional associations, the International Society for Performance Improvement (ISPI) and ASTD (formerly the American Society for Training and Development), present workshops and related learning events on performance improvement. Many excellent consulting firms also present workshops and other developmental experiences to prepare professionals for the performance consulting role.

The Certified Performance Technologist (CPT) designation demonstrates skills in the practice of HPT, one of the three areas of expertise of the performance consultant. The CPT designation is offered by ISPI (in affiliation with ASTD) to applicants who meet the rigorous Standards of Performance Technology (2002). ASTD is also developing certification for workplace learning and performance professionals, based on the *ASTD Competency Study* (2004).

Functioning as a Performance Consultant

It is up to each individual's judgment to determine when to claim the expertise of a performance consultant. Those who now make that claim (although their job titles may vary widely) have probably gone through several years of developmental activities.

But real life has a way of not waiting for full completion of one stage of development before moving on to another. It is very likely that performance improvement challenges will confront the emerging performance consultant before that individual is fully comfortable with claiming the title. This author's suggestion is to go for it! Don't shy away from a performance improvement challenge because of feeling not completely ready. We can always be of some help to clients, as long as we are *ethically clear* to our clients about our developmental status and committed to search for the expertise we lack when it is needed.

Testing skills on small projects is recommended. When a big project suddenly appears, acting as a support for an internal or external performance consultant can provide invaluable real-world experience with the joys and frustrations of the profession.

The next section explores, in some detail, the HPT process, which differentiates performance consultants from other varieties of the breed. All consultants share concerns about the client's complex system and about their own partnering and consulting skills, but only true performance consultants care deeply about HPT.

The Human Performance Technology (HPT) Process

An essential characteristic of a performance consultant is a commitment to HPT (sometimes referred to as HPI, human performance improvement) as the primary analytical and development tool for improving performance in complex organizational systems. The origins of HPT are in the work of Thomas Gilbert, author of *Human Competence: Engineering Worthy Performance* (1978). Over the years, Gilbert's ideas on what constitutes performance—and how it can be defined and developed—have been explored, tested, adapted, expanded, refined, and confirmed by many practitioners in a wide range of organizational settings. The current widespread focus on effective performance as the goal of every component of a complex organizational system is ultimately attributable to Gilbert's work and influence.

Overview of Human Performance Technology

Human performance technology (HPT) is a systematic, systemic, and scientific approach to obtaining desired accomplishments from performers by determining gaps in performance and designing cost-effective and efficient interventions (adapted from Harless, 1995, p. 75). Managers at every level (executives, top managers, supervisors, team leaders) and performance consultants are particularly important stakeholders who benefit from some knowledge of HPT. The HPT process helps them determine whether a performance intervention is needed, which interventions would be effective to improve performance, and whether the intervention is successful in achieving the desired performance.

ISPI identifies these important aspects of the HPT process (2005):

1. Emphasis on a rigorous analysis of present and desired levels of performance;

2. Identification of causes for a performance gap or opportunity for new performance;

3. Selection of the appropriate intervention(s) from a wide range of potential interventions to improve performance;

4. Guidance in the change management process; and

5. Evaluation of the results.

The HPT Process

The HPT process is covered in detail by several experts (Rummler, 2004; Stolovitch & Keeps, 1999; Van Tiem, Moseley, & Dessinger, 2004); they should be consulted for full background and comprehensive guidelines. Here we give only the basics of HPT's ten stages, shown in Figure 3.1. The ten stages are

---

Figure 3.1. The HPT Process

This figure is adapted from three sources: (1) the ISPI HPT model (www.ispi.org/services/whatshptmodel.pdf), which is from Van Tiem, Moseley, and Dessinger (2004); (2) Rummler (2004); and Broad (2002).

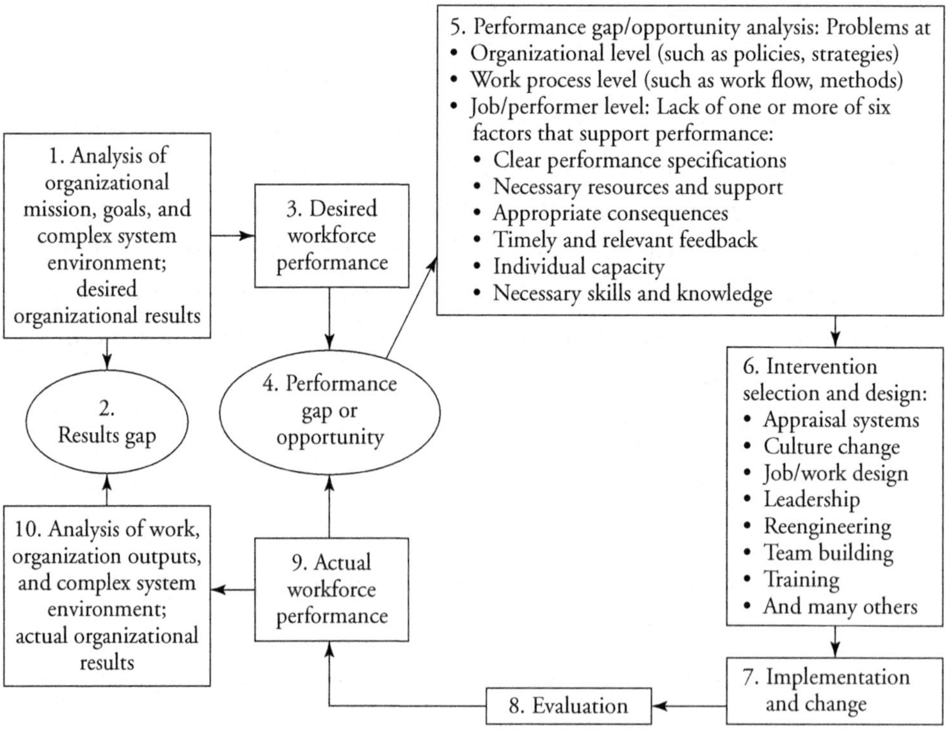

1. The mission and goals of the organization (or group or community) and its complex system environment are analyzed to identify *desired organizational results*. (Examples of typical *desired results* are specific metrics for market share, sales, customer satisfaction, number of repeat engagements, and retention of valued employees.)

2. These desired results are compared to *actual results* for the organization, and a *results gap* is identified if there are significant differences. (If there are no significant differences because *desired organizational results* are being achieved, no further intervention is needed. However, in today's world of global interconnectedness and constant change, chances are that a gap in results exists.) A results gap may be primarily due to problems not related to performance, such as lack of availability of resources. But even in these situations, performance problems may also exist.

3. If there is a significant organizational results gap, the *desired workforce performance* necessary to achieve the desired results is identified. (That is, what behaviors and accomplishments by employees would be necessary to produce the desired organizational results?)

4. The desired performance is compared to *actual workforce performance* to identify any significant differences. (If there are no significant differences between desired and actual performance when there were differences between desired and actual results, the organization must look at areas other than performance.) Performance differences may be one or more *performance gaps* between desired and actual performance. If the desired performance is new, caused by some new requirement, this is a performance *opportunity* that must be met. The HPT Stages 1, 2, and 3 that result in Stage 4, the performance gap or opportunity, are often referred to as *performance analysis*.

COMMON WORKFORCE PERFORMANCE GAPS

A 1994 study of 166 U.S. and European companies by the Conference Board (New York business and research nonprofit) found that 98 percent of the companies had problems (55 percent) or serious problems (43 percent) in getting desired levels of performance from their workforce (Csoka, 1994). It is unlikely that organizational performance problems have diminished significantly since that time.

5. The *performance gap* or *opportunity* is analyzed to determine the cause or causes. There are many possibilities for inadequate current performance. Managers, performance consultants, and other stakeholders should consider possible problems at three levels (Rummler & Brache, 1995):

   • The *organizational* level (problems such as outdated policies or strategies);

   • The *work process* level (problems such as inefficient work flow or redundant methods); and

   • The *job* and *performer* level (problems due to lack of one or more of the six necessary factors that support performance, previously mentioned in Chapter 2 and listed in Stage 5 of Figure 3.1). Almost inevitably, more than one factor will be found that should be strengthened. For example, if new knowledge or skills are needed, there often are lacks also in other factors such as provision of resources or timeliness of feedback to performers.

6. Based on determination of causes of the performance gap or opportunity, an intervention is selected. There are many *noninstructional* interventions at all three levels (organization, work process, and job/performer), such as organizational design, analysis of corporate culture, human resource selection, compensation systems, feedback, and workplace design. *Instructional* interventions, all at the job/performer level, include classroom instruction, mentoring,

distributed learning, and structured on-the-job training (Stolovitch & Keeps, 1999). The selection of the intervention depends on the careful analysis of the previous five stages of the HPT process (Figure 3.1).

7. The selected intervention is implemented. This must be carefully planned to align with analyses from the previous stages of the process.

8. The intervention is evaluated, both in terms of its development (formative) and outcomes (summative). Evaluation metrics and methods should be developed at the same time the intervention itself is designed so that the right data are collected at the appropriate time. (Evaluation is further discussed in Chapter 5.)

9. The actual workforce performance that follows the intervention is identified. This is compared with the desired workforce performance (Stage 3) to determine whether the intervention accomplished its purpose of closing the performance gap or meeting the performance opportunity. If there is still a significant performance gap or opportunity, the HPT process cycles back through Stages 5 through 9.

10. Actual organizational results, due at least in part to improved workforce performance, are identified. These are compared to the original desired organizational results (Stage 1) to determine whether the desired results have been achieved. If not, the HPT process cycles back through Stages 3 through 10.

HPT in Complex Systems

This brief outline of the HPT process gives a very high level view of what should happen in a project to improve performance. However, the basic HPT process description does not emphasize the *stakeholders* who should be involved in the various stages of the process. This essential collaboration of stakeholders at all stages of the HPT process is illustrated in Figure 3.2, showing stakeholder involvement added to the process shown in Figure 3.1.

Figure 3.2. The HPT Process Showing Stakeholder Involvement

This figure is adapted from three sources: (1) the ISPI HPT model
(www.ispi.org/services/whatshptmodel.pdf), which is from Van Tiem,
Moseley, and Dessinger (2004); (2) Rummler (2004); and (3) Broad (2002).

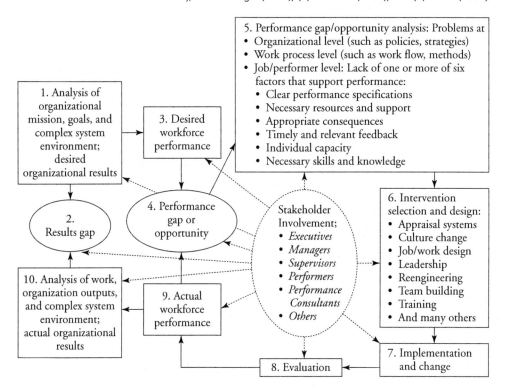

A basic premise of this book (Chapters 1, 2, and 4) is that, in complex organizational systems, the collaboration of key stakeholders is necessary to make any performance improvement effort successful. Primary stakeholders—and perhaps others—contribute to the data gathered at each stage of the HPT process, to related discussions, and to key decisions in many stages such as the following:

- *Stage 2:* Is there a significant gap between actual organizational results (such as sales and customer service ratings) and desired results?

- *Stage 4:* Is there a significant gap between actual performance (behaviors and accomplishments) and desired performance? Or is there a significant performance opportunity due to new requirements?

- *Stage 5:* Are there problems at the organizational level (such as outdated policies or strategies), at the work process level (such as work flow or methods), or at the job and performer level (such as lack of one or more of the six factors that support performance)?

- *Stage 6:* Which interventions are appropriate to address the problems at these levels?

- *Stage 7:* Is the project being implemented according to plan, and are stakeholders providing support to performers (addressing the six factors that support performance) as planned?

- *Stage 8:* Are data for formative and summative evaluations being gathered as planned?

- *Stage 9:* Has actual workforce performance closed the performance gap or met the performance opportunity (Stage 4)?

- *Stage 10:* Have actual organizational results closed the results gap (Stage 2)?

Each of the primary stakeholders in a performance improvement intervention (managers at one or more levels, performers, and performance consultants) needs some knowledge and abilities in HPT. The more that all stakeholders understand the basics of HPT, the better they will be able to contribute to decisions about effective performance improvement interventions. The following sections describe the knowledge and abilities needed by the primary stakeholders.

HPT Expertise for Performance Consultants

The HPT expertise required for performance consultants is very comprehensive. They must have detailed experience and insights into application of the HPT process. They must be able to apply HPT knowledge to a wide range of situations and to work in many supportive ways with stakeholders throughout the HPT process.

The first major column in Table 3.1 on HPT, one of the three major knowledge and skill areas for the performance consultant, is repeated (and slightly expanded) here as Table 3.2, to save the reader from having to flip pages back and forth. This table gives a wide range of reading resources, knowledge topics, and possible actions to explore and apply HPT. This might serve as a checklist on HPT for the experienced performance consultant or a developmental planning resource for less experienced performance consultants or managers who want to learn more about HPT. Other resources (such as Rummler, 2004: Stolovitch & Keeps, 1999; Van Tiem, Moseley, & Dessinger, 2004) should be consulted for more detailed information on the wide range of HPT expertise necessary for effective performance consulting.

Table 3.2. **Developing the Performance Consultant's HPT Expertise**

	Human Performance Technology (HPT)
Resources for Reading	*Performance Improvement* (ISPI's monthly publication) Broad (1997a, 2001, 2002) Broad & Newstrom (1992) Gilbert (1978) Hale (2003) Harless (1970, 1995) Hodges (2002) Langdon (1995) Mager & Pipe (1999) Phillips (2002) Rossett (1998) Rummler (2004) Rummler & Brache (1995) Stolovitch & Keeps (1999) Van Tiem, Moseley, & Dessinger (2004)
Knowledge Topics	Certified Performance Technologist standards (ISPI, ASTD) e-Learning Evaluation and measurement Factors that support performance at the individual level HPT process Instructional systems design Job aids Open systems Performance analysis Performance at organization, process, job/performer levels Performance interventions: instructional and non-instructional

Table 3.2. Developing the Performance Consultant's HPT Expertise, Cont'd

	Human Performance Technology (HPT)
Useful Actions	Analyze performance in unit Attend ASTD, ISPI, other professional conferences Complete HPT courses Offer performance analysis support to receptive managers Prepare for CPT certification Propose an HPT project for a performance problem Respond to training requests with performance questions Shadow an experienced performance consultant

HPT Knowledge and Abilities for Managers and Performers

The other primary stakeholders, managers at several levels and performers, also need to know enough about performance and the HPT process to be able to discuss performance improvement productively with other stakeholders. Suggested HPT-related knowledge and abilities for these two stakeholder groups are shown in Table 3.3.

Table 3.3. HPT Knowledge and Abilities for Managers and Performers

Managers and Performers Should Know . . .	*And Should Be Able to . . .*
Definition of Performance at the individual performer level: The combination of behaviors and the accomplishments (products and services) that are produced	Identify: • Their own behaviors and accomplishments and • The behaviors and accomplishments of co-workers and those whose performance they may oversee
Six Factors That Support Performance: • Clear performance specifications • Necessary resources and support • Appropriate consequences • Timely and relevant feedback • Individual capacity • Necessary skills and knowledge	Identify and discuss: • How each factor is apparent in the workplace • Which factors should be strengthened to support their own or others' performance

First, managers and performers should know the definition of *performance* at the individual performer level, that it is the combination of *behaviors* and the *accomplishments* (products or services) that are produced. Performers also should be able to identify their own *behaviors* and *accomplishments* and those of co-workers. Similarly, managers should be able to identify their own behaviors and accomplishments and those of others whose performance they may oversee.

Second, both managers and performers should know the six *factors that support performance,* as presented in Chapter 2 (modified from Rummler & Brache, 1995) and used in the model of HPT shown in Figures 3.1 and 3.2. Those two stakeholder groups should be able to identify and discuss, with performance consultants and other stakeholders, how those six factors are apparent in the workplace and which factors they think should be strengthened to support their own or others' performance.

HPT, as an essential expertise of the performance consultant, has been described in some detail above. The other two areas of expertise of the performance consultant, the client organization as a complex system and partnering and consulting with other stakeholders, are further described below.

Organizations as Complex Systems

The performance consultant must have significant expertise in analyzing the client organization as a complex system and in working with other stakeholders to help them recognize and identify important individuals, groups, and organizational units in the system. Chapter 1 of this book explored some of the characteristics of complex organizational systems.

Expertise in Complex Systems for Performance Consultants

Because working in complex systems is a relatively new concept to many organizations, there are no widely established guidelines on who needs to know what. The knowledge and abilities suggested here are definitely exploratory and at early stages of conceptualization. The second column of Table 3.1, earlier in this chapter, addresses resources, topics, and actions for performance consultants related to organizations as complex systems; it is repeated (and expanded a bit) here as Table 3.4 for the convenience of readers.

Table 3.4. Developing the Performance Consultant's Expertise in Organizations as Complex Systems

	Organizations as Complex Systems

Resources for Reading	*New York Times*
	Nonprofit Quarterly
	Time, Newsweek (and other weekly news periodicals)
	Wall Street Journal
	Conference Board reports
	Foundation reports and grants
	Government regulations and reports
	Industry trade journals
	Organizational reports:
	    Annual report
	    Customer service data
	    Financial reports
	    Strategic plan
	    Research reports
	    Reports of competitors
	Oshry (1996)
	Senge (1990)
	Senge, Kleiner, Roberts, Ross, & Smith (1994)
	Waldrop (1992)
	Wheatley (2001)

Knowledge Topics	Complex organizational systems
	Language of business and culture, including:
	    Competition
	    Downsizing, layoffs
	    Mergers
	    Operating revenue
	    Recruitment
	    Regulations
	    Return on Investment
	    Safety records
	    Stock prices
	    Strategic business and industry issues and trends
	    Technologies

(Continued)

Table 3.4. Developing the Performance Consultant's Expertise in Organizations as Complex Systems, Cont'd

	Organizations as Complex Systems
Useful Actions	Confer with internal and external stakeholder groups (with interests such as diversity, quality, environment)
	Diagram a complex system
	Help organize a conference on complex systems
	Interview key thinkers, organizational leaders
	Participate in task forces for highly complex systems
	Propose action learning projects
	Research systems issues and resources on the web
	Shadow a key manager or other leader in the system
	Volunteer for special assignments in system components

The suggestions in Table 3.4 can help performance consultants update their information, insights, and educated opinions on the contributions and interaction of the many organizational systems that make up our world. National boundaries no longer limit the extent of the information we need. Events and trends around the globe—environmental, political, and social—have enormous impact on our lives and futures. Constant inquiry, analysis, and application of new ideas have become requirements for the performance consultant in dealing with client organizations and other complex systems.

Rather than an attempt at a precise set of knowledge and abilities in complex systems for performance consultants, here are some suggested ways they might use ideas from Table 3.4 to learn about a particular client organization's complex system:

• Study a recent organization chart for a client organization and ask about higher and lower level organizations to which the client organization is linked. (For example, the National Weather Service is a component of the National Oceanic and Atmospheric Administration, which in turn is part of the U.S. Department of Commerce.)

- Explore the organization's website to learn about its mission, goals, history, products and services, contracts, and status in its industry. Read its recent annual report and look for issues raised by stockholders, regulators, and others.

- Research the archives of the *Wall Street Journal* and major daily newspapers for stories on the organization's recent acquisitions, disputes, or legal actions.

- In collaboration with stakeholder representatives (managers at several levels, performers, others), make a rough sketch of the complex system and its key internal and external components and relationships. Use this diagram as a tool—always open to refinement and revision— in discussions on performance and results issues and concerns with all stakeholders.

Knowledge and Abilities in Organizations as Complex Systems for Managers, Performers, and Other Stakeholders

Managers and performers also need to know something about complex systems as they collaborate in a performance improvement intervention. Table 3.5 suggests some knowledge and abilities that would help them make constructive contributions to the project. They should know the definitions of moderately and highly complex systems. They should be able to identify the important internal and external individuals, groups, and organizations that are stakeholders for the performance intervention in the system in which they function and be able to identify the lines of authority and influence that connect major components of the system.

Managers, performers, and other stakeholders also should be able to provide a wealth of information on the complex client system: its mission, vision, goals, operations, products and services, competitors, and many other aspects. They can suggest stakeholders who support or oppose achievement of a proposed performance improvement intervention and perhaps suggest how those stakeholders might be influenced to increase support or lessen opposition.

Table 3.5. Knowledge and Abilities for Managers, Performers, and Other Stakeholders in Organizations as Complex Systems

Managers, Performers, and Other Stakeholders Should Know . . .	*And Should Be Able to . . .*
Definitions of: • Moderately complex systems and • Highly complex systems	Identify, for a particular performance improvement intervention in a complex organizational system: • Important internal and external individuals, groups, and organizations that are stakeholders in the system, and • Lines of authority and influence that onnect major components of the system.
Mission, vision, goals, operations, products and services, competitors, and other aspects of the complex system in which they function	Suggest, for a particular performance improvement intervention: • Stakeholders who support or oppose achievement of the intervention, and • Ways that stakeholder support might be increased or opposition lessened.

Although many organization members will not have thought extensively about complex systems, they all have personal experiences that can illustrate the multiplicity of organizations involved and their interrelationships. An almost universally experienced example is the transportation system by which the individual arrives at the workplace, involving means such as walking on foot, taking a bus or subway, driving a car, or riding in a car pool. Components involved in this highly complex system include state and local governments and their highway and traffic authorities, managers and operators in bus and subway systems, police officers, weather reporters, the informal "slug" system that allows drivers to qualify for high-occupancy highway lanes by giving free rides, and many other components.

By using such a system as an example, performance consultants can help other stakeholders conceptualize and possibly diagram the complex system in which they function. They can also identify the major stakeholders who would be involved in a particular performance improvement intervention, the lines of authority and influence that link them to performers, and how stakeholders might be influenced to strengthen support or lessen opposition to the intervention's objectives.

Partnering and Consulting with Other Stakeholders

The performance consultant is, after all, a consultant, and needs all the skills that consultants use to make constructive contributions to client organizations. *Partnering and consulting with stakeholders* is the third area of knowledge and abilities that is important for the performance consultant. *Partnering* and *consulting* are linked together here because they are so closely linked in the work of the performance consultant. Chapter 6 in this book gives a suggested step-by-step process for developing and maintaining partnering and consulting relationships with managers and other stakeholders in the organizational system.

Some practitioners consider that partnering is a subset of the consulting process. That is a justifiable perspective. However, *partnering* and *consulting* are considered separately here for convenience; they emphasize different (though overlapping) skills and are directed at slightly different goals.

Partnering with a client means building a close working relationship with a stakeholder (usually a high level manager) over time, "founded on mutual trust, rapport, and credibility" (Robinson & Robinson, 1999, p. 714). A partnership focuses on many aspects of the client's business (products and services, desired results, workforce performance concerns, competitors, legal and regulatory issues, and so on) and is not based on specific projects. As Robb (1998) says, "When you communicate knowledgeably with clients about their business goals, measures of success, performance and learning needs, and work environment issues, you are establishing yourself as a strong business partner. If you are a strong proactive partner, the client is more likely to accept you as a member of his or her leadership team" (p. 235).

Consulting means coaching and guiding a client through a process of decisions and actions to meet a goal or objective. For the performance consultant, the process is HPT for a performance improvement intervention. The recommended role of the consultant (Block, 2000) is that of the *collaborator*. This includes helping managers make constructive decisions through involvement of primary stakeholders (and occasionally others) in gathering and analyzing data, considering options, establishing goals, developing action plans, evaluating outcomes, and sharing responsibility for outcomes. The collaborator role lays the groundwork for constructive stakeholder contributions to the performance intervention and buy-in for its results.

Partnering and Consulting Expertise for Performance Consultants

Developmental resources for performance consultants in *partnering* and *consulting* are presented in the third column of Table 3.1; this column is repeated here (slightly expanded) as Table 3.6 for readers' convenience. Again, these are resources and suggestions for developmental knowledge areas and actions. Universities, professional associations, and consultant groups present courses and workshops that address partnering and consulting expertise.

Table 3.6. Developing the Performance Consultant's Expertise in Partnering and Consulting with Stakeholders

	Partnering and Consulting with Stakeholders
Resources for Reading	Bellman (2002)
	Biech (1999)
	Block (2004)
	Brinkerhoff & Montesino (1995)
	Feldstein & Boothman (1997)
	Fuller (1997)
	Hale (1998)
	Robinson & Robinson (1995, 1998, 1999)
	Senge (1990)
	Senge, Kleiner, Roberts, Ross, & Smith (1994)
	Svenson (2004)
	Ulrich (1997)
	Weisbord (2004)
	Weisbord & Janoff (2000)

Table 3.6. Developing the Performance Consultant's Expertise
in Partnering and Consulting with Stakeholders, Cont'd

	Partnering and Consulting with Stakeholders
Knowledge Topics	Authenticity Champions Complex adaptive systems Consultant roles: collaborator, expert, "pair-of-hands" Consulting process Contracting Diagramming the system Identifying potential clients Interpersonal communications Learning organizations Networking Organizational culture Partnering: building ongoing, trusting, credible relationships
Useful Actions	Develop partnering relationships with key managers Look for formal or informal consulting clients Partner with colleagues and other stakeholders in projects Provide consultation to receptive managers, employee groups Provide pro bono consultation for community groups

Reading, exploring knowledge topics, and taking workshops can be very valuable. However, there is no substitute for the essential experiences of partnering and consulting with managers or other stakeholders. Prospective performance consultants can look for a manager who understands the value of focusing on performance and results and offer to partner with the manager to learn the business and help to analyze performance requirements. Those without direct consulting experience can look for a willing group in the organization or the community that would value consultant help in reaching a goal.

It is very important when beginning a consulting or partnering experience to be sure that your developmental status is very clear to your clients. If you are a beginner, be sure to make that clear and to assure your clients that you will seek and recommend more expert assistance if it is required.

Knowledge and Abilities in Partnering and Consulting with Managers, Performers, and Other Stakeholders)

Managers, performers, and other stakeholders need some information about partnering and consulting. Table 3.7 presents basic knowledge and abilities in these areas. Be sure that all stakeholders understand what *partnering* means and can describe its benefits to the organization. They should have the appropriate information on the terms and conditions of a consulting contract between performance consultant and client (usually a manager) for a specific performance improvement intervention and be able to discuss their expectations and commitment to participate.

Table 3.7. Knowledge and Abilities in Partnering and Consulting for Managers, Performers, and Other Stakeholders

Managers, Performers, and Other Stakeholders Should Know . . .	And Should Be Able to . . .
Definition of partnering: • Building a close working relationship between client and performance consultant over time • Focusing on aspects of the client's business (such as products and services, desired results, workforce performance concerns) • Not based on specific projects	Describe benefits of partnering to the client organization: • Obtain an ally in analyzing performance problems • Develop success measures for performance and organizational results • Make managers aware of factors to support performance in workplace • Make more informed investments in instructional and non-instructional solutions to performance problems
Basic terms and conditions of contract between performance consultant and client for a specific intervention	Discuss: • Their expectations for outcomes and processes during the intervention • Their commitment to participate throughout the intervention

**Table 3.7. Knowledge and Abilities in Partnering and Consulting
for Managers, Performers, and Other Stakeholders, Cont'd**

Managers, Performers, and Other Stakeholders Should Know . . .	And Should Be Able to . . .
Definition of consulting: • Coaching and guiding the client and other stakeholders through the HPT process for a performance improvement intervention • Consultant acting as collaborator (not expert or "pair-of-hands") • Helping decision-makers and other stakeholders to collaborate in gathering and analyzing data, considering options, establishing goals, developing action plans, evaluating outcomes, and sharing responsibility for outcomes	Describe how stakeholders will collaborate during the planning, implementation, and evaluation of the performance improvement intervention: • Assisting with data gathering • Contributing to discussions and decisions • Participating in analyses of evaluation data • Sharing responsibility for outcomes

Those stakeholders should also know the definition of consulting, particularly with the performance consultant in the collaborator role, helping to guide all stakeholders through the HPT process. They should be able to describe their roles as stakeholders and collaborators throughout the performance improvement intervention.

Summary of This Chapter

Performance consulting in complex organizational systems can be both energizing and daunting. It requires a significant shift from the traditional "trainer" perspective, which typically found a training solution for all performance problems. The three essential components of performance consulting are use of the HPT process, analysis of complex organizational systems, and partnering and consulting for effective performance improvement interventions.

In following the *HPT process,* the performance consultant guides the client—usually a high level manager—and other stakeholders to work collaboratively so that performance problems and opportunities are well analyzed and appropriate decisions are made. Educating stakeholders in HPT principles is an ongoing challenge, because they often wonder when you are going to give them what they originally expected, a quick training solution for a complex problem. The collaborative process almost always convinces stakeholders that the time taken to collaborate is well spent, with high payoffs in agreement and "buy-in" to the analysis of the problem, the selected intervention, and evaluation of outcomes.

Helping stakeholders analyze their *complex organizational system* also pays off by identifying those who should be involved in a performance improvement intervention and determining how support might be increased and opposition lessened. Stakeholders throughout the system can contribute the organizational information (missions, operations, products and services, competitors, and so on) that is needed by all participants to form the basis for sound decisions and actions.

The value of *partnering* for the organization lies in developing the performance consultant as a consistent and reliable ally. With increased familiarity with the organization's business issues and success goals, the performance consultant can help focus managers and performers on the factors that support performance in the workplace and on specific improvement possibilities.

Collaborative *consulting* underlies all the work of the performance consultant. Helping key stakeholders work together—so that each contributes necessary information and expertise collaboratively—greatly increases the chances of sound decisions and desired outcomes. The performance consultant combines the interpersonal strengths so necessary for partnering and consulting with more technical expertise in HPT and complex systems, to help groups and organizations achieve success.

This concludes the three chapters that provide the foundation for improving performance in complex systems. We have looked at complex organizational systems, their components, and the flow of authority and influence through them. We identified some important stakeholders in those systems and considered their responsibilities to provide factors that support performance. Finally, we explored the three main areas of expertise of the performance consultant—human performance technology (HPT), organizations as complex systems, and partnering and consulting with stakeholders to improve performance. In the next three chapters, Part 2, we consider some effective tools for stakeholders to use to support performance.

Suggestions for Further Reading

The performance consultant role is relatively recent. The resources listed below are very useful in understanding the role and how it is being fulfilled successfully in many organizations.

Block, Peter. (2000). *Flawless consulting: A guide to getting your expertise used* (2nd ed.). San Francisco: Pfeiffer. The classic guide for consultants is updated and still a classic for today and tomorrow.

Robinson, Dana Gaines, & Robinson, James C. (1995). *Performance consulting: Moving beyond training.* San Francisco: Berrett-Koehler. These authors coined the term "performance consultant" and describe the necessary knowledge and skills. The transition from the traditional training perspective to the performance consultant role is clearly outlined, with suggested analytical tools and scripts for how the performance consultant deals with clients.

Robinson, Dana Gaines, & Robinson, James C. (Eds.). (1998). *Moving from training to performance: A practical guidebook.* Alexandria, VA: ASTD, and San Francisco: Berrett-Koehler. This book is a guide for training and human resource departments in moving to a performance focus. Very substantive and thoughtful chapters are contributed by top people in the field (Rummler, Bellman, Elliott, and Stolovitch & Keeps, among others).

Tools for Stakeholders to Improve Performance

Now that we have established the foundation for our exploration of improving performance in complex systems in Part 1, we will focus our attention in Part 2 on several important tools. These equip the performance consultant, the manager, and other stakeholders to address performance challenges in some detail and with new expertise.

Chapter 4 looks more deeply at the role of stakeholders in supporting performance. Research over fifty years has shown convincingly that training alone is often very ineffective in producing desired performance. Research on the reasons for this consistent lack of effectiveness goes back many years as well, and consistently finds that lack of stakeholder support is a major part of the problem. Research-based strategies for stakeholders are essential tools that address many of the factors to support performance that were identified in Chapter 2. The strategies can be organized into another helpful tool, the transfer matrix.

In Chapter 5, we focus on evaluation for learning-related interventions. Evaluation is becoming widely recognized by managers
and other stakeholders as a very important tool for any intervention.
Recent additions to traditional evaluation approaches give us new
ways to support and encourage performance on the job, as well as
measure it.

Chapter 6 concludes Part 2. It presents a detailed, step-by-
step process—integrated with the HPT process—for performance
consultants to partner and consult with managers in leading a
performance improvement intervention. The process involves
key stakeholders throughout the important decisions and builds
their buy-in, as well as their information and expertise, into the
intervention.

4

Developing Stakeholder Strategies to Improve Performance

I N THIS CHAPTER, we concentrate on stakeholder strategies as tools to support improved performance in the workplace. These strategies are based, in large part, on research on desired performance following interventions and the stakeholder actions that helped support that performance.

This chapter focuses on:

- Low performance levels following training interventions
- Stakeholder support for performance following both instructional and noninstructional interventions
- Recommended stakeholder strategies to support performance

Low Performance Levels Following Training Interventions

Training consists of structured learning experiences to help a learner gain new knowledge and skills for use on the job. Training, at various levels of sophistication and cost, has been a staple of organizational life for many years. The original assumption was, "If they aren't performing the way they should, the solution is training." It took years for many learning professionals and managers to realize that the assumption was not holding true; frequently, the desired performance did not follow the training.

Research on Lack of Transfer of Training to Performance

As evaluation of training became more standardized (Kirkpatrick, 1998), two points became clear. First, training programs were often effective in helping learners gain the desired knowledge and skills. Second, evaluation of later job performance also often showed that the new knowledge and skills were not being applied. A literature survey (Baldwin & Ford, 1988) found, "There is growing recognition of a 'transfer problem' in organizational training today. It is estimated that while American industries annually spend up to $100 billion on training and development, not more than 10 percent of these expenditures actually result in transfer to the job" (p. 63).

The term "transfer of training" came into use, defined as "the effective and continuing application, by trainees to their jobs, of the knowledge and skills gained in training—both on and off the job" (Broad & Newstrom, 1992, p. 6). The studies and expert opinion in Table 4.1, from 1955 to 2000, identify consistently low levels of transfer of training to desired performance when training is given as the sole solution.

Table 4.1. Low Levels of Transfer of Training to Desired Performance

Researcher(s), Date	Focus of Research	Summary of Findings
Fleishman, Harris, & Burtt (1955)	Loss of desired behavior change following training	Study of International Harvester foremen, trained in leadership principles and techniques. Following training, most foremen exhibited desired behavior. After several months, most had reverted to original behavior. The few who continued to demonstrate desired behaviors worked for supervisors who also demonstrated the desired behaviors.

Table 4.1. Low Levels of Transfer of Training to Desired Performance, Cont'd

Researcher(s), Date	Focus of Research	Summary of Findings
Mosel (1957)	Minimal impact of training	Training often "makes little or no difference in job behavior."
Newstrom (1985)	Decrease in training content applied over time following training; barriers to transfer of learning to performance	Study of perceptions of learning specialists (members of ASTD). On average, they perceived: • Only 40 percent of training content was applied to job immediately following training; • Only 25 percent of content still applied to job after six months; and • Only 15 percent of content still applied to job after one year.
	Barriers to transfer of learning to performance include:	• Lack of reinforcement by supervisors on the job; • Difficulties in the work environment; • Non-supportive climate in the organization; • Learner perceptions of new skills as impractical; • Learner discomfort with change; • Separation from instructional provider; • Poor design and delivery of training program; and • Negative response to new behaviors by co-workers.
Baldwin and Ford (1988)	Survey of literature and research on transfer of training	Among other findings: Not more than 10 percent of the estimated $100 billion spent each year on training by American industries actually resulted in transfer to the job.
Kotter (1988)	Factors inhibiting success of management training	In a survey of top executives, more than half identified two factors that inhibited the success of training to improve performance of managers: (1) lack of involvement by

(Continued)

Table 4.1. Low Levels of Transfer of Training to Desired Performance, Cont'd

Researcher(s), Date	Focus of Research	Summary of Findings
		top managers in the change development process (71 percent of respondents), and (2) new improvement efforts centralized at top echelons of the organization but not accepted by lower-level participants (51 percent of respondents).
Tannenbaum & Yukl (1992)	Low levels of transfer of learning	In a review of the literature: transfer of learning to job performance was generally significantly lower than desired, with relatively few learners (as low as 5 percent) affirming that they had applied what they had learned to their job performance.
Stolovitch (2000)	Low transfer rates for training as sole intervention	In a study of best practices: Training alone is usually not effective in achieving on-job application. Low transfer rates for training alone range from 10 to 30 percent "with most on the low end."

The 1955 study by Fleishman, Harris, and Burtt in Table 4.1 is perhaps the first research study to identify problems of transfer of training to performance. Newstrom's 1985 study, thirty years later, tapped into the perceptions of early members of the emerging training profession and identified work environment problems that interfere with transfer to job performance. Baldwin and Ford's 1988 literature review, quoted earlier, is very comprehensive, with other findings related to training outcomes. Kotter (1988) found needs for involvement of both high level managers and lower level management training participants. Tannenbaum and Yukl (1992) did an updated review of the literature with findings of low levels of performance similar to those of Baldwin and Ford earlier. Finally, Stolovitch—as recently as 2000—still found low transfer rates for training alone as the solution to performance problems.

The reasons for the low performance levels in these studies are not clear. Undoubtedly, many of the training interventions studied or described in Table 4.1 were not designed by a process that looked at causes other than lack of knowledge and skills. Therefore, they may have been the wrong solutions for the performance problems. Rummler and Brache confirm the opinions of many in the field (as emphasized in Chapter 2), that "about 80 percent of performance improvement opportunities reside in the [work] environment" and are not due to lack of knowledge or skills (1995, p. 73). If some programs in Table 4.1 did address actual lack of knowledge and skills, they may not have provided support for other necessary factors supporting performance (Table 2.2 and Stage 5 in Figures 3.1 and 3.2).

Need to Involve Stakeholders

The need to involve stakeholders (primarily managers, learners, and trainers) in supporting transfer of training was a logical next step. Broad and Newstrom (1992, pp. 37–39) identified seven key decisions leading to and following from the decision to train, based on the work of Gilbert, Harless, Rummler, and others, in which these three key stakeholder groups should be involved. (The first three decisions parallel the performance analysis Stages 1 through 5 of the human performance technology [HPT] process.)

As HPT has become a widely practiced approach to solving performance problems, the need to involve a range of stakeholders for both instructional and noninstructional interventions has become more obvious to performance consultants and managers. Stakeholders support performance improvement in three ways:

- Managers at various levels, performers, and performance consultants help to analyze performance problems accurately, and select and implement the appropriate interventions.

- For the approximately 80 percent of performance opportunities that Rummler and Brache (1995) find are in the work environment, managers at several levels can provide what may be lacking (usually the first four factors at the job/performer level in HPT's Stage 5: clear performance specifications, necessary resources and support, appropriate consequences, and timely and relevant feedback).

- For the 15 to 20 percent of performance opportunities that require new or improved skills and knowledge (Rummler & Brache, 1995), managers at several levels and performers can contribute to the definition of desired performance and identification of other work environment factors that also need to be addressed.

Reports of low levels of performance following training should ring the alarm bells for those who are challenged to achieve strategically important performance goals and objectives. The important news: performance improvement solutions (both instructional and noninstructional interventions) are not likely to achieve their goals without organized support from stakeholders (including performance consultants).

The studies in Table 4.1 can be a useful tool as a group. Many performance consultants—and others as well—have used these studies to convince stakeholders that training alone is not enough and that their involvement is essential for interventions to pay off in desired performance.

New Definition of Transfer of Learning to Performance

Three factors lead to the need for a new definition of *transfer*. First, the growing emphasis on *performance* as the desired outcome of organizational learning activities has shifted the focus away from the type of intervention that produces the performance. We no longer accept input measures (such as numbers of training sessions or learners) as indicators of success for the traditional "training" function; success is now measured by *performance* on the job and organizational *results*.

Second, we now have many other learning interventions besides training that can lead to the desired performance: coaching, action learning groups, e-learning, and communities of practice, to name a few. It no longer is appropriate to name a specific learning method in our definition of *transfer*.

Third, we no longer want to limit our definition of transfer as applying only to "trainees." We may want to shape the performance of customers, suppliers, users of products and services, and the public in general.

The new definition bypasses all these limitations. *Transfer of learning to performance* is the full application of new knowledge and skills to improve individual and group performance in an organization or community (adapted from Broad, 2003, p. 98).

Caution about relying on training—or any other learning method—as the sole solution is particularly important as new learning technologies and approaches emerge and seem to be the long-desired "silver bullet" that handles all problems. A healthy cynicism, plus the research on stakeholder support below, can be very useful in countering reliance on silver bullets.

Stakeholder Support for Performance

The increasing awareness of organizations as complex systems and our previous examination of stakeholders in these systems suggest further attention to how stakeholders can support improved performance. Personal experience, although highly educational, must be balanced with more rigorous examinations of the impact of stakeholder support for both instructional and noninstructional interventions.

Stakeholder Support for Performance Following Learning Interventions

A growing body of research and best practices focuses increased attention on stakeholder support to ensure that desired performance follows learning interventions. The selected research studies and best practices discussions in Table 4.2 all focus on support from stakeholders. These include the four primary stakeholders (executives and higher level managers of performers for strategic interventions and supervisors, performers, and performance consultants for all interventions) and other stakeholders in the system, as appropriate.

**Table 4.2. Research on Support by Stakeholders for
Performance Following Learning Interventions**

Researcher(s) or Author(s), Date	*Research or Publication Title*	*Summary of Findings*
Mosel (1957)	"Why Training Programs Fail to Carry Over"	Three essential conditions for transfer of learning to performance on the job are that (1) training content must be relevant to the job; (2) learners must actually learn the content; (3) learners must be motivated to apply learning to the job.
Broad (1982)	"Management Actions to Support Transfer of Training"	In the first doctoral dissertation on transfer of training to performance, eighty-four ASTD chapter presidents identified seventy-one actions by managers and supervisors as important to support transfer of training to the job before, during, and after a training activity.
Baldwin & Ford (1988)	"Transfer of Training: A Review and Directions for Future Research"	A review of research on transfer of training identified: (1) trainee characteristics that support transfer, including ability, aptitude, personality, motivation; and (2) work environment character-istics that support transfer, including: supportive organizational climate; pre-course discussion with supervisor; opportunities to apply learning on the job; and post-course goal setting and feedback.
Baldwin & Magjuka (1991)	"Organizational Training and Signals of Importance"	Learners reported four indicators, all the re-sponsibility of managers, that tell learners how important it is to the organization that they transfer specific learning to their own perfor-mance: (1) learners are accountable for using new knowledge and skills; (2) learning programs are mandatory; (3) managers brief learners in advance on importance and need for transfer of new knowledge and skills to work performance; and (4) managers demonstrate involvement in the learning activity, investing their own time and effort in the program.

Table 4.2. Research on Support by Stakeholders for
Performance Following Learning Interventions, Cont'd

Researcher(s) or Author(s), Date	Research or Publication Title	Summary of Findings
Broad & Newstrom (1992)	*Transfer of Training: Action-Packed Strategies to Ensure High Payoff from Training Investments*	Based on research and best practices: (1) managers, trainers, and learners are three primary stakeholders in transfer of training, and (2) a list is presented of seventy-nine stakeholder strategies to support transfer of learning to job performance, organized by the three primary stakeholders and three time frames (before, during, and after training).
Brinkerhoff & Montesino (1995)	"Partnerships for Training Transfer: Lessons from a Corporate Study"	A controlled study looked at the value of supervisors providing prior information and follow-up support for transfer of learning to the job. Compared to learners in the control group, learners in the treatment group reported significantly higher levels of skills applied to their jobs. The treatment group's supervisors had (1) discussed importance of new skills with learners before and after the training; (2) provided frequent practice opportunities following training; and (3) held learners accountable for applying learning to their jobs.
Xiao (1996)	"The Relationship Between Organizational Factors and the Transfer of Training in the Electronics Industry"	Worker performance following training was compared for Chinese electronics companies (two state-owned and two private joint ventures). Variables related to higher levels of transfer were achievement in training; matching worker's knowledge, skills, and abilities with work requirements; and supportive supervision. Higher reductions in scrap rates occurred at joint ventures with close worker involvement and discussions with supervisors.

(Continued)

**Table 4.2. Research on Support by Stakeholders for
             Performance Following Learning Interventions, Cont'd**

Researcher(s) or Author(s), Date	Research or Publication Title	Summary of Findings
Feldstein & Boothman (1997)	"Success Factors in Technology Training"	Six critical factors (three by learners, three by managers) made a significant difference in performance of learners after training. Learners who rated themselves as high performers had (1) explored content in advance of training; (2) developed clear ideas of how to apply learning on the job; and (3) practiced new skills back on the job. Managers of high performing learners had (4) discussed importance of three learner steps with learners and followed up to be sure those steps were taken; (5) discussed expectations for learner performance after training; and (6) showed how learner performance would be measured on the job.
Seitz (1997)	"Transfer Strategies for Communities: Substance Abuse Prevention"	Significant increases in transfer of learning were found when performers and their managers collaborated to bid for training opportunities before training. The bids included analysis of organizational needs for new skills and specification of desired performance after training, and showed how performance change would be measured.
Holton, Bates, & Ruona (2001)	"Development of a Generalized Learning Transfer System Inventory"	Based on a range of research studies, the authors developed a learning transfer system inventory. Sixteen factors are related to four aspects (ability, motivation to transfer, environmental influences, and secondary influences) at three outcome levels: learning, individual performance, and organizational performance.
ASTD & MASIE Center (2001)	*e-Learning: If We Build It, Will They Come?*	Four critical success factors for participation in e-learning (as well as transfer of learning to performance) include: (1) strong internal marketing in advance by supervisors and others; (2) good

Table 4.2. Research on Support by Stakeholders for
          Performance Following Learning Interventions, Cont'd

Researcher(s) or Author(s), Date	Research or Publication Title	Summary of Findings
		support from technology, subject matter experts, and managers (including time for training without distractions); (3) incentives (training seen as valuable to learners' work, careers); and (4) training is mandatory (yields high registration and participation).
Pucel & Cerrito (2001)	"Perceptions as Measures of Training Transfer"	Assessment of trainees' perceptions of applicability of learning to job performance following training is a reasonable transfer measure if gathering direct information on later performance is difficult. Only two programs were studied. Immediately after training, learners were asked to rate their perceptions of quality of instruction (high for both courses); the applicability of learning to jobs (high for both courses); and whether they would recommend training to others (yes for both).
		Six months later, follow-up surveys showed high levels of application only for the course in which learners received strong encouragement for application to the job.
Yelon, Sheppard, Sleight, & Ford (2004)	"Intention to Transfer: How Do Autonomous Professionals Become Motivated to Use New Ideas?" (*Note:* This study is also discussed in Chapter 2.)	Autonomous workers: are not required to follow set procedures; are not closely supervised on performance; decide for themselves how to operate for some or all tasks; decide whether and when to apply new knowledge and skills to their performance. Three factors determine extent of transfer: (1) credibility of new skills for improving their performance; (2) practicality of new skills for ease of transfer to jobs; and (3) recognized need to improve their own performance. Stakeholders should emphasize these three factors in support strategies.

The studies and discussions presented here cover almost half a century (1957 to 2004) and include those that the author has found particularly important, informative, and applicable. All are worth further examination. However, several studies in Table 4.2 are of particular interest:

- Baldwin and Ford (1988) in their literature review (listed also in Table 4.1) had additional findings on characteristics of the work environment that supported transfer of learning to performance on the job: a supportive organizational climate, pre-course discussions about the training with the supervisor, opportunities to apply learning back on the job, and post-course goal setting and feedback.

- Baldwin and Magjuka (1991) found four indicators that learners reported as signaling that transfer of learning to performance was important to the organization: (1) learners are held accountable for using new knowledge and skills; (2) learning programs are mandatory; (3) managers brief learners in advance on importance and need for new skills; and (4) managers are directly involved in the learning activity.

- Broad and Newstrom (1992), mentioned earlier, also identified three primary stakeholders (managers, trainers, and trainees) and listed seventy-nine stakeholder strategies to support transfer of training to performance in three time frames (before, during, and after training).

- Brinkerhoff and Montesino (1995) found three strategies by supervisors that made a significant difference in skill levels later reported by learners: (1) discussing new skills with learners before and after training; (2) providing frequent practice opportunities after training; and (3) holding learners accountable for applying the learning to their job performance.

- ASTD and the MASIE Center (2001) found three critical factors in e-learning that supported transfer of learning to performance: (1) strong internal marketing of the program in advance by supervisors and others; (2) support from managers for distraction-free training time; (3) and making training mandatory.

- The study by Yelon, Sheppard, Sleight, and Ford (2004) on factors supporting application to the job by autonomous employees has been discussed in Chapter 2. It is included again here to make Table 4.2 a comprehensive resource for access to research on stakeholder support for performance.

The evidence is overwhelming that training efforts must be supplemented by significant and visible support from key stakeholders—before, during, and after a learning activity or on a continuing basis for continual learning situations—to ensure that the desired performance actually occurs on the job. This requirement is substantiated over and over by reports from practitioners in a wide range of organizational settings (Broad, 1997a, 1997b, 2000, 2001, 2002, & 2003). In a later section in this chapter, research results and best practices in Table 4.2 are incorporated into a matrix of commonly used effective actions by stakeholders to support performance on the job.

Support for Performance Following Other Nonlearning Interventions

Other approaches are emerging that have strong implications for enhanced performance but lie outside the usual boundaries of planned learning and performance interventions. The new approaches all bring the learning experience right into the work experience in some way. Three recent publications, and a sidebar in this chapter, describe the stakeholders involved and how new approaches—with built-in transfer support—serve to enhance performance. They are summarized in Table 4.3.

Table 4.3. Nontraining Learning Approaches with Built-In Support for Performance

Author(s), Date	Title	Summary of Key Points Linking Learning to Performance
Wenger, McDermott, & Snyder (2002)	*Cultivating Communities of Practice*	Communities of practice are networks of performers with common interests and expertise who create, share, and exchange knowledge and ideas. These are now supported by Internet resources that allow members to interact 24/7 across space and time boundaries, finding and developing resources for immediate and future job application.

(Continued)

Table 4.3. Nontraining Learning Approaches
with Built-In Support for Performance, Cont'd

Author(s), Date	Title	Summary of Key Points Linking Learning to Performance
Svenson (February 2004)	"Learning Systems for the New Millenium"	Learning opportunities beyond training are increasing; managers must play an active role in managing learning through a "balanced and integrated array of learning strategies" focusing directly on job performance. These may include: • Coaching by managers, co-workers, professional coaches; • Knowledge management systems; • Informal learning strategies to meet individual and group needs; • Holistic workplace learning strategies that bring learning directly into the workplace and involve whole teams; • Clear communication as a learning strategy; • Action learning to meet work challenges and develop learners; • Electronic performance support systems (EPSS); and • Performance-based job qualification systems.
Marquardt (2004)	*Action Learning: Solving Problems and Building Leaders in Real Time*	Bringing learning directly into work assignments, action learning involves teams of performers who explore organizational challenges. They work with a coach who guides them as they develop skills in reflective questioning and listening to resolve work issues and gain valuable organizational skills.
Finley (2005; sidebar in this chapter; not previously published)	"Stealth Training"	To improve performance of managers who evade direct training, the performance consultant can develop a form or mechanism to be used in following some new approach. During planning meetings the manager is "oriented" (via stealth training) to use of the new approach and receives coaching and feedback from the performance consultant as needed.

Communities of Practice

Networks of *performers* (within or across organizations) called *communities of practice* that coalesce around common interests and expertise are a longstanding custom that has greatly expanded with Internet support. These interactive groups have become an increasingly important component of a knowledge-focused organization. They offer long-range development opportunities through sharing information and ideas, as well as immediate just-in-time assistance to many performers who can seek answers to challenges on a 24/7 basis (Wenger, McDermott, & Snyder, 2002). (Also see the discussion of communities of practice in Chapter 9, e-Learning and Support for Performance.)

New Learning Systems

The rapidity of change requires *leaders* and *managers* in organizations to proactively accept responsibility for managing learning in new ways beyond more traditional training (Svenson, 2004). Similarly, performance consultants must stretch their capabilities to include new learning technologies and models beyond training. They must also support managers in learning about and developing *new learning systems* to meet evolving strategic requirements, including training, e-learning, and nontraining learning architectures such as Svenson suggests.

In the following list of strategies, titles (in bold) are reprinted from Svenson's article with ISPI's permission; the comments following each strategy title are my own descriptions and discussions of that strategy.

Coaching. As a recognized development strategy by managers, professional coaches, and co-workers, coaching may require new skills and work methods for managers and co-workers. It will also require acceptance throughout organizational systems as a useful resource for performance improvement.

Knowledge Management Systems. KM systems are now well established as essential resources for learning and performance in many organizations. They capture, organize, and make readily available the knowledge, skills, and experiences of performers throughout complex systems.

Informal Learning Strategies. Chat rooms, "brown bag" breakfasts and lunches, and ad hoc mentoring pair-ups are becoming common in many organizational systems. These informal strategies promote both general and issue-oriented collaborative learning.

Clear Communication as a Learning Strategy. Written, graphic, and spoken communication can make information delivery and performance guidance more accessible and efficient. Careful organization of content with the users' purpose in mind, plus effective use of charts, graphics, and other visual techniques, can deliver information clearly, rapidly, and precisely when needed.

Electronic Performance Support Systems (EPSS). These work site systems guide workers step-by-step through work applications. Learning may occur, but actual performance is the objective.

Performance-Based Qualification Systems. These systems prepare performers for specific performance requirements. They may also "certify" performers according to set criteria.

Action Learning

Introduced by Reg Revins in the Welsh and English coal mines in the 1940s, action learning is another well-developed approach gaining widespread application to address tough organizational challenges. It involves a team of performers, a coach, and processes for exploration, learning, and taking action. This approach provides a double payoff: gaining solutions to resolve organizational problems while developing highly valuable skills and abilities in reflective questioning and listening in individuals, teams, and organizations (Marquardt, 2004).

STEALTH TRAINING, ANOTHER NONLEARNING INTERVENTION
Ken W. Finley, Jr.

A vice president from a major industrial firm once stated, "Training is what upper management tells middle management to do to the rank and file." This effectively eliminates two-thirds of the organization structure from the benefits of training. Rarely have managers or supervisors found it necessary to attend the same training as their employees. Often, the perception is that the time requirement is too high or that the training is not correctly focused for management.

As a result, we lose manager support for transfer of learning to performance by their employees, in terms of motivation and commonality of language and objectives. Organizations have tried compressing days or weeks of training into a one- to four-hour overview for managers, usually with all the interactive stuff (polite word substituted) left out. This strategy almost never works out as hoped.

Enter "Stealth Training." This is getting people to exhibit the appropriate performance at the appropriate time, without telling them they are being trained. We do this with managers, first by developing tools for them to use and then by coaching them in their use under the guise of "planning meetings." (For employees, we would call this training, but not for managers.) An example of such a tool is shown in Figure 4.1.

Figure 4.1. Performance Analysis: Asking the Right Questions

By Kenneth W. Finley, Jr.

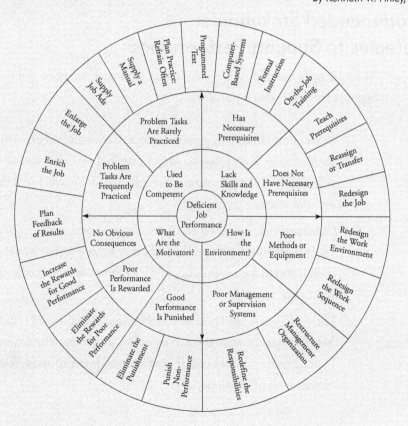

The second and equally important step is maintaining the expectation that managers have used the tools and setting subsequent meeting objectives to reinforce behaviors that can only be achieved by using the tools. The expectation and attitude that this is "what professionals do" reinforces the stealth training objectives and outcomes.

For the Stealth Training facilitator who wants to ensure transfer of this learning to performance, there is one caution—an absolute standard of facilitator performance. Never leave tools to be completed by managers at a later time. It rarely happens. Schedule a time and sit down with the manager(s) to complete the tool. It's just like conducting training by completing a job aid in class. But we won't tell them that.

Recommended Stakeholder Strategies to Support Performance

As we identify many possible stakeholder strategies, we need some way to organize them for several purposes.

1. As we communicate to primary stakeholders—and others—that their support is necessary to support desired performance, we must tell them what specific actions are envisioned, by which stakeholders, and when.

2. Important stakeholders then review the proposed strategies to select those most appropriate, add other strategies that would be useful, and make a commitment to act on those strategies at the right time.

3. The performance consultant, collaborating with primary stakeholders, uses the revised list of strategies to monitor the actions by stakeholders and to collect data as appropriate to assess the effectiveness of the strategies.

The Transfer Matrix, a Tool for Managing Stakeholder Transfer Strategies

A very flexible tool is a matrix of transfer strategies, successfully used by many organizations that recognize the need to involve stakeholders and plan and track their support actions (see examples in Chapters 7, 8, and 9 of this book and in Broad, 1997a, 1997b, 2000, 2001, 2002, 2003). An up-to-date recommended template of the transfer matrix is shown in Exhibit 4.1.

Exhibit 4.1. Recommended Template for the Transfer Strategies Matrix

Stakeholders	Before Intervention	During Intervention →| → After Intervention
Executives, Managers		
Supervisors, Team Leaders		
Performers		
Performance Consultants		
Evaluators		
Performance Partners		
Co-Workers		
Subject-Matter Experts		
Clients, Customers, Users		
Suppliers		
Regulators		
Union Representatives		
Special Interest Group Representatives		

(Continued)

Exhibit 4.1. Recommended Template for the Transfer Strategies Matrix, Cont'd

Stakeholders	Before Intervention	During Intervention →│→ After Intervention
Community Residents		
Mentors, Sponsors, Funders		
Others		

Adapted from Broad (2003).

Notes: (1) Many interventions now focus on ongoing performance improvement, with no definite break between "during" and "after" the intervention. Many transfer strategies may be carried over from "during" into "after," thus merging the third and fourth columns of the matrix. The exception is more traditional classroom training, which has a clear separation between "during" and "after" back on the job. (2) Primary stakeholders and other important stakeholders should be selected from those listed here for each performance improvement intervention, depending on the situation.

The transfer matrix has been a successful tool for communicating with stakeholders, capturing their revisions and confirming their commitments to act on the strategies, and tracking and managing implementation of stakeholder strategies for each intervention. In the template, the four primary stakeholders are listed in the left column. Other typical stakeholders are also listed; however, only those appropriate for the particular intervention and the organizational setting should be selected. There may be other stakeholders appropriate for that situation who are not listed on the template. The identification of key stakeholders is one of the first steps in managing performance improvement interventions in complex systems, discussed further in Chapter 6.

The other three columns of the template show stakeholder strategies before, during, and after a performance intervention. Note that the "during" and "after" columns are divided by a dashed vertical line. This reflects the fact that many interventions are ongoing. The resulting performance improvement is also ongoing, so the "during" and "after" time periods may merge. (A more traditional classroom intervention and many e-learning programs may have a clear "after" column for strategies back on the job.) Each stakeholder row of the template shows all strategies by a given stakeholder group across the three time frames.

This formulation of the transfer matrix has evolved over time, and the matrix may well continue to change to meet future needs. Key points in the evolution to date include:

- Lists of actions by managers to support transfer of training across time periods (pre-training, during training, job linkage, and follow-up) and an illustrative diagram (Broad, 1980);

- Lists of actions by managers to support transfer of training across time periods (pre-training, during training, job linkage, and follow-up) and suggestions on their use by human resource development practitioners (Broad, 1982);

- Lists of strategies by managers, trainers, and trainees to support transfer of training across time periods (before, during, following), illustrated by an unfilled nine-cell matrix diagram (Broad & Newstrom, 1992);

- A four-column matrix with multiple stakeholders listed down the first column and actions for each stakeholder to support transfer of learning entered in the next three columns (before, during, after) (Broad, 1997a, 1997b, 2000, 2001, 2002, 2003);

- A four-column matrix with multiple stakeholders in the first column and actions for each stakeholder to support performance improvement interventions in the next three columns (before, during, after), but with last two columns (during, after) separated by a dotted line to show possible merger of these time periods for ongoing performance improvement situations (Exhibit 4.1 in this chapter);

- A seven-column "transfer scaffold" for a primarily *noninstructional* organizational change intervention. The scaffold has four columns for stakeholders and support strategies (before, during, after), and three additional columns for information on "What's in It for Stakeholders," "Barriers to Actions/Success," and "Countermeasures" (in Hile's Chapter 7 in this book).

Transfer Matrix of Research-Based Strategies

The research studies and best practices shown in Tables 4.2 and 4.3 provide many suggestions for effective stakeholder strategies to support performance improvement interventions (instructional and noninstructional). Strategies from Table 4.2, and several from Table 4.3, are consolidated and organized into a transfer matrix of recommended strategies for primary stakeholders and evaluators (who are frequently involved in performance improvement interventions), Table 4.4. (The strategies suggested by Svenson in Table 4.3 are not included in Table 4.4; those strategies are very dependent on the culture of the complex system and should be included as appropriate.)

Table 4.4 provides a detailed list of many recommended strategies—before, during, and after an intervention—to support the desired performance. *Caution:* many of the strategies may not be appropriate for a particular complex organizational system, so stakeholders should review them and select those that fit the system. Also, there probably are strategies that would be effective in some organizational systems that are not listed here. Stakeholders should look for additional strategies that may be unique and very effective in their complex systems.

Most of the listed strategies in Table 4.4 are for use by the primary stakeholders (executives and managers of performers, supervisors and team leaders, performance consultants, and performers). Table 4.4 also adds recommended strategies for evaluators who are frequently involved in strategic interventions; these are not based on research, but result from the author's experience and that of experienced evaluators (Hodges, 2002; Phillips & Stone, 2002).

Possible strategies by *performance partners* and the many other potential stakeholders in Table 2.1 are not given in Table 4.4. These stakeholders and their strategies are very much dependent on the specific situation in the organizational system, so should be identified as a performance intervention is developed in that system. (See Chapter 6.)

**Table 4.4. Recommended Transfer Strategies
for Primary Stakeholders and Evaluators**

Stakeholders	Before Intervention	During Intervention	After Intervention
Executives, Managers of Performers	Approve performance intervention, provide funds Approve evaluation metrics Establish baseline performance data Communicate strategic importance of new performance objectives Emphasize credibility and practicality of new learning to performers Identify and involve other stakeholders Contribute to planning and design of intervention Make participation mandatory for performers Provide training in coaching skills to supervisors Establish rewards for desired new performance Establish online communities of practice for performers	Personally introduce sessions Provide attractive venue for intervention Reinforce strategic importance of new performance goals to other stakeholders Keep organization informed on progress of intervention	Regularly monitor progress of intervention Require briefings on evaluation metrics (Levels 1, 2, 3, 4 as needed) Monitor outcomes, results of new performance Applaud business units that show involvement, progress, and results Maintain alliances with other stakeholders Publicize success outside organization Request reports on usage of *communities of practice*
Supervisors, Team Leaders	Involve staff in performance gap analysis Identify specific performance requirements Select performers Brief performers on purposes, performance objectives	Lead or introduce sessions Participate in intervention's activities Protect performers from interruptions Assign performers' work to others while in intervention	Provide practice opportunities immediately, frequently Demonstrate new performance Discuss action plans with performers, co-workers

(Continued)

**Table 4.4. Recommended Transfer Strategies
for Primary Stakeholders and Evaluators, Cont'd**

Stakeholders	Before Intervention	During Intervention	After Intervention
Supervisors, Team Leaders (cont'd)	Emphasize credibility and practicality of new learning to performers Confer with performance consultants on barriers Provide time for performers to complete pre-work Plan with performers on applying new skills to job Demonstrate new skills Participate in *communities of practice*	Monitor attendance Encourage performers to participate actively Help performers develop action plans for applying learning to jobs Provide distraction-free time for learning Assist evaluators in collecting Levels 1, 2 data Support findings, proposals, and suggestions from *communities of practice*	Schedule briefings by performers to others Monitor performers' application of new skills, provide prompt feedback Remove performance barriers Arrange for coaching for performers as needed Assist evaluators in collecting Levels 3 and 4 data Continue support and participation in *communities of practice*
Performers	Participate in performance analyses, design, and briefings on intervention Confer with supervisor on performance objectives, barriers, applying skills to job Consider evidence of credibility and practicality of new learning Accept need for own performance improvement Complete all pre-work Participate in *communities of practice*	Attend all sessions Participate actively Discuss credibility and practicality of new learning Provide real work examples Identify barriers to application Develop realistic action plans Provide Levels 1 and 2 data Plan support groups on job Discuss support from *communities of practice*	Discuss action plan with supervisor Practice new skills promptly Assess own performance improvement Work with others to remove barriers, apply new skills Use job aids, materials on job Provide Levels 3 and 4 data Provide data on intervention to *communities of practice*
Performance Consultants	Involve executives, managers, supervisors, and performers in performance analyses, intervention design, barriers,	Lead or support sessions Integrate pre-work information into design, activities	Work with supervisors to plan support for performers Observe performers on the job to assess use of new skills

**Table 4.4. Recommended Transfer Strategies
for Primary Stakeholders and Evaluators, Cont'd**

Stakeholders	Before Intervention	During Intervention	After Intervention
Performance Consultants (cont'd)	performance objectives, metrics, evaluation plans Coach all stakeholders on transfer roles, strategies Develop pre-work materials Design relevant activities Emphasize credibility and practicality of new learning to performers Work with evaluators on instruments, plans Use good adult learning and organizational change methods throughout Suggest action learning projects Develop stealth training for managers	Involve performers in activities, use feedback to revise methods, materials Provide realistic job aids Aid performers in working on realistic exercises Provide individualized feedback to performers Help performers develop realistic action plans Assist evaluators in collecting Levels 1, 2 data Propose action learning projects to learners Provide stealth training for selected managers	Provide additional coaching as needed Maintain contact with performers and supervisors Assist evaluators in collecting Levels 3 and 4 data Review all evaluation data, revise intervention as needed Coach supervisors to remove barriers to performance Assess effectiveness of action learning projects, report to higher levels Evaluate success of stealth training projects, propose to higher-level managers as appropriate
Evaluators	Work with executives, managers, supervisors, and performance consultants on performance analyses, objectives, design, metrics, barriers, evaluation plans Develop instruments for Levels 1, 2, 3, 4 as needed Incorporate transfer support items into evaluation instruments	Brief performers on evaluation plans Plan good test environment Collect Levels 1 and 2 data Collect information from performers on barriers to application of new skills in the workplace, confidence in new skills	Collect Level 3 and 4 data Calculate ROI if wanted Assess use of stakeholder strategies before, during, and after intervention Assist in briefing executives, managers, supervisors, performance consultants, and performers on evaluation outcomes (Levels 1, 2, 3, 4, ROI) and use of stakeholder strategies

(Continued)

**Table 4.4. Recommended Transfer Strategies
for Primary Stakeholders and Evaluators, Cont'd**

Stakeholders	Before Intervention	During Intervention	After Intervention
Evaluators (cont'd)	Assist in documenting all stakeholder strategies for later assessments		Make recommendations on revision of intervention

Example of a Transfer Matrix

A transfer matrix currently in use to support a learning intervention in one complex organizational system is shown in Table 4.5. As mentioned in Chapter 2, the National Weather Service has launched an online synchronous and asynchronous training system for forecasters called Advanced Warning Operations Course (AWOC). The managers of the training system (the Warning Decisions Training Branch) identified eleven stakeholder groups or individuals, listed in the left column of the table. The strategies that they are encouraged or committed to take—before, during, and after forecasters are involved in the training—appear in the next three columns.

**Table 4.5. Transfer of Training Matrix, National Weather Service,
Planned AWOC Stakeholder Strategies (September 2004)**

AWOC Stakeholders	Before Training	During Training	After Training
NWS Director	Announce high priority of AWOC and stress strategic mission link to goals Participate in video that promotes AWOC	Receive progress reports of AWOC from Office/Regional Director	Report AWOC success stories to NOAA executives
Office of Climate, Water, and Weather Services Director (OCWWS)	Report to Corporate Board on metrics of AWOC completion	Authorize appropriate recognition and rewards for completion	Support additional measures to improve performance

Table 4.5. Transfer of Training Matrix, National Weather Service,
Planned AWOC Stakeholder Strategies (September 2004), Cont'd

AWOC Stakeholders	Before Training	During Training	After Training
Regional Directors	State high priority of AWOC, link to excellence of service (saving of lives and property) in warning program achievable through training in AWOC Ensure local office AWOC progress reports are submitted	Ensure that offices report progress	Report success stories Receive Level 3 evaluation reports
Meteorologists in Charge and Hydrologists in Charge (MICs/HICs)	State AWOC as one of top training priorities and best opportunities to improve warning performance in 2004—2005 Allow dedicated training time for all forecasters to complete training Put AWOC in local office training plans	Monitor office progress Schedule periodic briefings with the SOO (or DOH) Work with staff on scheduling and attendance commitments Provide dedicated training time to complete AWOC Provide regular reports to regional directors on status of AWOC completion	Report success stories Schedule periodic briefings with SOO (or DOH) on further performance requirements
Regional Scientific Services Division (SSD) Chiefs	Market AWOC Receive AWOC scheduling milestones	Track AWOC progress for each office (milestones are met) Encourage office completion Compare office to office completion rates	Report success stories

(Continued)

**Table 4.5. Transfer of Training Matrix, National Weather Service,
Planned AWOC Stakeholder Strategies (September 2004), Cont'd**

AWOC Stakeholders	Before Training	During Training	After Training
Office of Services (Training Division) Director (OS6)	Work with FRG (Field Requirements Group) to define future AWOC requirements and implementation	Work with FRG (Field Requirements Group) to define future AWOC requirements and implementation	Provide a centralized evaluation function for standardizing practices across OS6
Weather Decisions Training Branch (WDTB)	Provide orientation session to MICs and Regional HQs on importance of management support for successful AWOC training transfer Develop and distribute a video to advertise and promote AWOC Develop training Provide ample opportunities in scheduling teletraining sessions Develop evaluation practices and instruments	Deliver training Collect Level 1 and 2 evaluation measures Report rates of completion	Collect Level 3 data on performance measures Provide reinforcement exercises to maintain proficiency
Development and Operations Hydrologists and Science and Operations Officers (DOHs/SOOs)	Attend Facilitator Workshop Go through AWOC Help assess learner needs Choose appropriate lessons in each track	Facilitate AWOC Track course completion of each forecaster via LMS Schedule periodic briefings with the MIC on student performance Report success stories	Support Level 3 evaluation collection process Meet with each forecaster to discuss additional training needs Reinforce AWOC objectives with seasonal drills

Table 4.5. Transfer of Training Matrix, National Weather Service, Planned AWOC Stakeholder Strategies (September 2004), Cont'd

AWOC Stakeholders	Before Training	During Training	After Training
Warning Coordination Meteorologists at Local Offices (WCMs)	Market AWOC internally and externally	Take AWOC training Help SOO monitor progress of students in AWOC	Solicit feedback from customers on NWS performance Work with MIC, SOO to assess forecaster performance issues Record local success stories of warning performance
Forecasters	Plan with SOO how to best complete the course	Work with co-workers and local management on scheduling and attendance commitments Complete training requirements Complete Level 1 and 2 evaluation Develop a personal action plan to correct weak areas	Complete 2 WES simulations Implement action plan to improve personal performance
Union Representative	Review AWOC plan for 2004–2005 with WDTB		

Note: Strategies *before* and *after* training are usually to support *performance*. Strategies *during* training are usually to support *learning*.

Initial delivery of AWOC is underway as this book goes to press, so the matrix must be considered a work in progress. Revisions in stakeholder strategies are likely during delivery (through September 2005), as reinforcement exercises are developed and used, and as evaluations are completed of participant reactions, learning, and performance on the job. (Evaluation of organizational results may be undertaken in the near future.)

Summary of This Chapter

Many research studies pinpoint the low levels of desired performance that organizations typically experience, often following some intervention designed to heighten that performance. This common experience of many organizations, with performance well below desired levels even after efforts to improve it, should heighten the awareness of performance consultants and other organizational change experts on the need to bring key stakeholders into the intervention processes.

A growing body of research demonstrates the importance of stakeholder support for improved performance. The studies summarized in this chapter provide many useful strategies for stakeholder support to improve the payoff from performance interventions. Recommended strategies, based on research, have been organized into a transfer strategies matrix for the four primary stakeholder groups. The strategies are clustered according to time periods, before, during, and after the intervention, with the "during" and "after" time periods merging for ongoing performance improvement interventions. Of course, there will probably be other useful transfer support strategies for stakeholders in a specific organizational system, and stakeholders are encouraged to search for these.

Recommended strategies for evaluators, a common additional stakeholder group, have been added to the matrix of recommended transfer strategies. Evaluators should be involved as stakeholders from the beginning of planning for any intervention that will have an evaluation component, as many strategic interventions will. The evaluator strategies shown in the matrix are not necessarily research-based; they are included as best practices based on the experience of evaluation experts.

In almost every performance improvement intervention, there will be additional stakeholders who can provide valuable support for performance following the intervention. Performance consultants, who generally are most aware of the need to involve key stakeholders, should work with the other primary stakeholders to identify and bring other stakeholders into the intervention's planning and implementation. Suggestions on enlisting stakeholders are given in Chapter 6.

In the next chapter, we look at evaluation as a tool to support performance. Evaluation can measure the impact of an intervention in several ways. Recent developments in evaluation approaches can also give direct support for performance. Finally, the evaluator can be a supportive stakeholder in strengthening the intervention itself.

Suggestions for Further Reading

There are relatively few resources in performance improvement that address stakeholders as essential players in complex systems. Some that may be useful to readers are listed below.

Broad, Mary L., & Newstrom, John W. (1992). *Transfer of training: Action-packed strategies to ensure high payoff from training investments.* New York: Perseus Books Group. This volume is the first to our knowledge to address the transfer problem. Of particular interest to readers may be the list of seventy-nine strategies by primary stakeholders in Appendix A, and Chapter 3, "Managing Transfer of Training."

Greer, Michael. (1999). Planning and managing human performance technology projects. In Harold D. Stolovitch & Erica J. Keeps (Eds.), *Handbook of human performance technology* (2nd ed.). San Francisco: Pfeiffer. This chapter addresses primarily the tasks of the project manager, but also identifies key stakeholders (sponsors, project team members, subject matter experts, suppliers, regulators, and the public) and their roles.

Hale, Judith. (2003). *Performance-based management: What every manager should do to get results.* San Francisco: Pfeiffer. This book is aimed at first-line managers and supervisors as well as performance consultants, and it includes a CD with tools to modify for the reader's use. It provides techniques and guidelines, plus examples, on helping people be more productive.

5

Evaluation to Measure and Support Performance

EVALUATION IS an increasingly important tool for the performance consultant and the manager. Current and emerging evaluation approaches can precisely measure outcomes of instructional performance improvement interventions. They also can support performance on the job by helping performers analyze their work situations and plan—and later assess their success in—application of new knowledge and skills on the job.

This chapter focuses on:

- Evaluation as a tool to measure and support performance
- Levels of evaluation of training interventions
- The role of evaluators in supporting learning and performance

Evaluation as a Tool to Measure and Support Performance

The old saying holds true: "You don't get what you *expect,* you get what you *inspect.*"

There is only one way to know whether our instructional interventions are effective in achieving *learning* (changes in behavior), are well applied by transfer of learning to *performance* (behavior and accomplishments on the job), and have the desired impact on organizational *results*. We must measure responsibly in each of these areas. Evaluation and measurement are essential components of any effort to improve performance in organizations, communities, and other settings.

Increased Focus on Both Measurement and Support

Stakeholders, including organizational decision-makers, are giving growing attention to evaluation to measure outcomes, particularly for expensive training interventions to improve workforce performance (Phillips & Stone, 2002). More often than in the past, they recognize that investments in improving strategically important performance should be measured to gauge their effectiveness, just as other strategically important organizational efforts such as product development, delivery of services, safety, and security are measured.

Recent extensions of evaluation into actual support and encouragement for improved performance add another level of value to the usual evaluation process. These evaluation approaches encourage stakeholder support and gather additional data from learners that can help them plan and implement their learning more effectively (Hodges, 2002; Lanigan, 2001; Phillips & Stone, 2002).

This chapter addresses evaluation approaches that have been developed primarily to assess the value of *instructional* interventions to improve performance. It is likely that similar evaluation approaches could be applied to *noninstructional* interventions at the individual, group, and team performer level, because those interventions are also aimed at improving performance and are often necessary to support instruction.

In this chapter we will not attempt to cover the entire field of evaluation. There are many excellent resources that present wide-ranging and up-to-date learning-related evaluation concepts, procedures, and examples (such as Hodges, 2002, & Phillips & Stone, 2002). We will summarize basic evaluation principles and focus on new developments that support improved performance as well as measure it.

Why Evaluation Is Important for Learning and Performance

Performance consultants and managers increasingly recognize that the evaluation process lends rigor and credibility to performance improvement interventions in several ways. First, the fact that outcomes will be "inspected" (evaluated, measured, monitored, or assessed) heightens the attention that all stakeholders—performers, managers, performance consultants, and others—give to carrying out their roles in the performance improvement intervention.

The human performance technology (HPT) process, described in Chapter 3, heightens this attention by building evaluation into an intervention from the beginning (see Figure 3.1). Stages 1 and 2 of the process define a significant gap in organizational results to be addressed (such as inadequate sales, high levels of rework, or low customer satisfaction ratings). Stages 3 and 4 define the gap between the desired workforce performance to produce those results and actual performance. Then specific metrics are established to measure each desired performance and results (in terms of frequency, number, length of time, ratings, and so on).

Second, initiating the evaluation process early in project planning emphasizes the need for measurable outcomes at the planning stages and supports thorough analysis and decision-making throughout the planning, design, and implementation of the intervention. Developing evaluation methods and metrics as the project is designed focuses close attention on the desired performance and organizational results that are the project's objectives.

Third, gaining stakeholder agreement for the time and resources necessary for the evaluation process indicates that stakeholders are serious about the purposes and goals of the intervention. Also, approval by stakeholders of the metrics for the evaluation means that they hold themselves accountable for performing their roles in supporting outcomes (learning or work environment changes by the end of the intervention, subsequent performance on the job, and organizational results).

Incorporating evaluation (at the appropriate levels) into important performance improvement initiatives also gains recognition for performance consultants and evaluators as business partners, valued for their contributions to attaining the organization's strategic and lesser goals. This opens the door to further acceptance by the organizational system that evaluation is an important component of any performance-related intervention. The more detailed discussion of the various levels of evaluation below provides guidelines and examples of ways to gain valuable information that strengthens evaluation's impact.

Levels of Evaluation of Training Interventions

The most widely used approach to evaluation of training is Kirkpatrick's four-level framework (1998, first introduced in 1959). This framework remains in use primarily because it is straightforward and easy for stakeholders to understand. Many more sophisticated evaluation approaches have been developed to fill in particular niches or gaps in the framework (such as formative evaluation, return on investment, and forecasting). To summarize Kirkpatrick's four levels and their current frequency of use:

- Level 1 (the most frequently used evaluation level) measures participant reaction to and satisfaction with the learning intervention;

- Level 2 (occasionally used) shows the extent of learning by participants at the end of the learning intervention;

- Level 3 (not often used) measures the extent of application of learning by participants to job performance; and

- Level 4 (even more rarely used) measures organizational results following the learning intervention.

An important point: Whatever the highest level of evaluation used for an intervention, evaluations at each lower level must also be done. For example, an intervention evaluated at Level 4 must also be evaluated at Levels 1, 2, and 3.

Limitations of Kirkpatrick's Four-Level Framework

There are two important points to consider about the Kirkpatrick framework. First, it is widely assumed that there is a causative link between the levels. That is, users new to the framework assume that good Level 1 ratings are important in order to have good Level 2 results, and that these imply good

Level 3 measures of transfer of training on the job and good Level 4 measures of organizational results. However, extensive research (Holton, 1996) has shown no direct causal links between the levels; good ratings at one level do not necessarily lead to good ratings at another level.

Second, it is also widely assumed that Level 3 data (extent of transfer of learning to job performance) are measures of the effectiveness of the training intervention. However, research and analyses since 1955 show that there are many factors in the organization and work environment that affect transfer of learning to job performance, only one of which is the quality of the training program (Broad & Newstrom, 1992; Rummler & Brache, 1995; Rummler, 2004). Level 2 evaluations measure effectiveness of the training program at supporting performance in the classroom or learning situation. Level 3 evaluations should be considered as measures of effectiveness of workplace support for performance, as well as possible measures of the training program's effectiveness in supporting performance.

In recent years, experienced evaluators have added another level to Kirkpatrick's traditional four levels. This is called Level 5, Return on Investment (ROI), the monetary value of organizational results due to training compared to costs (for example, Phillips & Stone, 2002). These five levels, the information gathered, and their uses in supporting learning and performance are shown in Table 5.1.

Table 5.1. **Levels of Evaluation of Training, Information Gathered, and Uses to Support Learning and Performance**

Level of Evaluation	Information Gathered	Uses to Support Learning and Performance
1	Learner's identification of: • Reaction to and satisfaction with program • Level of confidence in transferring new learning to job performance	• Can be somewhat useful to improve program design and delivery • Suggests need for more practice, coaching, or program revision

(Continued)

Table 5.1. **Levels of Evaluation of Training, Information Gathered, and Uses to Support Learning and Performance, Cont'd**

Level of Evaluation	Information Gathered	Uses to Support Learning and Performance
	• Action plans to transfer new learning to job performance • Potential workplace barriers to transfer of learning to performance • Use of support strategies by other stakeholders before and during program	• Provides motivation for later transfer of learning to job performance • Motivates stakeholders to remove potential barriers • Motivates stakeholders to use planned stakeholder strategies before and during program
2	Learners' accomplishment of program's learning objectives at end of program	• Reinforces learners for learning gained • Motivates learners to close any learning gaps found
3	Learners' identification of: • Learners' transfer of learning to job performance after short time on job • Implementation of action plans • Actual workplace barriers to performance, if they were removed and by whom • Strategies by other stakeholders to support performance on the job	• Identifies extent of transfer of learning to job performance; if low, raises questions on worksite support for performance, effectiveness of program • Measures completion of action plans; reminds learners to complete action plans • Identifies actual barriers found; motivates managers to act promptly to remove barriers • Measures use of planned stake-holder strategies after program; reminds stakeholders to use strategies
4	Organizational results	• Identifies improved organizational results due to program • Motivates performers to maintain new performance

Table 5.1. Levels of Evaluation of Training, Information Gathered,
and Uses to Support Learning and Performance, Cont'd

Level of Evaluation	Information Gathered	Uses to Support Learning and Performance
5	Return on investment (ROI)	• Identifies costs compared to benefits (improved organizational results) in monetary terms • Motivates performers to maintain new performance

Levels 1 through 4 are adapted from Kirkpatrick (1998). Level 5 is adapted from Phillips and Stone (2002).

All training interventions need not be evaluated at the same levels. Phillips and Stone (2002, p. 19) give an example of the way one large company sets evaluation targets:

- All interventions are evaluated at Level 1 (reaction, satisfaction, plus action-planning).

- About 50 percent of the interventions are evaluated up to Level 2 (learning by the end of the intervention).

- Some 30 percent of interventions are evaluated up to Level 3 (extent of application to job performance).

- Only 20 percent of interventions are evaluated up through Level 4 (organizational results).

- Only the most important training interventions (about 10 percent of the total) are evaluated at all levels up through Level 5, ROI.

These percentages match the ease and cost of the evaluation: easiest and least costly for Level 1, most challenging and most costly for Level 5.

The following sections discuss the information gathered at each of the levels. Recent advances in information gathered at some levels have added strength to the evaluation process for both measuring and supporting learning and performance.

Level 1 Evaluation

Typically, data for Level 1 evaluations are gathered at the end of the learning intervention, before learners have had an opportunity to apply their new knowledge and skills to their work. These evaluations focus on getting learners' opinions about the program: How good or useful was the content? How effective the methodology? How skillful the facilitator? and so on. This information has some utility in suggesting possible areas for program revision, but does not provide a sound basis for making decisions (Phillips & Stone, 2002). Therefore, Level 1 evaluations—although relatively easy to collect—have frequently been dismissed as not providing much significant or useful information.

However, recently developed additions to typical items in Level 1 instruments immediately following the program (such as Lanigan, 2001) can provide very usable information in areas that support job performance:

- Learners' levels of confidence in applying new learning to the job;

- Learners' action plans for transferring learning to job performance;

- Learners' perceptions of potential workplace barriers to transfer of new learning; and

- Learner reports on use of support strategies by other stakeholders, before and during the program.

Please note that the following examples of items for each of these four Level 1 areas are suggestions only, meant to be adapted or reformulated to suit the specific learning situation.

Learners' Level of Confidence in Applying New Skills

Learners can be asked to assess their level of confidence in transferring new learning to job performance after they complete a learning intervention. This may provide some suggestions on possible revisions to the program. It may also signal a need for more practice, coaching, or other stakeholder support for the individual to improve the likelihood of effective performance on the job. Exhibit 5.1 shows two examples of items on confidence levels. (Also see Phillips & Stone, 2002.)

Exhibit 5.1. Examples of Level 1 Items on Learner's Level of Confidence

Example 1: Estimate your level of confidence (as a percentage) in performing the new skills you learned in this program. (Complete confidence = 100 percent; No confidence = 0 percent)

My level of confidence is _____ percent.

Example 2: Below are listed the important learning objectives for this program. For each objective, please indicate your level of confidence, as a percentage, in applying that learning on your job. Then, for any confidence levels below 75 percent,* please suggest actions by yourself or others that could increase your level of confidence in applying that learning.

Learning Objectives	*My level of confidence (%)*	*For confidence levels below 75 percent, suggest actions by self or others to increase confidence level*	
		Action	*By whom*
1.			
2.			
3.			
4.			

*Note that the 75 percent confidence level in Example 2 is arbitrarily chosen; a different percentage could be identified as the confidence level below which actions should be suggested.

Learners' Action Plans for Applying New Learning on the Job

Learners can be asked to specify how they plan to transfer their new learning to the job. Developing action plans helps learners become very specific on their planned application of new skills, and thus provides motivation for transferring learning to job performance. This can be used also as the "before" question for a later Level 3 "after" question on how well they were able to implement their plan (Hodges, 2002). The Level 1 question could be open-ended or more specifically linked to program objectives. Exhibit 5.2 shows three examples of relatively simple items on action plans for Level 1 instruments. A more complex action plan is presented and discussed in Chapter 8 in this book (Exhibit 8.2 and related text). More extensive and detailed action plan examples are provided in many evaluation resources in the literature, such as Hodges (2002) and Phillips and Stone (2002).

Exhibit 5.2. Examples of Level 1 Items on Action Plans

Example 1: What do you plan to do differently on your job, to apply what you have learned in this program?

Example 2: Select one of the learning objectives for this program that is particularly important for you in your job, and summarize it briefly here:

Please indicate the steps you will take to apply this learning on your job:

Step Number	Action	Proposed Completion Date

Exhibit 5.2. Examples of Level 1 Items on Action Plans, Cont'd

Example 3: The learning objectives for this program are listed in the table below. For each objective, please indicate one or two actions that you plan to take to apply that learning on your job.

Learning Objectives	*Actions I Plan to Take*
1.	a. b.
2.	a. b.
3.	a. b.

Learners' Perceptions of Potential Barriers in the Workplace

Learners can be asked to identify any potential barriers in the workplace that might interfere with their transfer of learning to performance (Phillips & Stone, 2002). Two examples of such items are in Exhibit 5.3. If significant patterns emerge from learners' responses, performance consultants and managers can use Table 2.2 (Factors That Support Performers in Complex Systems) to identify the stakeholders who can help to eliminate barriers (often the managers or supervisors themselves). Then Table 4.4 (Recommended Transfer Strategies for Primary Stakeholders and Evaluators) can help stakeholders (again, often managers or supervisors) identify strategies that would eliminate or lessen the impact of those barriers and improve the likelihood of effective performance on the job.

Exhibit 5.3. Examples of Level 1 Items on Potential Workplace Barriers

Example 1: In your workplace, are there any conditions or barriers that might interfere with the application of your learning to your job? List them below.
Be as specific as possible.

Example 2: Please check any of the following potential barriers on your job that you
believe might interfere with your application of your learning. Check all
that are likely to occur in your situation.

___ Lack of practice opportunities   ___ Lack of time to plan application

___ Lack of support by supervisor   ___ Lack of support from co-workers

___ Interference from other tasks   ___ Lack of necessary information

___ Lack of equipment, technology   ___ Negative consequences

___ Other barriers (be as specific as possible):

_____

_____

_____

_____

_____

_____

_____

_____

_____

_____

Learner Reports on Stakeholder Support Strategies Before and During the Program

Learners may be asked to identify any stakeholder support strategies that they observed before or during the program. Knowing that this question will be asked in the evaluation is a strong motivator for stakeholders to be sure to carry out the support strategies they had planned. The examples in Exhibit 5.4 should be tailored to include the specific stakeholder strategies that were planned for each program that is being evaluated.

Exhibit 5.4. Examples of Level 1 Items on Support Strategies by Other Stakeholders

Example 1: Did your supervisor or manager brief you about the learning program in advance of the start of the program? ___ Yes ___ No

If "Yes" please indicate one or two points that you recall from that briefing:

1. _____

2. _____

Example 2: Did any of the following events occur before or during the program you just completed? Please check all that may apply.

Before the program started:

___ My supervisor or manager briefed me about the program's importance.

___ My supervisor indicated how I would be expected to apply what I learned.

___ The program facilitator gave me pre-work to be completed before the program.

___ One or more co-workers and I were scheduled to take the program together.

(Continued)

Exhibit 5.4. Examples of Level 1 Items on Support Strategies by Other Stakeholders, Cont'd

During the program:

___ My supervisor assigned my work to others, so I would not have a backlog when I returned to my job.

___ My supervisor protected me from work-related interruptions during the program.

___ My manager or supervisor introduced the program.

___ My manager or supervisor participated in one or more portions of the program.

Note: The "before" and "during" items should be tailored to the stakeholder strategies planned for the specific learning intervention.

Level 2 Evaluations

Level 2 evaluations measure the extent of the learner's accomplishment of learning objectives at the end of the intervention. The measures often include pre-tests (that measure how much of the program's content the learner already knows before being involved in the intervention) and post-tests (that measure how much more of the content the learner has gained by the end of the intervention). Level 2 measures (both pre and post) should be as close as possible to the actual work performance and setting so that they accurately measure accomplishment of the desired knowledge and skills.

Level 2 post-test results for all participants in an intervention are essential before attempts at Level 3 evaluations are made, for if the participants did not learn from the intervention, they will not be able to perform in the workplace. If they did learn the necessary knowledge and skills from the intervention, then inadequate performance on the job is most likely a result of inadequate workplace support and not a measure of effectiveness of the intervention.

The outcomes of Level 2 pre-tests should be communicated clearly to each individual as an incentive to accomplish the desired learning throughout the program. Post-test results should also be communicated to each individual as feedback on what has been learned. This provides reinforcement for learning and an incentive to close any remaining learning gaps that are found.

Level 3 Evaluations

The extent of transfer of skills and knowledge to performance in the work setting is measured by Level 3 evaluations. Data for these evaluations are typically gathered three to six months after the intervention, although other time frames can be selected as appropriate. Phillips and Stone (2002, p. 122) show several data-collection methods often used for Level 3 evaluations: follow-up questionnaires and surveys, observations on the job, follow-up interviews and focus groups, work assignments, action planning, performance contracting, and follow-up sessions. These methods are widely covered in the evaluation literature.

Anecdotal information can be a powerful addition to more complete evaluation data at Level 3. Stories of instances of performance on the job can illustrate both challenges and successes in developing new behaviors and new accomplishments. Stakeholders should keep an eye out for good stories to round out the picture of the intervention as it is implemented.

If transfer of new skills to performance is lower than hoped, questions are raised about the extent of work site support for performance and the work-relatedness of the program. Here we will limit the discussion to three areas:

- Extent of accomplishment of action plans (one of the data collection methods listed by Phillips and Stone);

- Actual workplace barriers to application of new learning observed by performers; and

- Use of support strategies by other stakeholders after the program, as observed by performers.

Requests for information in all three areas can be included in any Level 3 data-collection method. Again, knowing that these questions will be asked on a Level 3 follow-up evaluation can motivate key stakeholders (such as managers and supervisors) to act promptly to eliminate barriers and provide support.

Extent of Accomplishment of Action Plans

The discussion of Level 1 evaluations earlier in this chapter included items on development of action plans (Exhibit 5.2), which help learners plan and describe the steps they will take to apply their learning back on the job. In Level 3 evaluations, learners can be asked to document the extent to which they were able to carry out their action plans. Exhibit 5.5 gives two examples of these items, which serve as reminders to learners of the importance of completing their action plans. The Level 3 item (such as Exhibit 5.5) should follow the style and content of the earlier Level 1 item (such as Exhibit 5.2) for that intervention.

Exhibit 5.5. Examples of Level 3 Items on Accomplishment of Action Plans

Example 1(a): At the end of your training, did you prepare an action plan to apply your learning to the job? ___ Yes ___ No

Example 1(b): If you answered "Yes," please rate the extent to which you were able to carry out your plan on the job:

___ Fully

___ Very much

___ Very little

___ Not at all

Example 2: As an alternative to (b) above, use the following:
(b): If you answered "Yes," please list one or more objectives of your action plan in the table below. Then check the extent to which you accomplished each objective.

	Action Plan Accomplished			
Action Plan Objectives	Fully	Very much	Very little	Not at all

Actual Workplace Barriers That Interfere with Performance on the Job

Learners may be asked to identify any actual workplace barriers that interfered with their ability to apply their new learning to performance on the job. Examples of items on barriers are shown in Exhibit 5.6. These are almost identical to the items on potential barriers, Exhibit 5.3 for Level 1 evaluations, but also include questions on possible removal of barriers. Information on actual barriers can help performance consultants and managers identify stakeholder strategies that may prevent or eliminate the barriers. Knowing that these items are being asked can motivate stakeholders to act promptly to remove barriers if they occur.

Exhibit 5.6. Examples of Level 3 Items on Workplace Barriers

Example 1(a): In your workplace, did you find any conditions or barriers that interfered with the application of your learning? Be as specific as possible.

Example 1(b): Were any of the barriers then removed? How and by whom? Please be as specific as possible.

Example 2(a): Check any of the following barriers that you found on your job that interfered with your application of your learning. Check all that occurred.

    ___ Lack of practice opportunities   ___ Lack of time to plan application

    ___ Lack of support by supervisor   ___ Lack of support from co-workers

    ___ Interference from other tasks   ___ Lack of necessary information

    ___ Lack of equipment, technology   ___ Negative consequences

    ___ Other barriers (be as specific as possible):

Example 2(b): Were any of the barriers then removed? How and by whom? Please be as specific as possible.

Strategies by Other Stakeholders to Support Performance on the Job

Learners may be asked to list any support they actually received from other stakeholders in the workplace, following the learning intervention, which helped them transfer their new knowledge and skills to performance on the job. Examples of these items are shown in Exhibit 5.7. (These are related to the items on stakeholder strategies before and during the training intervention in Exhibit 5.4 for Level 1 evaluations.) Again, knowing that learners will be asked about support they received on the job can motivate stakeholders to follow through on committed support strategies.

Exhibit 5.7. Examples of Level 3 Items on Strategies by Other Stakeholders to Support Performance on the Job

Example 1: Did your supervisor or manager discuss the learning program with you after you completed the program? ___ Yes ___ No

If "Yes" please indicate one or two points that you recall from that discussion:

1. _____

2. _____

Example 2: (*Note:* Tailor the "after" items below to the stakeholder strategies planned for the specific learning intervention.)

Did any of the following events occur after the program you just completed? Please check all that may apply, and add any other support or encouragement you have received for applying the program to your work.

After I completed the program:

___ My supervisor or manager discussed the importance of applying the program with me.

___ My supervisor indicated how I am expected to apply what I learned.

___ The program trainer or facilitator has discussed my application of what I learned to my job.

___ I have discussed how to apply the program with co-workers who are taking or have completed the program.

Exhibit 5.7. Examples of Level 3 Items on Strategies by Other Stakeholders to Support Performance, Cont'd

___ My supervisor asked me to contact him/her if I have any difficulties in applying what I have learned.

___ Other support or encouragement I have received for applying the program:

Support or Encouragement	Provided by:
1.	
2.	
3.	

Level 4 Evaluations

Organizational results due to the performance intervention—such as reductions in waste, increased sales or repeat engagements, and many other metrics—are the focus of Level 4 evaluations. The desired results are established, and their metrics defined, early in the HPT process. In general, metrics that are already important to the organizational system are easiest to obtain and most credible in use for evaluation.

Of course, great care must be taken to identify any other factors that may also affect organizational results, besides a learning intervention. Performance consultants gain credibility with their clients when they search for, and estimate the impact of, other organizational events or actions that may have an impact on the desired results. Not claiming more impact from a learning intervention than can be justified is a prudent course that pays off in more solid relationships with clients.

If desired results are not realized, the intervention has not been successful, no matter what changes in performance have been gained. The intervention must be rethought from the beginning to identify the disconnect between desired performance and desired results.

On the other hand, when desired results in terms of business outcomes are achieved through the desired performance, performers gain validation for their efforts to achieve new behaviors and accomplishments. Their new performance is likely to be maintained. Business results, then, are important information that should be regularly shared by managers with performers, performance consultants, and other stakeholders in order to reinforce the connections between desired performance and desired business results.

Anecdotes can also be very useful Level 4 information. Stories about specific results, such as performer satisfaction in avoiding a safety threat following an intervention, can add a powerful personal quality to otherwise less dramatic statistics.

Level 5 Evaluations

Level 5 evaluations, return on investment (ROI), are the Level 4 results translated into monetary values. The standard formula for calculating ROI is

$$\text{ROI} = \frac{\text{Program Benefits} - \text{Program Costs}}{\text{Program Costs}}$$

This result is multiplied by 100 to show the ROI as a percentage. Level 5 information should also be shared with performers as reinforcement for achieving an important goal or, if the ROI is not as high as hoped, as motivation for increased performance.

For all evaluation levels and data, sharing of information with performers and other stakeholders is important to build ownership of results, good or bad. If managers, performance consultants, and other stakeholders have established effective partnering relationships (as discussed in Chapter 3), sharing of all levels of evaluation will be part of the relationship.

The Role of Evaluators in Supporting Learning and Performance

Evaluators are shown as important stakeholders in Chapter 2 (Table 2.1). They may be internal to the organization (such as performance consultants who specialize in evaluation) or external evaluation specialists. In both cases, they should have demonstrable skills and knowledge in current, widely accepted evaluation methods (such as Hodges, 2002, and Phillips & Stone, 2002).

When evaluators are included as stakeholders at the planning stages of a performance improvement intervention, they can make several important contributions in partnership with performance consultants:

- Educating stakeholders (if necessary) that *training* and other performance improvement interventions are the initial inputs in a sequence that is designed to produce *learning* or *new behaviors* of some sort, *desired performance* in the workplace, and *desired organizational results*;

- Educating stakeholders that good scores at one of the five evaluation levels are not indicators of good scores at another level; all must be measured separately;

- Emphasizing the need to follow the HPT process rigorously to ensure that decisions are based on the most complete information and that important stakeholders are involved throughout the process;

- Coaching other stakeholders in the identification of appropriate metrics for all objectives, and in identifying and capturing needed baseline performance data before the intervention occurs;

- Assisting stakeholders in deciding which evaluation levels are appropriate for various interventions, and educating them on the meaning of the data gathered and valid implications that can be drawn; and

- Helping to educate stakeholders on the research on stakeholder strategies necessary to support performance following training and on the specific strategies that each type of stakeholder can provide.

This chapter has focused primarily on evaluations of instructional interventions. Evaluators can play important roles also in helping to evaluate performance outcomes and organizational results for other noninstructional interventions at the job/performer level, such as motivation and incentive programs, feedback systems, and use of job performance aids. Interventions at the work process level (such as work process or work site redesign) and organization level (such as organization redesign or policy changes) can also be evaluated to see if desired performance and organizational results have occurred.

Evaluators can be strong partners with performance consultants (Hodges, 2002). For all strategically important interventions, and for many others, evaluators should become part of the project team at the initial stages in order to support the HPT process from the start.

Summary of This Chapter

Evaluation has become an expected and valued component of important performance improvement interventions. Increasing sophistication of evaluation methods strengthens the HPT process for all stakeholders. These newer evaluation methods have also strengthened the long-used four-level evaluation framework and added to the expertise provided by evaluators.

The five levels of evaluation now commonly used in learning evaluations are all important in both measuring and supporting workplace performance following an intervention. Advances in collection of data from learners at Levels 1 and 3 are particularly useful in supporting and encouraging them to apply what they have learned to their work performance. Some of these advances in evaluation also serve as motivators for other stakeholders to provide more complete and timely support for performers in the workplace.

Whenever possible, evaluators should be involved from the beginning of the planning process for an important performance improvement intervention. As partners, they can provide expertise, ideas, and appropriate methods and techniques to help the intervention meets its goals.

However, performance consultants must treat evaluators as they would any stakeholder group, educating them if necessary on new developments to achieve performance goals in complex systems. Evaluators also may need insights into the complex organizational system in which the desired performance is important and the various stakeholders who may provide necessary support for that performance in the workplace.

The next chapter completes Part 2, which has focused on important tools for stakeholders to use in supporting performance. It provides a tool that pulls together much of the previous five chapters, a process for managers and performance consultants to partner—in conjunction with other stakeholders—to develop and implement successful performance improvement interventions.

Suggestions for Further Reading

Several resources mentioned throughout this chapter are referenced below, with additional resources added. The evaluation literature is growing, and much of it is tailored to use by performance consultants and managers as they plan performance improvement interventions.

Hale, Judith. (2002). *Performance-based evaluation: Tools and techniques to measure the impact of training.* San Francisco: Pfeiffer. This book describes well-tested methods and provides practical guidance on their use. A CD with over forty tools is included.

Hodges, Toni. (2002). *Linking learning and performance: A practical guide to measuring learning and on-the-job application.* Boston: Butterworth-Heinemann. Hodges provides a good overview of evaluation principles, with many useful tools for less-experienced users. She also has unusually strong insights into problems of transfer of learning to performance.

Lanigan, Mary. (2001). *Creating evaluation instruments to predict behavior transfer: A new theory and measures in training evaluation.* Tinley Park, IL: Third House. This book won ISPI's Award of Excellence in 2002. Lanigan provides guidance and examples for effective "reactionnaires" and self-efficacy instruments to measure on-the-job behavior and ROI.

Phillips, Jack, & Stone, Ron. (2002). *How to measure training results: A practical guide to tracking the six key indicators.* New York: McGraw-Hill. Phillips has been a major force in defining and promulgating useful evaluation approaches. This book has clear descriptions of evaluation principles and methods and examples applicable to many situations.

6

Partnering and Consulting with Managers

A **MAJOR TOOL** for performance consultants, and for the stakeholders they support, is the combined process of *partnering and consulting* with managers to improve performance in a complex organizational system. This process is based on the three foundation blocks we explored in the first three chapters of this book: organizations as complex systems, the roles of stakeholders in supporting performance, and the performance consultant who helps the organization to achieve the performance it needs for success. The process of partnering and consulting with managers to improve performance also incorporates the tools addressed in Chapters 4 and 5: developing stakeholder strategies to support performance, and using evaluations to both measure and support performance.

This chapter focuses on:

- Establishing partnering relationships with managers
- Consulting with managers on a performance improvement intervention
- Supporting the performance of stakeholders in performance improvement interventions

Establishing Partnering Relationships with Managers

In Chapter 3, we discussed partnering with managers as an important skill for the performance consultant. Our definition of *partnering* is building a close working relationship with a stakeholder (usually an upper level manager) over time, focused on the partner's business (products and services, desired results, workforce performance concerns, competitors, and other issues), and not based on specific projects. (The performance consultant shifts into a *consulting* relationship with the stakeholder when a specific intervention is undertaken, leading the client through the decisions and actions of the HPT process.)

Partnering with the performance consultant is equally important for managers who seek improved performance by the workforce as an essential part of the organization's success. Performance consultants must take the initiative to show managers the new role for the traditional "training department" as valued partners on performance improvement, not just "order takers" delivering training programs (Stolovitch & Keeps, 2004).

Steps to Partner with Managers to Improve Performance

The shift in role is significant, from delivering training to partnering with managers on performance improvement on an ongoing basis, and consulting with them on specific interventions. Making that shift requires initiative, planning, effort, and flexibility from performance consultants. In the following pages, we will work through a sequence of actions by the performance consultant to make the shift: to analyze the complex system, develop a partnership with a manager with performance improvement concerns, and—when specific projects arise—move into a consulting relationship with that manager through the entire human performance technology (HPT) process to achieve the desired performance and the desired organizational results. Figure 6.1 presents a flowchart of suggested steps for performance consultants. Throughout this chapter, we will go through the steps one by one to suggest ways to accomplish each step.

The suggested steps assume that the performance consultant builds the *partnering* relationship first, and then moves into a *consulting* relationship when a specific performance improvement intervention becomes a possibility. Of

Figure 6.1. Steps to Partner and Consult with Managers to Improve Performance

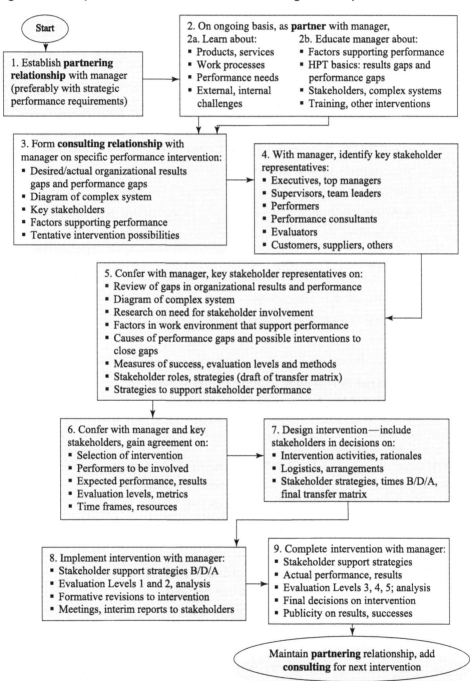

course, the reverse may happen; the consulting opportunity may appear before the partnering relationship is established. A simple shift of gears (to which any performance consultant is quickly accustomed) moves Steps 1 and 2 of the flowchart to later in the process, perhaps in parallel with other steps.

An important qualifier: The flowchart in Figure 6.1 suggests a specific sequence of actions and events during the performance improvement process. We have already noted a possible shift of Steps 1 and 2. The sequence of other steps in reality is also likely to be different. Events and opportunities occur in unexpected ways, and both the performance consultant and the manager must be ready to shift from one part of the suggested sequence to another to take advantage of new information and new possibilities. For example, it may make sense to combine two steps in the flowchart into the same session with stakeholders. So the flowchart's sequence should be considered a flexible guideline, not a prescription.

The resources in this book that refer to the steps in Figure 6.1 are summarized in Table 6.1. This serves as a quick reference aid to readers in applying the steps and as resources in consultation with clients and other stakeholders.

Table 6.1. Resources in This Book to Support Involvement of Stakeholders for Steps in Figure 6.1

Step in Figure 6.1	Resources in This Book
1. Establish partnering relationship with manager	Table 3.6, Developing the Performance Consultant's Expertise in Partnering and Consulting Table 3.7, Knowledge and Abilities in Partnering and Consulting for Managers, Performers, and Other Stakeholders
2. Learn and educate on ongoing basis	Table 2.1, Typical Stakeholders in Performance Improvement Interventions Table 2.2, Factors That Support Performance in Complex Systems Table 2.3, Factors Supporting Autonomous Performers in Applying New Knowledge and Skills

Table 6.1. Resources in This Book to Support Involvement of Stakeholders for Steps in Figure 6.1, Cont'd

Step in Figure 6.1	Resources in This Book
	Figure 6.2, The HPT Process Showing Stakeholder Involvement
3. Establish consulting relationship with manager on specific performance intervention	Figure 6.2, The HPT Process Showing Stakeholder Involvement Figures 1.3, 1.4, Diagrams of Complex Systems Table 2.1, Typical Stakeholders Table 2.2, Factors That Support Performance
4. Identify key stakeholder representatives	Table 2.1, Typical Stakeholders Figure 6.2, The HPT Process Showing Stakeholder Involvement
5. Confer with manager and key stakeholder representatives	Table 2.1, Typical Stakeholders Figure 6.2, The HPT Process Showing Stakeholder Involvement Table 2.2, Factors That Support Performance Table 5.1, Levels of Evaluation of Training Table 4.4, Recommended Transfer Strategies
6. Again, confer with manager and key stakeholder representatives	Figure 6.2, The HPT Process Showing Stakeholder Involvement Table 5.1, Levels of Evaluation of Training
7. Design intervention and include stakeholders in decisions	Table 4.4, Recommended Transfer Strategies
8. Implement the intervention	Table 4.4, Recommended Transfer Strategies Table 5.1, Levels of Evaluation of Training
9. Complete intervention	Table 4.4, Recommended Transfer Strategies Table 5.1, Levels of Evaluation of Training

Step 1: Establish a Partnering Relationship with a Manager

The first step is easier said than done. Establishing a partnering relationship with a manager does not happen just by wishing it to be so. The qualifying phrase in Step 1 of the flowchart, "preferably with strategic performance requirements," is added because these requirements are the most important to the organizational system, and thus the easiest around which to generate key stakeholder involvement. (Needless to say, helping to meet strategic performance requirements will gain performance consultants significant attention and access to additional clients.)

There are two ways to find a client/manager willing to become a partner:

- By *searching* for a manager with strategically important requirements for improved performance, and

- By *marketing* performance consulting skills throughout the complex system so managers contact the performance consultant when they have such requirements for improved performance.

Both ways should be used simultaneously, when the performance consultant feels prepared to undertake the partnering role.

Searching for a potential partner means learning the components of the organization's complex system (Chapter 1) and finding out which parts of the organizational system have important performance requirements that are not yet met. This is a significant part of the performance consultant's preparation, learning about the organization as a complex system (Chapter 3) by studying internal and external reports, news items, industry publications, and other sources.

Marketing performance consulting skills can be attempted when the performance consultant's basic preparation is completed (Chapter 3). Examples of marketing are publicizing the kinds of questions that managers should ask when faced with a performance problem, giving examples of answers to those questions and subsequent decisions, and—when possible—providing endorsements by satisfied users. Potential partners will almost inevitably be an executive or upper level manager (a primary stakeholder, Table 2.1), although initial contacts may be with lower level stakeholders.

Early conversations with managers who are potential partners should include three areas:

- The *purpose* of working together and benefits to both parties;
- The *roles* that both partners take on; and
- The *process* of partnering, how it works (Bellman, 1998; Stolovitch & Keeps, 2004).

Although specific projects are not the goal of the *partnering* relationship, they will certainly become possibilities for a *consulting* relationship as managers become educated about performance and how it can be improved. Helpful resources for Step 1 (listed in Table 6.1) are Tables 3.6 (Developing the Performance Consultant's Expertise in Partnering and Consulting) and 3.7 (Knowledge and Abilities in Partnering and Consulting for Managers, Performers, and Other Stakeholders).

Step 2: Learn and Educate on an Ongoing Basis

As the *partnership* gets under way, both parties learn and share information with each other. The performance consultant learns in greater detail about the work of the manager/partner's organization: its complex system, products and services, work processes, performance needs (both urgent and ongoing), and various external and internal challenges that must be faced. External challenges may include new products from competitors and new regulatory constraints. Internal challenges may include difficulties with internal suppliers of information or other resources and longstanding organizational policies that interfere with new work processes.

Meanwhile, the performance consultant is taking every opportunity to educate the partner and other managers and performers in the partner's organization about key concepts:

- Various stakeholders in complex systems (Table 2.1);
- Factors that support performance (Table 2.2);
- Factors that support autonomous performers in applying new knowledge and skills (Table 2.3); and
- The HPT process with stakeholder involvement. (The earlier diagram of this process is reproduced here as Figure 6.2. for easy reference.)

Figure 6.2. The HPT Process Showing Stakeholder Involvement
This figure is adapted from three sources: (1) the ISPI HPT model
(www.ispi.org/services/whatshptmodel.pdf), which is from Van Tiem,
Moseley, and Dessinger (2004), (2) Rummler (2004), and (3) Broad (2002).

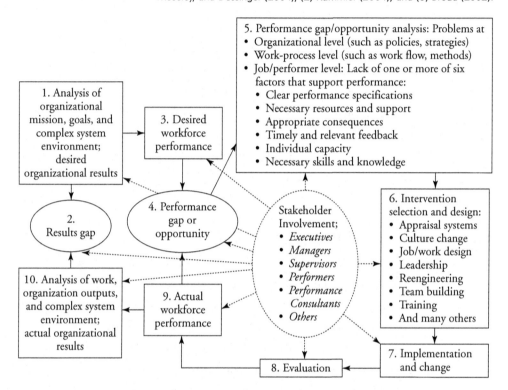

As this exchange of information and ideas between the performance consultant, the manager/partner, and others in the partner's organization continues, specific projects are bound to surface. This leads to discussion of the possibility of developing an intervention to improve a specific performance problem.

Consulting with Managers on a Performance Improvement Intervention

As specific project possibilities surface, the tone and style of the interaction between the partner and the performance consultant changes somewhat. The mutual education and interactions of the partnering relationship continue.

However, the partner and performance consultant also begin to move toward a consulting relationship to discuss desired outcomes, time commitments, responsibilities, resources, and other aspects of a particular intervention to improve a specific performance.

Step 3: Form a Consulting Relationship with Manager on a Specific Performance Intervention

The partners meet to discuss a possible intervention to improve a specific performance problem. The performance consultant now takes on the *consultant* role, leading and supporting the client through the decisions and actions of the HPT process (Figure 6.2). The desired outcomes for this meeting should include discussions of:

- Important gaps: desired versus actual organizational results (Stages 1 and 2 in Figure 6.2) and desired versus actual performance (Stages 3 and 4 in Figure 6.2);

- Components of the complex system that are important for closing the gaps and a tentative diagram of the system (Chapter 1, Figures 1.2 or 1.4 as examples);

- Key stakeholders (by position or component in the complex system diagram; selected from Table 2.1 plus possible others) who can support or possibly undermine an intervention to improve performance. These will always include the appropriate primary stakeholders and probably others who can affect performance improvement efforts;

- Factors in the performers' work environment that support performance (Table 2.2); and

- Some tentative possibilities of interventions that might be useful to close gaps in performance and results (Stage 6 in Figure 6.2).

With this information in hand, the manager and performance consultant can decide whether to pursue the intervention possibility. If they agree to proceed, they plan to bring other stakeholders promptly into the discussion.

Step 4: Identify Key Stakeholder Representatives

The performance consultant and manager should identify specific persons, if possible, who are representatives of important stakeholder groups that will be invited to one or more meetings described in Step 5. These stakeholders should be people who can support a possible intervention, or can undermine it if not supportive. Table 2.1, listing typical stakeholders, and the diagram of the complex system can be useful in identifying stakeholders.

Primary stakeholders often include executives and managers (for a strategic performance requirement) and always include performers (the focus of the intervention, whose performance must be developed or improved), their managers and supervisors, and performance consultants. Representatives of all these primary groups should participate, as appropriate, in all ten stages of Figure 6.2. Additional stakeholders can be important as well, including evaluators if the intervention's desired outcomes are to be measured. Key stakeholders contribute to planning, analyzing, approving, designing, delivering, evaluating, and maintaining accomplishments from the intervention.

Involvement of key stakeholder representatives is essential for eventual success of the intervention for two reasons. First, stakeholders in complex systems know much more about the realities, opportunities, and pitfalls in the system than a manager in one component of the organizational system or the performance consultant who is internal or external to the system. Key stakeholders can help everyone see the big picture, not just a segment.

Second, stakeholders in complex systems can support interventions that they understand, to which they can contribute ideas and information, and that they believe will benefit the whole system. They can also undermine interventions that they do not favor or understand, through lack of support, inattention, or opposition. The Federal Aviation Administration (FAA) provided an excellent example in 2004 of involvement of stakeholders who could make or break an agreement that had repercussions throughout a highly complex system (see sidebar).

GAINING STAKEHOLDER AGREEMENT:
FAA AND AIRLINES

The Federal Aviation Administration reached a precedent-setting agreement with stakeholders in the U.S. aviation system in August 2004 that was expected to cut airline delays significantly at O'Hare International Airport in Chicago, Illinois. The agreement was hammered out through several sessions with key stakeholders (including a two-and-a-half-day strategic planning Future Search led by Marvin Weisbord and Sandra Janoff).

Stakeholders included: representatives of commercial airlines, unions (pilots, attendants, mechanics), airport managers, general aviation, the U.S. military, FAA managers, and others. The stakeholders, some originally contentious, eventually came to agree that current practices that benefited one or another stakeholder group actually undermined the whole system's effectiveness and that sacrifices by many stakeholders would benefit all by supporting improved system performance (Federal Aviation Administration, 2004).

Step 5: Confer with Manager and Key Stakeholder Representatives

Face-to-face meetings are useful but becoming rarer in today's complex systems. In the first contact with key stakeholders about the proposed intervention, both manager and performance consultant should be directly involved if at all possible, to orient stakeholders to the organizational priorities and the complex web of necessary performance support anticipated. Later meetings or other contacts may be initiated or chaired by either manager or consultant as project leaders, with stakeholders separately or as a group.

Agenda items include a repeat of much that the client and performance consultant have already discussed in Step 3, to gain stakeholder views and involvement on those important topics: gaps in organizational results and performance, a diagram of the complex system, key stakeholders, factors in the work environment, and tentative intervention possibilities. All of these are likely to evolve and become more useful as stakeholders help to shape the initiative.

Additional agenda items for these key stakeholder meetings include:

- Possible factors in the work environment that may cause performance gaps (Table 2.2) and possible interventions to close gaps (Stage 6 in Figure 6.2);

- Levels of evaluation, information gathered, and uses to support learning and performance (Table 5.1);

- Stakeholder roles (Table 2.1)

- Strategies to support performance (a transfer matrix, adapted from Table 4.4, Recommended Transfer Strategies, following the template in Exhibit 4.1; see example at Table 4.5, the NWS transfer matrix).

Step 5 in Figure 6.1 also lists, as its last item, strategies to support stakeholder performance. This recognizes that the *performance of stakeholders* must also be supported, using factors in Table 2.2, to help them identify and follow through on commitments to support learner performance. In the next section of this chapter, guidelines are discussed to help performance consultants and managers guide and support all stakeholders in living up to their commitments to support learning and performance in the work environment.

Step 6: Again, Confer with Manager and Key Stakeholders

After the performance consultant (and other stakeholders as appropriate) have completed the analysis of performance gaps and identified an appropriate intervention and before the design is begun, it is important to gain agreement from key stakeholders on the proposed intervention. They should be briefed (together if possible) on the analysis process and its outcomes and on the rationale for the proposed intervention. Their agreement is important on:

- Final selection of the intervention, based on the analysis up to Stage 6 in Figure 6.2;

- Performers to be involved as learners from one or more parts of the organization;

- Expected performance and results following the intervention;

- Evaluation levels (Table 5.1) and specific metrics to assess success; and

- Time frames and other necessary resources required.

Step 7: Design the Intervention and Include Stakeholders in Decisions

Performance consultants (with other assistance as necessary) design the intervention. It is important to continue to brief the manager, and other stakeholders as appropriate, on the rationale for specific intervention activities, logistics, and other arrangements.

Also, this is the time to develop the proposed transfer matrix tailored for this intervention, an adapted version of Table 4.4, listing the proposed strategies by each stakeholder group. The strategies are arrayed in three columns—before, during, and after the intervention (or, if ongoing performance improvement is the goal, the "during" and "after" columns may be merged). The proposed tailored transfer matrix should be reviewed by each stakeholder group to approve or revise the strategies they are expected to follow to support transfer of learning to performance on the job.

Step 8: Implement the Intervention

As the intervention is implemented, the performance consultant should make sure that several activities occur at appropriate times:

- Stakeholders implement their specific support strategies in the tailored transfer matrix—before, during, and after the intervention;

- Level 1 and 2 evaluation data are gathered and analyzed at appropriate times (Table 5.1);

- Recommendations are given to stakeholders on any formative revisions to the ongoing intervention that Level 1 or 2 evaluation data suggest; and

- Meetings are held to share important information, and other kinds of interim reports are given to stakeholders as appropriate.

Stakeholders themselves may participate in overseeing and managing some of these activities, depending on the situation.

Step 9: Finish the Intervention

The intervention may be ongoing, or it may have a finite conclusion. The performance consultant, and manager if appropriate, should continue to oversee important activities:

- Stakeholders implement "after" strategies as planned in the tailored transfer matrix;

- Stakeholders stay focused on actual workplace performance and organizational results;

- Level 3, 4, and 5 evaluation data are gathered and analyzed (Table 5.1), with additional anecdotal information (which can be powerful) if available;

- Recommendations are given to stakeholders on summative revisions or changes in intervention plans that evaluation data suggest; and

- Reports and publicity are disseminated, as appropriate, on results and successes related to the intervention. Again, anecdotal information can be a powerful supplement to more precise evaluation data.

This completes the sequence for performance consultants and managers to involve other key stakeholders in performance interventions. Table 6.1 summarizes the resources in this book available for each of the steps for involving stakeholders in Figure 6.1. As pointed out earlier, probably no intervention will ever follow the suggested sequence exactly. Performance consultants, their clients, and other stakeholders should stay flexible, seize opportunities, and resolve unexpected challenges as they occur.

Following completion of an intervention, performance consultants and their clients continue their *partnering* relationship to educate and learn from each other. They move in and out of the *consulting* relationship as specific interventions are considered.

Supporting the Performance of Stakeholders in Performance Improvement Interventions

We have addressed, in some detail, the parts that stakeholders play in supporting a performance improvement intervention—from planning through implementation, evaluation, and reports of success. An important part of their orientation to their roles has been their introduction, through the performance consultant, to the factors that support performance.

Not long ago, in a blinding flash of the obvious, the need for support for *stakeholder performance* became apparent. We give stakeholders a lot of new information about their roles to support performance, and then expect them to perform accordingly—without much further support or practice. So it seems useful to go over the same factors that support the performance of people going through a performance improvement intervention and to apply these to support stakeholders in their own performance.

Table 6.2 presents the six factors supporting performance (from Table 2.2), plus the three factors supporting autonomous performers in applying new knowledge and skills (from Table 2.3). For each factor, actions are suggested for performance consultants and managers to support the performance of stakeholders.

Table 6.2. Factors and Actions by Performance Consultants and Managers to Support Performance of Stakeholders

Factors	Actions by Performance Consultants and Managers to Support Stakeholder Performance in Supporting Transfer of Learning to Performance
Factors That Support Performance (from Table 2.2)	
1. Clear performance specifications	Clarify, for each stakeholder group and individual, exactly what they are expected to do to support transfer of learning to performance.

(Continued)

**Table 6.2. Factors and Actions by Performance Consultants
and Managers to Support Performance of Stakeholders, Cont'd**

Factors	*Actions by Performance Consultants and Managers to Support Stakeholder Performance in Supporting Transfer of Learning to Performance*
2. Necessary resources and support	Provide each stakeholder group and individual with necessary information and materials to give support.
3. Appropriate consequences	Give appropriate recognition to stakeholders who carry out their commitments. Note that performance of learners on the job will be posted and compared across organizational components.
4. Useful feedback	Give reminders in advance, and confirmation afterward, for actions that stakeholders agreed to take.
5. Individual capacity	Clarify (if appropriate or necessary) that all stakeholders are expected to be fully capable of carrying out their commitments.
6. Necessary skills and knowledge	Educate and coach all stakeholders in: • Research on stakeholder support for performance; • High priority of top management for transfer of learning to performance for this intervention; • Evaluation metrics that will measure performance of learners on the job; and • Evaluation strategies that will ask learners if they received stakeholder support.

*Factors Supporting Stakeholders as Autonomous Performers
in Applying New Knowledge and Skills (from Table 2.3)*

7. Credibility of stakeholder actions	Provide positive comments on learner performance and results from other stakeholders who provided support.
8. Practicality of stakeholder actions	Provide examples of effective support provided by other stakeholders.
9. Recognized need to improve their own stakeholder performance	Help stakeholders review their past practices to continue useful support actions and build in new support actions.

The performance consultant and manager can use Table 6.2 to confer with stakeholders themselves—separately or together—on what the stakeholders need to support their own performance in providing support. Clarifying expectations for all nine factors on that table with stakeholders themselves can strengthen their understanding and commitment for taking support actions.

For the six factors supporting performance (Rummler & Brache, 1995; Rummler, 2004), the manager and performance consultant can

- Give clear specifications on exactly what stakeholders are supposed to *do* to support transfer of learning to job performance;

- Give all stakeholders the necessary information and materials to provide support;

- Give stakeholders *recognition* for carrying out their commitments to act before, during, and after the intervention, and let them know that the resulting job performance of learners will be publicized across the organization;

- Remind stakeholders in advance of actions they agree to take, and confirm completion afterward;

- Clarify, if necessary, that all stakeholders are fully capable of providing support (or help them plan to fill any capability gaps); and

- Give stakeholders all the information and guidance they need to provide necessary support to performers to apply their learning to the job.

For the three factors that support autonomous performers (which many stakeholders may be) in applying new knowledge and skills to their work (Yelon, Sheppard, Sleight, & Ford, 2004):

- Emphasize the *credibility* of the support they will provide by telling them the positive experiences and impact of other stakeholders who have supported transfer of learning to performance;

- Confirm the *practicality* of their giving support by giving examples of support successfully provided by other stakeholders; and

- Help stakeholders *recognize their need* to improve their own stake-holder performance by reviewing their past practices and finding new and useful support actions to take.

Summary of This Chapter

In this chapter we have presented suggestions and guidelines for building partnering and consulting relationships between performance consultants and managers, so they can work together effectively to support improved work-place performance. These relationships can help managers address perfor-mance challenges in many day-to-day interactions with employees, as well as in longer range performance improvement interventions throughout the orga-nizational system. The relationships can also help performance consultants gain access to higher level managers to demonstrate valuable performance improvement services of which many managers may be unaware.

The rationale for involvement of performance consultants with other stakeholders in improving performance is compelling to many organizations and consultants who have followed these paths. Of course, there is much still to be learned about gaining effective involvement with managers, perform-ers, and other influential stakeholders. The profession of performance con-sulting is relatively new, as are the rapidly evolving technologies of designing and implementing learning and other kinds of interventions to improve per-formance. New evaluation methods and metrics have appeared to address new intervention designs. Meanwhile, of course, the forms and complexity of the organizations and communities we serve are changing more quickly than ever. So all stakeholders have much to learn about best practices in supporting per-formance improvement in complex organizational systems.

Two of the following three chapters give detailed case studies of applica-tions of support for performance following learning interventions in very dif-ferent complex systems. The third provides an analysis and gives examples of the strong support that e-learning can give to performance by delivering the learning right to the work site. The expertise and creativity of these applications, and many others, are exciting and provocative; they clearly illustrate that human performance is forever challenging us to learn and experiment and find new ways to be effective. That is a sign of growing maturity in our profession, as well as a spur for improvement of our own skills and abilities.

Suggestions for Further Reading

The literature on partnering and consulting relationships of performance consultants with managers and other stakeholders is growing rapidly. The books listed here have given the author much information, insights, and occasional confirmation of hunches. Although they differ in tone and approach, each contributes very helpful perspectives on the value of informed and thoughtful performance consulting assistance to managers and other stakeholders in our complex organizational systems.

Hale, Judith. (1998). *The performance consultant's fieldbook: Tools and techniques for improving organizations and people.* San Francisco: Pfeiffer. Clear, straightforward, no-nonsense discussions of models, performance barriers, real-life examples, and guidelines for how to diagnose, select interventions, and measure results, plus a disk with more than twenty tools.

Robinson, Dana G., & Robinson, James C. (1995). *Performance consulting: Moving beyond training.* San Francisco: Berrett-Koehler. The book that coined the term "performance consulting" is still very valuable for its descriptions of appropriate consulting roles and the differences between training and performance perspectives. A focus on organizational results and performance, business needs, work environment factors, plus guidelines, case studies, and worksheets, keep this a most useful volume.

Robinson, Dana G., & Robinson, James C. (Eds.). (1998). *Moving from training to performance: A practical guidebook.* Alexandria, VA: American Society for Training and Development, and San Francisco: Berrett-Koehler. Excellent articles on partnering and consulting throughout the performance consulting process, phase by phase, by experts and practitioners (Rummler, Bellman, Elliott, Stolovitch & Keeps, LaBonte, and more).

Stolovitch, Harold C., & Keeps, Erica J. (2004). *Training ain't performance.* Alexandria, VA: ASTD Press. A very lively, exercise-filled discussion of performance-related concepts and practices including partnering and consulting, with loads of pithy information and references. Chapter 6, From Training Order-Taker to Performance Consultant, is excellent.

PART 3

Applications of Performance Improvement in Real-World Systems

Part 1 of this book established the foundation for performance improvement in complex systems. Chapter 1 presented organizations as complex systems and suggested ways to conceptualize and visualize them for stakeholders' information. Chapter 2 looked at the many stakeholders in complex systems, particularly those most closely involved with performers who are the focus of a performance improvement intervention. Chapter 3 examined important areas of expertise of the performance consultant, a change agent role that is becoming widespread.

In Part 2, with the foundation in place, we explored several important tools for stakeholders to use in supporting performance improvement interventions. In Chapter 4, we looked at research on lack of success of training as a sole intervention and at tools for stakeholders who can supply the factors that support performance. Chapter 5 presented evaluation as an important set of tools to measure and to encourage performance. Chapter 6 gave a process tool, a set of *partnering* and *consulting* steps for performance consultants and managers, in collaboration with other stakeholders, to analyze performance problems and to develop, implement, and evaluate a performance improvement intervention.

Now in Part 3 we look at applications of these foundation blocks and tools for performance improvement in real-life settings. Each of the following three chapters was written by a colleague with particular expertise in one type of complex system and equal expertise with the focus on performance and necessary support from stakeholders.

Chapter 7, by Julie Hile, presents an organizational change process in a major complex railroad system that is not primarily learning-related. This change process involved many stakeholders in developing and implementing enhanced system-wide safety rules and operations.

In Chapter 8, by Rick Sullivan, we learn about a highly complex international system—with important learning components—to improve healthcare for women and children in countries with low resources.

Chapter 9, by Ken Finley, gives the case for e-learning's support for performance by bringing learning into the workplace, supported by stakeholders and technology advances. These applications give readers a wide range of options and possibilities to consider as they plan performance improvement interventions in their own organizational systems.

7

Sleuthing Out Performance Consulting's Best Partners

SAFETY AND HEALTH AS A CASE IN POINT

Julie S. Hile

ONCE PERFORMANCE CONSULTANTS have the foundation blocks and tools of our trade in hand, we do well to seek out our *best* organization stakeholders—people with whom we can most reliably effect transformative organizational change. To illustrate this point, in Chapter 7 we peel back and examine the mutual benefits found in the strong working partnership between strategic stakeholders: performance consultants and Safety and Health (S&H) professionals. We highlight a highly stakeholder-driven, major intervention led by these partners, one that advances deep change in a tradition-steeped safety culture.

This chapter focuses on:

- The call for performance consultants' best stakeholders
- Lessons from the performance consulting/S&H partnership
- The case in point: Canadian National Railway U.S. Operation's safety rule book revision process

The Call for Performance Consultants' Best Stakeholders

As performance consultants focusing on *performance* as the goal, our views of important organizational partners have changed significantly over recent years. More than a decade ago, Broad and Newstrom (1992) began to emphasize the need for *transfer of training,* identifying partnerships among *managers, trainers,* and *learners.* Their work led many aspiring performance consultants to build a credible business case for active manager involvement in training support and to plan with customers those detailed actions the customers might most productively take before, during, and following training.

Shortly thereafter, Robinson and Robinson (1995) raised the question: "Who is the performance consultant's customer?"—leading people in organization performance to newly complex, proactive conversations with their operational colleagues. In 1997 Broad challenged us once again, this time to consider an expanded range of possible stakeholders, including top decision-makers, team leaders and members, learning professionals, strategic planners, union officials, quality specialists, finance and budget experts, customers, suppliers, and others. We have since deepened our knowledge of the vast array of interventions in which we might involve those stakeholders in efforts to close performance gaps. All of this points to the healthy maturation of performance consulting as a profession.

The time has come to ask: "Who—among the scores of people with whom we have worked projects and processes—are performance consultants' *best* stakeholders?" Who out there in our working worlds are the partners we work with most productively, most efficiently, to generate performance improvements that are transformative, deeply systemic, hooked into results for the long haul? Who shares our values? Who recognizes and seeks out multiple stakeholders and contributing factors, engineers blended solutions to performance issues, assesses outcomes both qualitatively and quantitatively? Or if they don't operate this way today, who can most quickly and powerfully gain such an orientation and pick up and apply the requisite skills?

The partnership between performance consultants and S&H professionals, who are noted in Chapter 2 as *performance partners* with interests in particular kinds of organization performance, is one that has shown significantly positive results. An examination of this partnership offers important lessons about how organization-wide performance improvement can be realized for those of us who seek to re-cast our stake in organizational outputs toward earlier, more varied, and more strategic impact on how and why people and processes perform as they do.

Lessons Learned from the Performance Consulting/S&H Partnership

The performance consultant/S&H partnership comes into strategic alignment around four significantly complementary areas: key shared values; parallel history and evolution; mutually beneficial knowledge, skill, and ability (KSA); and mutually validating KSAs. These areas synergize into a potent formula for mutual understanding and long-term collaboration. In reading on, consider where in your organization network such complementarity exists, pointing you toward your own high-potential stakeholder partnerships.

AREAS OF COMPLEMENTARITY FOR HIGH-IMPACT PERFORMANCE PARTNERSHIPS

- Key shared values
- Parallel history and evolution
- Mutually beneficial knowledge, skill, and ability (KSA)
- Mutually validating KSAs

Key Shared Values

Who among your potential stakeholders stands with people, continuous improvement, and performance complexity? Performance consultants and S&H share, as a primary responsibility, the nurturing and protection of the human element—people's quality of performance and work life and the return of their bodies and minds, healthy and whole, to families and friends at the end of each work cycle. We both champion human behavior—what people *do*—as the fulcrum of organization performance. Our functions share an abiding interest in and need for the coherent and continuous improvement of work processes across systems. Finally, we are at our best when our performance assessments capture the messy, multi-causal, multidimensional complexity that comes from analysis models of performance support factors such as that of Rummler and Brache (discussed in Chapter 2).

PROSPECTIVE BEST PERFORMANCE PARTNERS FOR PERFORMANCE CONSULTANTS

Look for best prospective performance partners such as those below:

- S&H professionals who engage with the human element and in root cause analysis;

- Operations leaders who see and think systemically and innovatively;

- Quality people who seek out qualitative and quantitative performance data;

- Marketing colleagues with a consultative sales orientation;

- Customer relations people who understand that a known, heard, satisfied customer is better than one who always gets his or her way without question; and

- HR professionals focused beyond regulatory compliance on organization goals and achievements.

Parallel History and Evolution

Who among your potential stakeholders has learned lessons like those you have learned along a path from reactive to proactive, programmatic to process-driven? As a long-time practitioner in both the performance consulting and S&H fields, I have seen strikingly parallel lessons learned in the transition of Human Resources (HR)/Training to performance consulting and of S&H from administrators to safety professionals.

Historically, both functions were initially isolated as sole stewards of a particular organization activity—in HR/Training's case, training interventions; in S&H's case, safe work conditions and environments. Both functions have moved through to staffing and career paths, reporting requirements, function outputs, and indicators of success. Throughout, both functions have been perceived as primarily administrative, irrelevant to front-end business development and strategy, and excluded from initial discussions framing performance-based issues. HR/Training and S&H attitudes and behaviors within this context have blocked our ability to engage with full performance improvement. The sidebar lists obstructing behaviors in which both functions have long engaged.

OUR OWN WORST ENEMIES: HOW WE RESIST ENGAGING WITH FULL PERFORMANCE IMPROVEMENT

Compare your current professional practices to those listed below to assess ways in which you may be preventing yourself from transitioning to full performance improvement:

- A focus on what people know rather than on what they can *do;*

- Plate overloaded with activity not linked to performance results;

- Too few visits to the field to learn the operation and build systems knowledge, credibility, and relationships;

- Reactive, go-it-alone mentality: "Leave training/safety to us. Just call.";

- Analysis of performance gaps and root causes that leads to dis-integrated countermeasures;

- Overuse of one-shot, too often training, too often blaming solutions; and

- Emphasis on quantitative indicators that show activity (for example, number of classes, number trained) not linked meaningfully with performance.

Safety's evolution toward process- and behavior-based performance improvement, led by Dan Petersen (1975) and others, tracks with HR/ Training's Broad/Newstrom/Robinson's path described earlier in this chapter in its calls for us to ask why behavior occurs and to analyze the usually complex chains of human error contributing to performance outcomes. Other parallel developments included calls for integration of performance issues into operations; greater supervisor involvement in and accountability for performance; and the reorganization of large corporate functions into agile, flexible, field-based teams that require high stakeholder involvement.

Mutually Beneficial Specialized Knowledge, Skill, and Ability (KSA)

With which potential stakeholders are you most likely to enjoy high-impact symbiosis? Applying their respective KSAs, performance consultants and S&H can steer one another toward performance work that saves time, effort, budget, and face, in addition to narrowing performance gaps significantly the first time out. In driving Frequency Severity Indices (the combined measure of recordable injuries per 200,000 person-hours worked) and Lost Time Days *down* and quality processes, job outputs, and morale *up*, performance consultants in our practice have taught their S&H counterparts consulting theory and practice, cognitive psychology and facilitation practices, and performance-driven models of evaluation and authentic assessment. We have introduced transfer of learning to key S&H stakeholders and facilitated their collaborative creation of transfer "scaffolds" (shown in Table 7.1), the expanded, multi-dimensional version of the transfer matrix described in Chapter 4. Transfer scaffolds take their name from the strategically placed, carefully constructed, multi-layered, temporary structures used in construction and repair.

Representative intervention stakeholders are listed in the far left-hand column of the transfer of learning scaffold. The earlier transfer matrix format for each stakeholder (Exhibit 4.1) had three columns for actions before, dur-

Table 7.1. Tranfer of Learning Scaffold

Stakeholder	What's In It for Stakeholder (WIIFS)	Actions Before	Actions During	Actions After	Barriers to Actions/Success	Counter-Measures

ing, and after the intervention. The scaffold adds three more columns: the "What's In It for Stakeholder" column second from the left and the "Barriers to Actions/Success" and "Countermeasures" columns to the far right. The analysis and strategy that inform completion of these columns equip people engaged in performance improvement to raise key stakeholders' awareness of how they will benefit from an intervention's success. It also guides project planners to document outcomes that align with stakeholders' needs, even as it holds those stakeholders accountable to doing what they have said they will do to move the intervention forward.

Finally, our six question adaptation of Rummler and Brache's (1995) organization performance factors morphed in Safety Committee members' hands into a tool that helps workers analyze and adjust safe work choices on the spot, sometimes—remarkably—at the behest of their peers.

Getting "in there"—into day-to-day business practices—ranks among the performance consultant's greatest challenges. S&H's significant contribution to performance consultants begins with the provision of prime sites of practice, including access to senior decision-makers in whose personal and professional networks S&H has long enjoyed a reliable berth. Invaluable coaches in the initiation and sustenance of credible organization relationships, our safety colleagues have taught us how to build compelling business cases from statistics related to the high cost of injury—the $80K saved by prevention of a single back injury is a real attention-getter—and corralled the significant resources needed to jump-start major cultural change. Last,

S&H has instilled in us their sharp detection of the observable, concrete, often spare indicators of safety performance that, when worked, bridge to deep performance change.

Mutually Validating KSAs

What possible performance partnership in your world confirms for both stakeholder partners—coming from disparate disciplines and research arenas—the important, basic tenets of performance management? There is much to appreciate in the parallels between performance consultants' gap analysis and S&H's root-cause analysis, between our human factors focus and S&H's behavior-based safety. Figure 7.1 shows the parallels and overlaps in KSAs for both groups.

Figure 7.1. Performance Consultant and S&H Mutually Beneficial and Mutually Validating KSAs

In examining the performance consulting-S&H example, assess the KSAs you share with prospective performance partners and those you will benefit from sharing with/learning from those colleagues.

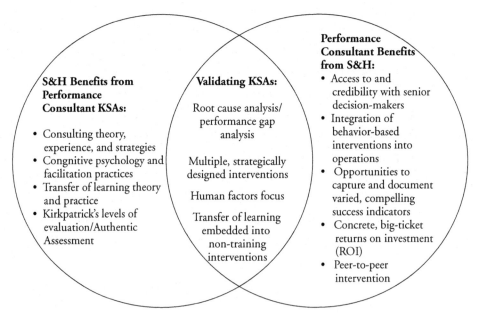

S&H Benefits from Performance Consultant KSAs:

- Consulting theory, experience, and strategies
- Congnitive psychology and facilitation practices
- Transfer of learning theory and practice
- Kirkpatrick's levels of evaluation/Authentic Assessment

Validating KSAs:

Root cause analysis/ performance gap analysis

Multiple, strategically designed interventions

Human factors focus

Transfer of learning embedded into non-training interventions

Performance Consultant Benefits from S&H:

- Access to and credibility with senior decision-makers
- Integration of behavior-based interventions into operations
- Opportunities to capture and document varied, compelling success indicators
- Concrete, big-ticket returns on investment (ROI)
- Peer-to-peer intervention

In the case study that follows, note the presence and interplay between performance consultants and S&H professionals of the four complementary areas described above. Consider how the performance partners serve as powerful, mutual, best stakeholders—customers, coaches, and organizational allies—in the project of improving workplace performance. Where in your performance consulting work might you connect and collaborate with such colleagues?

THE CANADIAN NATIONAL RAILWAY U.S. OPERATION'S SAFETY RULE BOOK REVISION PROCESS

"Live Injury-Free Everyday (the 'L.I.F.E.' safety rule book) is a breath of fresh air. It is one thing that brings us, that forces us, to come together."

—Gordon Trafton, Senior VP, Canadian National Railway,

U.S. Region, in April 2004 safety meeting

CN U.S. Operations Background

Canadian National Railway (CN) is the fifth largest Class One railroad in North America, its U.S. Operations employing 6,700 people in management and four professional crafts: Clerical, Engineering, Mechanical, and Transportation. The U.S. organization runs on approximately 10,122 miles of track.

At the turn of 2000, CN began expanding its U.S. territory significantly, shaping a U.S. Operations that today includes the former Grand Trunk Western Railroad in Michigan and Ohio, the former Illinois Central, which spans the length of the Mississippi River, and the former Wisconsin Central railroad. Add to this CN's company headquarters in Montreal, Quebec, Canada, and its Canadian Operations, spanning the country east to west, and the carrier is the North American continent's most geographically connected railroad, linking Canada, Mexico, and the United States and serving ports on the Atlantic, the Pacific, and the Gulf of Mexico. CN generates more than one billion Canadian dollars annually from its transport of finished vehicles, automotive parts, chemicals, petroleum, coal, fertilizer, grain, forest products, metals, and minerals.

By 2001, CN's U.S. Operations had acquired and was reorganizing the Illinois Central and Grand Trunk railroads away from small, familial operations and toward CN's expansive corporate culture. U.S. Ops wanted to head off reorganization-driven spikes in incident and injury, advance its core safety culture in the ways described in the previous section, and unify its new locations and associates within that culture.

While each new property had voiced its commitment to operating as safely as possible, each was also protective of the programs and processes it believed had served well up to its purchase. The U.S. Ops' 2001 Frequency Index showed a 2.89 (114 recordable injuries) for the former Illinois Central and a 4.32 (83 recordable injuries among a far smaller work force) for the former Grand Trunk. CN U.S. Ops' AVP of Safety and Regulatory Affairs, Bob Keane, wanted his diverse stakeholders to coalesce around a unified safety effort.

Keane contacted the Hile Group, seeking the results of its well-known safety rule book revision process: credible review of current safety rules; consistent, clear application to specific operations; clarification of mandatory versus recommended work practices; rules that are distinct from procedures; simple, accessible, user-friendly text and layout; a bridge to at-home safety, wherever appropriate; and, importantly, "buy in" to rulebooks from both management and unions.

Performance Gap Analysis

In keeping with human performance technology (HPT) principles, the performance consultants probed for fuller information about what was happening in CN's U.S. Operations that made the safety team think a safety rule book revision was in order. This also turned out to be solid validation of S&H's orientation to root-cause analysis. Tapping into that orientation in a critical, although informal, performance intervention, consultants pushed Keane and his S&H colleagues to further develop their thinking about their performance situation: What changes were they out to create in U.S. Operations' larger performance picture?

While the safety rule book process would indeed produce high-quality safety rule books, we warned, it would also initiate dynamic changes to CN U.S. Ops' safety culture. In producing the longed-for realistic, accurate, accessible rules, we would build intense, positive, working momentum among co-authors from the field, management, and safety. Associates throughout the workforce would gain long-term critical engagement about what makes a safety rule a safety rule as well as in the continuous improvement of safety practices.

Another key change would have CN redefine its framework for communicating its safety expectations to people by confirming with mandatory safety rules situations when railroaders were to follow orders and with a new convention, "recommended practices" when they were to decide whether a job would be most safely done as recommended or following a practice they knew to be as safe or safer. Recommended Practices would, without precedent, call on associates to assert their informed, professional judgment in deciding the safest way to work.

Beyond buy-in to the books, the safety rule book revision process would create grassroots support for and ownership of a practical, shared, and empowering safety movement. Were Keane and his team prepared to tackle sometimes sacrosanct elements of the whole system? Keane intoned that whole-system engagement was precisely his intention. Values were lining up.

So Keane launched the project with performance gap/root-cause analysis, which further mapped out CN U.S. Ops' performance needs. Conducted by the project's Planning Team made up of select CN managers and safety professionals supported by the performance consultants, the analysis results clustered insights around organization climate, management/leadership performance, and safety rules. You will see among them evidence of the second area of complementarity mentioned earlier: S&H's history at CN U.S. Ops, its early efforts to transition to a full operating partner, and its need for a planned implosion of longstanding barriers in order to effect real change.

Organization Climate

U.S. associates were wary. The continuous reassignment of key senior leaders to accommodate organization growth was making people uncomfortable. Trust, never an easy commodity to create in this strong union environment, was shaky.

Management/Leadership Performance

As new people came into the CN fold from smaller, emotionally closer environments, CN managers' demands of immediate respect, open communications, and standardization often felt dogmatic and rigid. Old, industry-wide supervisory habits of controlling people's behavior through fear and intimidation were alive and well in pockets across the organization. Further, some managers limited their work to operational oversight, expecting HR/Training to deal with "people" issues and S&H to handle safety.

Safety Rules

The U.S. territory had *eleven* safety rule documents in play. These documents were dramatically disparate in rule quality, tone, scope, depth, clarity, accuracy, currency, accessibility, and in the degrees to which they focused specifically on safety. Within the documents, distinctions among policies, programs, procedures, work practices, training content, rules, and regulations were unclear. Many safety rules were charged emotionally and politically, written in the "blood" of colleagues to prevent recurrence of incidents from which workers had suffered injury and worse. Some safety rules forced noncompliance, requiring people to work in physically impossible ways.

The "hanging books," as many people called them, offered numerous "just-out-to-get-you" rules that were interpreted, enforced, and complied with inconsistently by managers and associates in the field. Loopholes routinely bolstered reprimand, punishment, and legal arguments by CN attorneys, plaintiffs' attorneys, and union officials in courts of law. New hires moving from job orientation into the field were often admonished by co-workers to put their safety rules away because "that's not the way we do things out here in the real world." Table 7.2 shows the Planning Team's use of the six-question adaptation of Rummler and Brache in the safety rules component of its performance gap analysis.

The Planning Team rooted Keane's initial thinking in performance data and decided that this particular safety rule book revision process, with its broad reach and strategic blend of diverse interventions, was CN U.S. Ops' performance solution of choice.

With key shared values and parallel history and transition now confirmed, the performance consultant/S&H partnership plunged into a highly charged give-and-take driven by mutually beneficial and mutually validating KSAs.

Table 7.2. Results of Safety Rules Portion of Performance Gap Analysis as CN U.S. Operations, 2000

Performance Expectations (Do people know what they are supposed to do?)	Gap: Performance expectations were being set variously and inconsistently by supervisors, new-hire orientation facilitators, safety committees, and safety rules documents. Non-enforcement of safety rules redefined expectations as noted in "Performance Feedback" below.
Necessary Support (Do people have what they need to do what they are supposed to do?)	Gap: Safety commitment and message were compromised by multiple rules documents, inconsistent supervisor performance, sometime production pressure, and co-workers who modeled and coached unsafe work practices.
Appropriate Consequences (What happens when people do what they are supposed to do?)	Gap: Unclear performance expectations limited the system's ability to hold people accountable, as did confusing, indefensible, and unsupported safety rules documents.
Performance Feedback (How do people know whether they are doing what they are supposed to do?)	Gap: Safety rules were enforced inconsistently. Some supervisors resisted providing proactive feedback on individual performance; they often lacked the skill to provide it effectively. (See "Knowledge/Training/Education" below.)
Knowledge/Training/ Education (Do people know what they need to know to do what they're supposed to do?)	Gap: Supervisors lacked safety leadership skills. Field associates lacked skills in peer-to-peer intervention. Everyone needed to better understand performance gap analysis, transfer of learning, and what makes a safety rule a safety rule.
Capacity (*Can* people do what they are supposed to do?)	Adequate: All involved had the physical, emotional, and intellectual capacity needed to get the job done safely.

Adapted from Rummler and Brache, 1995.

Safety Rule Book Revision Process Plan

The revision process would pull all eleven safety rule books into review and revision by a cross section of organization stakeholders who would test the rules with a rigorous safety rule sorter over a fourteen-month period during 2000 and 2001. A description of the process, organized into stages, follows.

Stage 1: A cross-craft Core Team—made up of stakeholders from all functions, management and unions, and representative geographic locations and job classifications—drives the revision process. The Core Team negotiates "Core Safety Rules," which apply to all associates, and makes decisions throughout the process about how the revision project engages with the rest of CN U.S. Ops.

Stage 2: Craft-specific Satellite Teams coordinate and lead the writing of Safety Rules (mandatory) and Recommended Practices (strongly supported but not mandatory) for their respective crafts (Clerical, Engineering, Mechanical, and Transportation).

Stage 3: Drafts of the Core and Craft-specific Safety Rules and Recommended Practices (RPs) are exchanged among the four crafts for review and comment by other crafts also affected.

Stage 4: Solid drafts of the books are "shopped" with CN U.S. Ops colleagues in the field for accuracy, currency, enforceability/ability to comply, and clarity of language. Field colleague recommendations are considered by the Core Team, with appropriate changes being made before the books head into layout and production.

Stage 5: The revised books are implemented in the field.

The Transfer of Learning Scaffold

The Planning Team began identifying project stakeholders and building the transfer of learning scaffold in earnest (template shown in Table 7.1). Stakeholders included the five analyzed in Tables 7.3 through 7.7—division vice presidents, Safety and Health and Risk Management, Core and Satellite Team members, performance consultants, and middle managers.

In reviewing the tables, consider the interplay between complementary and validating performance consultant and S&H/Risk Management KSAs as we engaged crucial stakeholders in senior leadership, the Core and Satellite Teams, and middle management in culture change. A rapid scan of the five tables will afford you a snapshot of the transfer scaffolding that coordinates various stakeholders' work. A more

Table 7.3. Application of Rule Book Revision Transfer Scaffold to S&H/Risk Management

Stakeholder(s)	WIIFS* (Stakeholder)/ Return on Investment	Actions Before	Actions During	Actions After	Barriers to Actions/Success	Countermeasures
Safety and Health/Risk Management	• Reductions in incidents • Clarification of safety-related requirements vs. recommendations • Safety-only rule books • Craft-specific rule books • Current, accurate rule books • Broad network of cross-organization safety advocates • Improved ROI on safety	• Build relationship with performance consultant (PC) • Learn safety rule book process • Sell process strategically inside organization • Ensure project budget • Build baseline performance data • Consult with key stakeholders to configure Core and Satellite Teams • Meeting logistics • Provide safety rule source documents to PC • Arrange executive visit to kick-off meeting	• Lead Core Team participatively • Endorse and partner with PC • Hold back; resist dominating • Demonstrate support, especially for core rules (CRs) and recommended practices (RPs) • Listen, learn, build relationships • Just-in-time support for PC • Track down answers to questions that arise • Model safety culture and rules enforcement	• Ensure high-saturation roll-out • Ensure flawless book distribution • "Catch the wave" of momentum from Safety Committee roll-out meetings • Protect safety rule books from unilateral edits • Teach leadership re process and book as new kind of management tool • Develop and launch interventions/processes from Tracking Document • Accept suggestions from field and call for review of new books when suggestions reach critical mass • Capture and communicate success indicators at 3-, 6-, and 12-month intervals	• Access to executive leadership • Time it "should" take to write a safety rule book • Defensiveness about current book, rules-generation process • Focus-on/focus-off nature of project work • Credibility compromised by split role between safety and risk management (mitigation of company losses due to incidents) • Lack of performance management skills	→ Align project business case with organization goals and WIIFVPOs; sell up-front → Build and communicate transfer scaffold → Focus on culture change elements of project; work calendar → Exploit inquiries about project status/timeframe as learning opportunities → Grow confidence in Core and Satellite Teams → Talk to industry colleagues who have used the process → Stay organized and pull on PC → Demonstrate that Safety and Risk Management can be both/and rather than either/or; ensure fairness in court of law; support safety rules that cut out "gotcha's" and loop holes → Build PC skills

*WIIFS = What's In It For Stakeholder

Table 7.4. Application of Rule Book Revision Transfer Scaffold to Performance Consultants (Hile Group)

Stakeholder(s)	WIIFS (Stakeholder)/ Return on Investment	Actions Before	Actions During	Actions After	Barriers to Actions/Success	Countermeasures
Performance Consultant (PC)	• Opportunity to influence process: culture, priorities, resources allocation • Enhanced morale, reduced turnover • Movement toward authentic, grass-roots oriented culture change in safety and beyond • Clarification of safety-related requirements vs. recommendations • Broad network of cross-organization safety advocates • Cost reduction for injuries and incidents • Improved ROI on CN-U.S. shares	• Build relationship with S&H/RM and project planning team • Teach Rummler and Brache questions and apply them to safety performance gaps • Orient S&H/RM to safety rule book process • With S&H/RM lay out project time line, milestones, deliverables, success indicators • Support creation of business case to sell process inside organization • Ensure project budget • Ensure validity of baseline performance data • Consult with key stakeholders to configure Core and Satellite Teams • Review and analyze safety rule source documents • Design facilitation and materials for project meetings	• Foster open discussion • Teach consensus • Build team rapport • Listen and learn • Shape current rules text for review and calibration of CT and STs to rule sorter • Model rule writing by scribing CT decisions on flip charts • Build facilitator and writer skills for ST leadership • Provide virtual support for ST work • Hold to rule sorter • Maintain strong interface with S&H/RM and other key stakeholders • Capture CT and ST outputs in working drafts • Support development of non-rule text: intro and front material, glossary, other • Build shopping/roll-out plans; coordinate them with S&H/RM, CT, STs • Ensure final drafts to printer	• Support high-saturation roll-out • Reinforce Safety Committee roll-out meetings with follow-up system safety coaching • Reinforce management skill building around use of new rule books • As contracted, develop and launch interventions/ processes from Tracking Document • Facilitate lessons learned • Document and communicate success indicators at 3-, 6-, and 12-month intervals	• Access to and credibility with executive leadership • Disorganization on the part of project lead • Lack of systems safety/PC skills in project leadership • Safety professionals who struggle with relinquishing control and authority over safety rules • Tight time frames • Cross-craft inability to come to consensus on "same work, same rule" • Confusion at ST writing level	→ Align project business case with organization goals and WIIFVPOs; provide S&H/RM with evidence of project potential and progress to goals → Build project work plan and transfer scaffold early on → Mentor skills for project leadership, and capitalize on questions about/ snags in project as some of your most legitimate and impactful consultative work → Infuse interface with project players with 5- to 20-minute learning interventions → Define and refine the issues at hand, pushing for rearticulation of mental models and cultural breakthroughs → Provide continuous virtual support for STs

Table 7.5. Application of Rule Book Revision Transfer Scaffold to Division Vice Presidents

Stakeholder(s)	WIIFS (Stakeholder)/ Return on Investment	Actions Before	Actions During	Actions After	Barriers to Actions/Success	Countermeasures
VPs Operations, Midwest and Gulf Divisions	• Cost reduction for injuries and incidents • Enhanced morale, reduced turnover • Movement toward authentic, grass-roots-oriented culture change in safety and beyond • Demonstration that management has employees' best interests at heart • Improved ROI on CN-U.S, shares	• Provide consistent, full financial support for rule book revision process, including cross-function employee participation • Understand and support TIME requirements • Review existing safety rule books	• Align management team to support process • Drop in on Core and Satellite Team working meetings to observe, listen, learn how to better support the effort • Provide rewarding and re-directive feedback to management and craft leaders • Participate in shopping process, reviewing and commenting closely on drafts of new books	• Comply with new safety rules and RPs • Continue to build relationships with and listen to rule book revision project members • Champion project with President and Board of Directors • Protect processes put in place • Charge all performers with continuous improvement of processes • Demonstrate safety leadership	• Subordinates will not "tap the boss on the shoulder" from all • $ pressure, lean staffing • TIME, competing priorities • Workforce resistance to new systems • Long tradition of division superintendents unilaterally changing safety rules through bulletins • Uncertainty about how current skill set fits with total safety culture	→ Ask for and respond graciously to taps from all → Build the safety business case → Build transfer scaffold, communicate VPO actions needed early and often → Steward change in Supt. Bulletin system, requiring that rule changes go through Core Team and rule sorter process → Build skills that integrate safety into day-to-day work of self and of all employees → S&H/PC orient VPO to performance consulting strategy

Table 7.6. Application of Rule Book Revision Transfer Scaffold to Core and Satellite Team Members

Stakeholder(s)	WIIFS (Stakeholder)/ Return on Investment	Actions Before	Actions During	Actions After	Barriers to Actions/Success	Countermeasures
Core and Satellite Team Members (Note that these key players come by design from other stakeholder groups.)	• Opportunity to influence process: culture, priorities, resources allocation • Career growth • Leadership development • Building of personal network across organization • Increased credibility on all sides for participation in a successful collaborative effort	• Comply with current safety rules • Learn about safety rule book process • With Safety/RM help, build boss's support for time to be spent on the project • Review current safety rule book	• Comply with current safety rules • Assess and work through own biases re safety rules • Listen • Build cross-function, cross-title, cross-location relationships • Comply with current safety rules • Test authenticity of process • Learn and apply skills for rule writing • Learn other crafts' unique safety contexts	• Comply with new CRs, craft-specific rules, and RPs • Participate as advocate of rules revision process and culture change in roll-out • Solicit suggestions for new/revised rules, teaching rule-writing logic • Stay in touch with CT/ST colleagues • Seek out new opportunities for collaboration • Initiate/support post-rule-book development and implementation of Tracking Document action items	• Reputation to maintain as tough negotiator • Conviction that a new safety rule is the best method for preventing recurrence • Lack of middle manager understanding and support of time needed for project • Cross-craft, cross-location, cross-title history, tensions • The way we've always done it • Own safety practices • Fear of betraying injured/killed co-worker by deleting rule written in his/her blood • Writing anxiety	→ Use safety rule sorter consistently and fairly → Apply Rummler and Brache organization performance factors to group analysis of unsafe acts' root causes → VPO endorsement of project with specific support expectations → Educate middle managers → Facilitate disagreement to consensus, celebrating/codifying/ deconstructing successes → Ask tough questions in the context of rules negotiations; CT/ST peer pressure → Affirm desire to honor incidents with systemic countermeasures, blended performance solutions → Facilitate toward participant skill sets, openly affirming dislike of "languaging"

Table 7.7. Application of Rule Book Revision Transfer Scaffold to Middle Managers

Stakeholder(s)	WIIFS (Stakeholder)/ Return on Investment	Actions Before	Actions During	Actions After	Barriers to Actions/Success	Countermeasures
Middle Managers (MMs): Trainmasters, Yardmasters, Mechanical, and Clerical Supervisors	• Reductions in incidents • Increased efficiency • Reduction in paperwork • Less subjective rules • Clarification of safety-related requirements vs. recommendations • Safety-only rule books • Craft-specific rule books • Current, accurate rule books • Positive safety results for personal performance plan • Positive salary treatment	• Model strong commitment to safety • Hear VPO orientation to and expectations for support of project • Forward questions/concerns to S&H/RM • Consent to CT/ST participation	• Listen to and learn from project status reports • Support CT/ST member participation/time in project • Participate in shopping process, offering reactions/ suggestions • Interface with peers who are CT/ST members to think through implications of safety rule/RP framework for own and collective practice	• Build working knowledge of new books • Support and participate in roll-out • Comply with and enforce new rules according to safety rule/RP framework even in the face of production pressure • Endorse, coach, teach • Report suggestions for changes in rules/RPs to S&H/RM for review • Help document performance outputs relative to the new rule books and communicate them to S&H/RM	• Production pressure: meat grinder location in overall system • The way we've always done it • Personal investment in rules s/he has written • Preference for lots of rules • Habit of responding to incident with rule violation charge • Personal skill set and reputation for pacesetter/ coercive leadership style • No knowledge of transfer of learning • Product over process, efficiency-or-safety orientation	→ Key middle managers on CT → Check-ins regarding rule books impact at 2-, 4-, 6-week intervals → Positive consequences for improved safety performance → Use of MM performance outputs data to reinforce project business case → VPO accountabilities re noncompliance/unacceptable performance → Support MM learning curve through supervisory skill building that defines rule book flash points and builds knowledge of how to use book into the muscle

comprehensive reading will, among other things, point up the access that transfer scaffolding opens to systems thinking and plain effective planning.

Scaffolds were also developed for other stakeholders: the President of CN, Legal, HR/Training, track supervisors and foremen, safety committees, union associates in the field, the Federal Railway Administration, families at home (see sidebar), and other railroad sector organizations. S&H's authority and standing with key project stakeholders, both up and down the food chain, preempted political hurdles and infused our efforts with positive energy. Interest in the project and momentum were mounting. As U.S. Region Risk Management Officer Ronald Ester observed, "That's the whole company. Man, it's the whole *industry*. Safety is everybody. Every place. All the time."

FAMILIES AT HOME: HIGH-IMPACT STAKEHOLDERS FOR SAFE WORK PERFORMANCE

- "Everybody buckled up? Alright, let's go."
- "Safety glasses and steel-toed shoes might be hot when you're out there mowing the lawn, but you'll be glad for them if the mower blade nicks your foot."
- "Hey, Dad, work a safe day, okay?"
- "Watch the weather out there in the yard tonight. See you when you come home. I love you."

Canadian National Railway has seen that safe behavior at home correlates strongly with safety at work. Who better than family to remind railroad professionals of the value of working safely? CN appeals to spouses, life partners, and children to reinforce their loved ones' safety commitment and behavior. *Live Injury-Free Everyday* (the *L.I.F.E.* book) used this icon to remind users that the safety issue being addressed was applicable at home as well as on the job:

Figure 7.2. "Home" Icon for *L.I.F.E.* Book

The Planning Team drafted elements of the transfer of learning scaffold up-front and, over the course of the project, vetted and re-vetted pieces of it with relevant stakeholders in brief coaching sessions. These interactions clarified the Planning Team's expectations and needs of these stakeholders and ensured their commitment to the project. The entire safety rule book scaffold served as one of the central structures in the project's architecture—and it was a work in progress.

Rule Book Revision Project Finish, Outputs, and Results

After four Core Team meetings and five sets of Satellite Team writing sessions (April 2000-January 2001) and a robust shopping process (February-April 2001), four safety rule books—one each for the Clerical, Engineering, Mechanical, and Transportation crafts—went to press in June 2001. Performance consultants and S&H were working tightly in tandem; draft rule books were touched in some way by more than five hundred CN colleagues in hand. A strong leading indicator of fundamental change underway in CN U.S. Ops' safety culture was the title of the new books, coined by Charlie Scholes, a Core Team member and machine operator from Effingham, Illinois. Instead of "hanging books," the new books were called *Live Injury-Free Everyday*, the *L.I.F.E.* books.

Other representative upstream indicators included fundamental changes in Core and Satellite Team members, who dropped career-long "us" versus "them" attitudes and kept pressure on the project as a top priority for themselves and for management. The teams consistently worked well past meetings' quitting time, starting with and sustaining high intensity, stewardship of detail, candor, commitment to consensus, and professional courtesy noted by most drop-by stakeholders. Core Team members—who began with the hope of gutting the safety rules—asserted the *need* for rules that would support raised safety standards in some areas and increased regard for the well-being of the associates working there. Further, senior union representatives in politically sensitive positions eliminated safety from the bargaining table, putting their personal reputations on the line to endorse the revision process and educate the field about the new safety culture.

The *L.I.F.E.* books themselves reflected transformative change in both the *quality* and the enormous reduction in the sheer *volume* of the rules. CN U.S. Ops' initial 900+ safety rules evolved into eighteen Core Safety Rules, those applicable to all crafts. The Transportation Department had the greatest reduction (85 percent) in craft-specific rules. The Engineering Department, whose function manages by far the most significantly diverse safety-related operational details, had the lowest reduction (a still hefty 65 percent). Reductions in the Clerical and Mechanical Departments' craft-specific rules fell somewhere in between.

Notably, most job requirements that had accommodated inconsistent safety standards from one craft to another were made consistent across all crafts. "Gotcha" rules, those enforced most often as post-incident evidence of non-compliance rather than as proactive job tools, were eliminated from all *L.I.F.E.* books.

Organizationally, the safety rule book revision process was awarded the CN President's Award, given to organization initiatives that produce performance improvements with dramatic impact and system-wide reach. CN Corporate brought the project Core Team together, post-distribution of the rule books, to deconstruct features of the process in order to import them into other efforts with whole culture change in mind.

CN Risk Manager Ron Ester describes the rule book revision project as "one of the most magical experiences of my life." He reflects further on the process in the sidebar.

S&H PARTNER RON ESTER INSIGHTS: CN U.S. OPS' SAFETY RULEBOOK RESULTS

It was the hard work and passion that these Core and Satellite Teams put into their rules that made the rule books truly great documents. Not just because they put in long and arduous hours, but because after a while they made it difficult to determine during various debates who was management and who was craft. Safety became the sole objective in drafting the new safety rule books.

The employees on the Satellite Teams ultimately wrote the safety rule books, with some guidance and assistance from the Core Team. The Satellites' charge to develop all content led to a broad group experience of ownership, pride, and ultimately trust in the process. Satellite Team confidence soared as their suggestions, new ideas, and deletions from the old rule books become the new, craft-specific books.

Most reluctance came from a segment of the management team who felt the changes would adversely affect productivity. Union officials were also skeptical and felt that there would be no changes in how discipline is meted out in safety-related issues. However, during the two months prior to implementation, when the books were shopped around the properties and informational training sessions on how to use the new rulebooks were held, acceptance of the finished product became overwhelming.

The Challenge of Evaluation

Performance consultants and S&H professionals agree that clear correlation between safety rule book revision and safety outputs are difficult to confirm. Discrete success indicators are muddied by the revision process's pragmatic call for rapid post-launch clean-up of text removed from original rule books and for action to be taken on issues raised during Core and Satellite Team rules discussions. The CN U.S. Ops process triggered follow-on interventions in capital improvement, job procedures manuals, education, and technological enhancements.

The Planning Team saw that deep stakeholder investment in the process, engineered through our extensive transfer scaffold, stood to largely compromise stakeholders' ability to assess rule book revision process results reliably. Bob Keane put the temptation to confirm the outcomes we hope for this way: "I can change it on paper, but that doesn't change it in the field. It takes real integrity to put the true story out there. In the end, you'll only fool yourself. It's like buying a smaller shirt. The guy who's trying to sell it to you says you look great. In the store you think you look great. But you get home, put the shirt on, look in the mirror, and see the real deal. And you know that in the end that's what other people will see, too."

What *is* clear is that CN U.S. Ops' safety rule book revision was the standard bearer for a suite of performance interventions between the high-hazard reorganization years of 1999 and 2003. During this time the Illinois Central Railroad, which had foreseen a potential spike in incidents and injuries due to dramatic organizational change, experienced only a mild 1.5 percent increase in its Frequency Index (FI); the Grand Trunk saw a 45 percent improvement in FI and received the FRA's Continuing

Safety Improvement award; and the Wisconsin Central saw a 22 percent FI improvement. Costs associated with derailment were reduced by 50 percent during this time period.

Other representative lagging performance indicators for the revision process include acknowledgement of the *L.I.F.E.* books by rail industry safety professionals as an industry best; consistent correlations between strong safety committee performance and injury reduction for the work groups they represent; and more willing and open communication between management and craft employees (including union leadership), as evidenced by the initiation of a streamlined "Resolution Process" for union-management-Federal Railway Administration negotiation of organization issues.

Two Years Later: *L.I.F.E.* Book Review

In mid-2004, CN U.S. Ops reconvened the rule book revision Core Team, augmented with representatives of more newly acquired properties, to revisit the first edition *L.I.F.E.* books. Calls from the field for changes to the books were minimal. Core Team newcomer Craig Peachy saw the *L.I.F.E.* book as "one of the most impressive things about Canadian National Railroad. A real shot in the arm for the small guy who's just been bought."

The review quickly assimilated new team members into the process and, by extension, into CN safety culture. Core Team alumni acknowledged the challenge of having new team members open issues that those involved in the first edition had battled over in 2000. "I feel a responsibility to protect the integrity of work done by hundreds of my colleagues who were involved in the first *L.I.F.E.* book," alumni David Lustig mused.

Core Team members applied their now considerable performance gap analysis skills to assessment of how the *L.I.F.E.* first edition has functioned. They zeroed in on the frequent relocation of new untrained supervisors to new work groups as a previously undetected barrier to consistent knowledge and application of safety rules and RPs throughout the system. The Core Team is currently working with HR/Training and Operations to make sure supervisors know what they need to know to use the *L.I.F.E.* books effectively and to continue expanding the network of tightly connected CN people who care greatly about one another's well-being.

Summary of This Chapter

Much is to be gained by performance consultants, performance partners like S&H, and the organizations we serve from the forging of strategic relationships that acknowledge and capitalize on our mutual stakeholder status. In the case study offered here, performance consultants and safety professionals walk the same theoretical and practical path. Surely there are other equally complementary functions out there with which we can interconnect and accomplish transformative work. Finding and learning these functions—and moving into powerful relationships with them—is an important step in our profession's evolution.

Finally, performance interventions like the safety rule book revision model described here take their successes not just from identification and inclusion of who does or should care about the effort once it is already underway. The interventions are deeply *defined* according to the web of interrelationships and insights of stakeholders whose lives, in the case of workplace safety, the processes literally hold in the balance. This is not incidental, nice-to-have work. It is the essential mission of those of us who earn our way by shaping organization performance.

Suggestions for Further Reading

Below are additional sources of information on one set of *performance partners*—safety and health professionals—that performance consultants may want to contact. They could be potential partners to support certain performance improvement interventions.

Geller, E. Scott. (2001). *Working safe: How to help people actively care for health and safety* (2nd ed.). Boca Raton, FL: CRC Press. A no-nonsense call for early inclusion of stakeholders at all organization levels in safety processes with lots of excellent tips for helping those stakeholders invest successfully.

Petersen, Dan. (2003). *Techniques of safety management: A systems approach.* Chicago: American Society of Safety Engineers. An important primer in safety-based systems thinking with a basic orientation and tone that correspond well with the Robinsons' performance consulting texts. This fourth edition has a nice, transferable section on measuring performance. The book complements *Safety Management: A Human Approach* well.

Petersen, Dan. (2001). *Safety management: A human approach.* San Francisco: American Society of Safety Engineers. An accessible, complete overview of a participative, behavior-based safety process with significant applicability throughout organizations. A great help for performance consultants interested in partnering with safety.

8

Implementing Transfer of Learning to Performance in a Complex International System

Richard L. Sullivan

IN THIS CHAPTER we focus on a highly complex system in which support for performance following instructional interventions from stakeholders in several key system components has become an essential part of the performance improvement process. The settings are particularly challenging: low resource countries with the support of the United States Agency for International Development, which provides reproductive healthcare training to healthcare personnel. The major topics for this chapter are

- An international complex system
- Moving from training to performance improvement
- Transfer of learning to performance
- Summary and lessons learned

An International Complex System

The mission: "Expanding quality healthcare for women and families globally." Sounds clear enough. Of course, we—the external consultants—need to do this internationally in countries with limited resources, significant cultural differences between us and our clients, and where our consultant organization works from outside the healthcare system. Now it sounds a bit more complicated. This has been the mission and challenge of JHPIEGO, an affiliate of Johns Hopkins University, since its beginning in 1973. In this chapter we look at how to involve stakeholders to support transfer of learning to performance in a highly complex international system. Although JHPIEGO works in healthcare, the implementation principles presented in this chapter will apply to many organizations working internationally. (In its early years, JHPIEGO stood for the "Johns Hopkins Program for International Education in Gynecology and Obstetrics." For many years, the organization has been known simply by the initials.)

The healthcare delivery system in any country is complex. This is especially true in a government-run healthcare system in a country with limited resources. When you add the United States Agency for International Development (USAID) and other international donors, as well as organizations such as JHPIEGO assisting stakeholders with implementing programs to improve healthcare, the system becomes very complex. JHPIEGO's international clients have included healthcare systems in over thirty countries in Africa, Asia, the Middle East, Latin America, and the Caribbean. Figure 8.1 shows a photograph of a typical outdoor training session in Kenya.

Figure 8.1. Typical JHPIEGO Outdoor Training Session in Kenya

Copyright © Rick Sullivan.

The primary focus of the system is the client and community. Community members receive health services at delivery sites that are typically linked to a national or subnational supervision system. Many sites are also connected to the pre-service education system that prepares healthcare providers, as well as to an in-service training system that ensures that practicing providers maintain the knowledge and skills required to provide quality services. At the national level are ministries of health and education as well as licensing and accreditation bodies.

The typical complex international healthcare system shown in Figure 8.2 will give some idea of what we are facing. Note in Figure 8.2 that arrows indicate the direction of the relationship between two parts of the system, solid lines indicate a direct interactive relationship, and dashed lines indicate an indirect informative relationship. The components of this system as well as the relationships vary from country to country.

Figure 8.2. A Typical Complex International Healthcare System

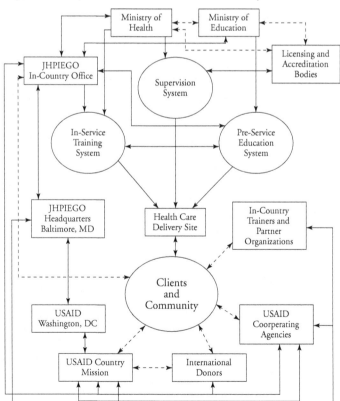

Moving from Training to Performance Improvement

One of JHPIEGO's core competencies is the ability to improve the performance of healthcare providers and the systems within which they work. This means that we work at the level of the healthcare delivery site as well as with in-service training, supervision, and pre-service education. Applying principles of transfer of learning to performance to our in-service training approach and connecting the training and supervision systems have proven to be very effective in ensuring that healthcare providers are able to provide quality services in their local areas. Before our approach within a complex system is outlined, it may be useful to describe how we moved from a focus on *training* to a focus on *performance.*

In the Beginning There Was Training

When we first opened our doors more than thirty years ago, the plan was to bring physicians from developing countries to Johns Hopkins University to be trained and to work in the clinics with proficient clinicians. Once we realized that this approach was very expensive and would take a long time to train each doctor individually, we reversed the direction and sent clinical trainers to the field to conduct training courses. Although this approach was very effective, it was not cost-efficient or sustainable. We needed to build the capacity within the country to train healthcare providers.

Training systems development became the primary focus for JHPIEGO for many years. Using the framework shown in Figure 8.3, we followed a relatively standardized process:

1. We began with a traditional *needs assessment* (or training needs assessment as it was often called).

2. Using *current international resource materials,* we updated the knowledge and skills of national stakeholders to better prepare them to make decisions related to strengthening their healthcare system.

3. We worked with national stakeholders to strengthen or develop their *national healthcare policies and guidelines* for service delivery.

Figure 8.3. Framework for Integrated Health Training

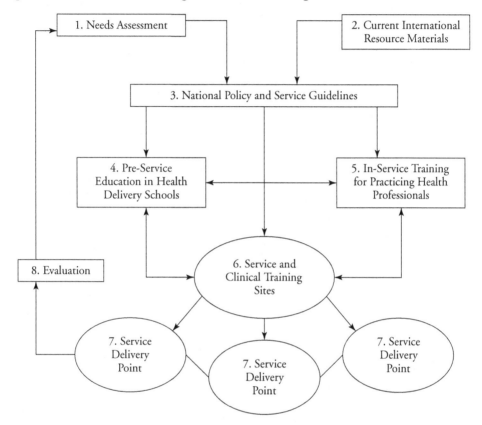

4. We worked with ministries of education and faculty within schools
    to strengthen curricula and faculty classroom and clinical teaching
    skills in *pre-service education* institutions (such as medical, nursing,
    and midwifery schools).

5. In *in-service training,* we worked with stakeholders and in-country
    partners to design, deliver, and evaluate training interventions to
    improve provider performance.

6. *Service delivery and clinical training sites* were common to pre-service
    education and in-service training. These were strengthened sites
    providing services according to the national guidelines, to give

pre-service education students and in-service training participants opportunities to practice in a model service delivery setting.

7. After completion of their education or training, individual providers then provided services at *service delivery points* (such as hospitals and clinics).

8. We did continuous *evaluation* of the quality of the providers' performance and service delivery in order to make changes in the training system.

Although this framework and the associated interventions served us well, over time it became apparent that, even when providers were highly trained, they occasionally were not providing quality services. During follow-up and monitoring visits, we found that some of those completing in-service training courses were not using their new knowledge and skills on the job. Why not?

We first looked at our training interventions. Were the designs valid? Did we have high-quality materials? Were trainers delivering the training as designed? Did we have the correct participants? We soon realized that our focus was just on training. Maybe we needed to be looking at what helped or hindered "performance on the job" instead of looking only at training. This led us to the performance improvement process.

JHPIEGO's Performance Improvement Process

For years we had believed that training was the primary way to improve worker performance. Although training is certainly one way to improve performance, it is rarely the only way. To have a lasting impact, training cannot be an isolated event. Instead, we needed to employ an integrated process that identifies the most appropriate solution by first defining what desired performance is and what is inhibiting the achievement of that performance. So we started looking at the factors that affect worker performance (JHPIEGO, 2004; Sullivan, 1998). Working with several other USAID cooperating agencies, we determined that the primary factors affecting health worker performance are those shown in Exhibit 8.1. (These factors were adapted from the work of Rummler & Brache, 1995.)

Exhibit 8.1. Primary Factors That Affect Health Worker Performance

- Having clear job expectations
- Receiving feedback on performance
- Being motivated
- Receiving organizational support
- Having the equipment and supplies to do the job
- Having the knowledge and skills to do the job (the primary factor requiring training)

Note that these factors were identified by JHPIEGO and other USAID organizations, based partially on G.A. Rummler and A.P. Brache (1995), *Improving Performance: How to Manage the White Space on the Organization Chart.*

Recognizing the importance of looking at worker performance and considering other factors that affect this performance, we began to move from a training focus to a focus on performance improvement (PI). The PI process being used by several USAID agencies (including JHPIEGO) is shown in Figure 8.4. (The model is based on the work of Van Tiem, Moseley, & Dessinger, 2000.)

Figure 8.4. JHPIEGO's Performance Improvement Process

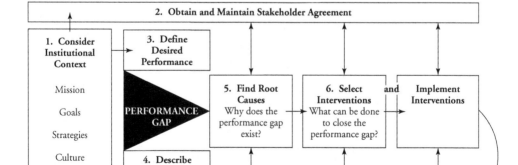

The PI process involves a series of steps that are repeated until the desired performance is achieved. The series of steps can be used to identify solutions for any type of performance gap. In our business, these gaps may be found in practices for infection prevention, management of stocks, counseling, overcrowding of wards, and lateness of employees. The PI process has the following steps.

Step 1: Consider the Institutional Context

Become familiar with the mission of the client country's healthcare system, its goals and current strategies, and the culture within which it functions. For a particular healthcare situation, identify the client system and key perspectives and concerns of the local community.

Step 2: Obtain and Maintain Stakeholder Participation

For the PI process to be implemented, buy-in from all stakeholders is necessary. Stakeholders are the people who have an interest in improving worker performance and the quality of services at the healthcare facility or within the organization where the PI process will be applied. Stakeholders may include workers, community members, supervisors, and representatives of different levels of the healthcare system, as well as representatives of JHPIEGO, USAID, and other collaborating organizations.

In developing countries, the community is the largest component of the stakeholders in healthcare services. The services of a healthcare facility are most effective when the community is involved from the beginning in the process of improving performance and the quality of services. Getting stakeholders to agree on using the performance improvement process (and then keeping them informed about the services at the facility) is the first big step in implementing the process.

Step 3: Define Desired Performance

For workers to perform well, they must know what they are supposed to do. This means that performance standards must be available. Workers must know not only what their job duties are, but also how to perform them. Desired performance should be realistic and take into account the resources (including the number of workers, training, budget, equipment, transport, supplies) at the facility. Desired performance should be based on common goals of stakeholders, including the expectations of the community.

Step 4: Describe Actual Performance

The supervisors (or those managing the PI process) should continually describe and assess how the workers and the facility are performing compared to how they are expected to perform. This assessment can be done on an ongoing, informal basis or more formally on a periodic basis. Methods to assess performance include conducting self-assessments or peer assessments, obtaining feedback from clients, and/or observation by supervisors or other staff.

Step 5: Find Root Causes of Performance Gaps

A performance gap exists if the supervisor and workers find that what workers are actually doing (Step 4) does not meet the set standards of performance (Step 3). If a gap is found, then the supervisor needs to carefully explore with workers why the gap is there. What is preventing the desired performance? Sometimes the reasons for poor performance are not immediately clear. It may take some time to find the real causes (which relate to one or more of the six factors affecting performance in Exhibit 8.1).

Step 6: Select and Implement Interventions to Close Performance Gaps

Once the causes of the performance gap have been identified, the supervisor and workers need to develop and implement ways to improve performance. Steps may be planned to improve the knowledge and skills of workers. There may be ways to improve the environment or support systems that make it possible for workers to perform well. There are many different ways to improve worker performance, including training. It is important to select methods that match facility resources.

Step 7: Monitor and Evaluate Performance

Once interventions have been implemented, it is very important to determine whether or not performance has improved. Is the worker now closer to meeting the established standards? If not, the PI team will need to go back to Step 3 of the PI process and consider again what is preventing the desired performance. It is important that the interventions be targeted at the real cause of the performance gap. If performance has improved, it is important for the supervisor to continue monitoring to make sure that the desired level of performance is maintained.

Applying the PI process has helped us to make better decisions about training. Because many of the factors that affect worker performance relate to the worker's supervisor (for example, job expectations, feedback on performance, having the tools to do the job), PI has also helped us to link training to supervision. That was when we discovered the missing link—transfer of learning to performance.

Transfer of Learning to Performance

When the acquisition of knowledge and skills (sixth primary factor in Exhibit 8.1) is identified as one of the solutions to a performance problem at a work site, training or other learning interventions will be used to improve the knowledge and skills of healthcare workers. Further efforts by stakeholders will be required to ensure that learning is transferred to job performance.

Transfer of learning to performance is defined in Chapter 3 as "the full application of new knowledge and skills by learners to effective performance on jobs, in communities, or in other settings." The goal is for learners to transfer 100 percent of their new knowledge and skills to their jobs, resulting in a higher level of performance and an improvement in the quality of services at their facilities.

The key stakeholders involved in this process include:

- *Supervisors*—responsible for monitoring and maintaining the quality of services and ensuring that healthcare workers are properly supported in the workplace;

- *Trainers*—responsible for helping healthcare workers acquire the necessary knowledge and skills to perform well on the job;

- *Healthcare workers*—responsible for the delivery of quality services; and

- *Co-workers*—responsible for supporting learners while they are engaged in training and as they apply new knowledge and skills at the work site.

Why Focus on Transfer of Learning to Performance?

In JHPIEGO's PI process, transfer of learning to performance (hereafter often shortened to "transfer to performance") is important for supervisors, trainers, learners, and co-workers because it is in the best interest of clients. Healthcare workers participate in a learning event to acquire new knowledge and skills to better meet the needs of their clients. Improving workplace performance enhances the quality of services—and may lead to increased client satisfaction.

Supervisors may not be proficient in all of the clinical services provided by the health workers they supervise. Being closely involved in the transfer to performance process can help them stay up-to-date.

Trainers are more likely to prepare interventions that meet the specific needs of learners and healthcare delivery sites when they have become invested in the outcome of training. Learning interventions can be expensive; improving transfer to performance helps to protect these investments.

Learners—and their supervisors—are more accountable for implementing what is learned if there is early agreement about what will occur after training (often as outlined in an action plan).

Learners are motivated to perform well at their jobs when they are able to apply what they have learned. The support and guidance of supervisors, trainers, and co-workers can encourage and empower learners to make changes and improve performance.

What Is the Process for Transfer to Performance?

JHPIEGO modeled our process for transfer to performance on the original transfer of training approach developed by Broad and Newstrom (1992). Our process is an interrelated series of tasks performed by supervisors, trainers, learners, co-workers, and sometimes others (such as government regulators and clients) before, during, and after a learning intervention in order to maximize transfer of knowledge and skills and improve job performance. The process is usually represented in a *matrix* that outlines the specific tasks performed by supervisors, trainers, learners, and co-workers.

What Is the Matrix for Transfer to Performance?

The matrix shown in Table 8.1 is a useful means of presenting stakeholder strategies for transfer of learning to performance (Broad, 1997a). The JHPIEGO matrix is designed for use in the complex healthcare systems in which we work. It includes suggested strategies adapted from the research literature (see Table 3.4) and the experiences of supervisors, trainers, and learners in the international healthcare field (JHPIEGO and PRIME II, 2002). The suggestions can be adapted to fit many international healthcare situations, including the use of different types of learning interventions (such as classroom, on-the-job, e-learning, and self-directed) and various sorts of supervisory arrangements (internal supervisors onsite or periodic external supervisory visits).

Table 8.1. JHPIEGO's Matrix for Transfer of Learning to Performance

	Before Learning	*During Learning*	*After Learning*
Supervisors	Recognize, describe the performance need Participate in any additional assessments required for training Influence selection of learners Communicate with trainers about the learning intervention Help learners create a preliminary action plan Support and encourage learners	Participate in or observe training Protect learners from interruptions Plan post-training debriefing Provide supplies and space and schedule opportunities for learners to practice	Monitor progress of action plans with learners and revise as needed Conduct post-training debriefing with learners and co-workers Be a coach and role model—provide encouragement and feedback Evaluate learners' performance Stay in contact with trainers

Table 8.1. JHPIEGO's Matrix for Transfer of Learning to Performance, Cont'd

	Before Learning	*During Learning*	*After Learning*
Trainers	Validate and supplement the results of the performance needs assessment Use instructional design and learning principles to develop or adapt the course Send the course syllabus, objectives and pre-course learning activities in advance	Provide work-related exercises and appropriate job aids Give immediate and clear feedback Help learners develop realistic action plans Conduct training evaluations	Conduct follow-up activities in a timely manner Help strengthen supervisors' skills Facilitate review of action plans with supervisors and learners Share observations with supervisors and learners Maintain communication with supervisors and learners
Learners	Participate in needs assessments and planning Review course objectives and expectations and prepare preliminary action plans Begin establishing a support network Complete pre-course learning activities	Participate actively in the course Develop realistic action plans for transferring	Meet with supervisor to review action plan Apply new skills and implement action plan Use job aids Network with other learners and trainers for support Monitor your own performance
Co-Workers and Others	Participate in needs assessments and discussions of the training's intended impact Ask learners to bring back key learning points to share with the work group	Complete learners' reassigned work duties Participate in learning exercises at the request of learners	Be supportive of learners' accomplishments

(Continued)

Table 8.1. JHPIEGO's Matrix for Transfer of Learning to Performance, Cont'd

	Before Learning	*During Learning*	*After Learning*
Ministry of Health	The primary role of the MOH related to transfer of learning is to establish national policy and service delivery guidelines, manage the in-service training system, and support the national supervision system.		
Ministry of Education	The primary role of the MOE related to transfer of learning is to strengthen the pre-service education system to graduate and deploy competent healthcare providers pursuant to licensing requirements.		

It may not be appropriate or possible to implement all of these suggestions as part of any one learning intervention. Some of the suggestions in the matrix may represent a radical change from current policies and procedures at a specific facility. However, if just a few of the ideas described in the matrix can be adapted and implemented, JHPIEGO's experience shows that this improves the likelihood that new knowledge and skills will be applied on the job. The more ideas and suggestions being implemented, the stronger the transfer of learning will be.

What Are Other Actions to Improve Transfer to Performance?

In addition to the specific suggestions included in the matrix, the following actions by some or all of the key stakeholders (supervisors, trainers, healthcare workers, and co-workers) are essential for transfer to performance:

- Exploring and recognizing the relationship of knowledge and skills to the other factors that affect performance at the work site (Sullivan, 2002);

- Establishing and maintaining structures that support desired performance (including using nontraining interventions to influence other factors that affect performance, such as constructive feedback, provision of necessary equipment and supplies, and clear protocols);

- Working collaboratively with all individuals who can support (or might hinder) desired on-the-job performance;

- Using action plans or similar devices to set and maintain clear performance objectives and expectations and to document progress and challenges; and

- Creating a supportive environment in which all workers appreciate their potential to improve services by acquiring new skills and knowledge.

What Is an Action Plan?

In JHPIEGO's transfer to performance process, an action plan is a written document that describes the steps that supervisors, trainers, learners, and co-workers will complete to help maximize the transfer of learning to performance. An action plan is initiated *prior to the training intervention* so that everyone who can support the transfer to performance is involved from the beginning. The plan is *refined* during the training event and usually is *not completed* until after the event, when learners are implementing new skills on the job. Action plans are essential to implementing transfer to performance. The content and layout of an action plan should support the users of the plan, especially the learners. In developing and using an action plan, keep in mind these important points:

- Write activities as discrete steps that are realistic, measurable, and attainable;

- Identify clear responsibilities for learners, supervisors, co-workers, and trainers;

- Develop a specific time schedule for completing activities;

- Identify resources necessary to complete the activities, including plans for acquiring those resources;

- Send blank action plans to the supervisors and learners in advance of training and ask that they describe specific areas to improve and problems to overcome, and ask that the learner bring the partially completed action plan to the training course;

- Afford learners an opportunity to publicly share their completed action plans before the last day of training so that they can modify their plans based on feedback and ideas from their peers; and

- Provide a copy of the completed action plans to trainers for follow-up purposes and to each learner and the learner's supervisor for their ongoing use.

An example of an action plan is provided as part of the following example of a JHPIEGO performance improvement intervention.

THE CASE OF IMPROVED INFECTION PREVENTION PRACTICES

In Ecuador during 1999–2000, JHPIEGO worked with a nongovernmental organization with health facilities providing reproductive health and family planning services for members of local communities. Two steps of the JHPIEGO PI process (Figure 8.3) had been established for this intervention. In Step 1 the Ecuadorian institutional context had been explored at national and local levels. In Step 2 the required relationships and agreements for involvement had been established with key stakeholders, including the central management team, clinic supervisors, clinic directors, staff, and members of the community.

In order to define the desired performance (Step 3) and to describe the actual performance (Step 4), data was collected during visits to local health facilities. The performance needs assessment determined that there were problems related to infection prevention (IP) practices, resulting from inadequate physical facilities (such as lack of sinks, lack of space, poor traffic flow), lack of supplies (including chlorine), and the outsourcing of cleaning and laundry services.

Results of the root-cause analysis (Step 5) determined that one of the root causes of the problem was that health workers lacked the necessary knowledge and skills to provide appropriate IP practices. In addition, there was a need to strengthen IP guidelines and protocols at the central level of the healthcare system.

Stakeholders, working to select and implement interventions (Step 6), decided to provide health workers with the required knowledge and skills during a four-day IP training course. Part of the design of this training intervention included activities to facilitate the transfer of learning to performance.

The first offering of this course included twenty-two health workers and supervisors from ten local health facilities from eight different cities. Involving the supervisors in the training was part of the transfer of learning strategy. The training design also involved interactive training methods, including small-group activities, demonstrations, case studies, simulations, and observation visits to clinical sites.

Before training began, a conference call with key stakeholders stressed the importance of their support in the improvement of IP practices at the facility level. The specific strategies each stakeholder would take (adapted from the JHPIEGO Matrix for Transfer of Learning to Performance, Table 8.1) were discussed and agreed to.

Also before training took place, a performance matrix (Table 8.2) was developed as a means to collect information in advance of training about the performance need and potential causes of IP problems at the facility level. The performance matrix was sent to supervisors at the target clinics to help them to facilitate discussions with their health workers before the workers and selected supervisors attended training.

Table 8.2. JHPIEGO's Performance Matrix

Gaps Related to IP	Potential Causes	Potential Solutions	Strategies for Implementation

Early in the training course, representatives from each health facility presented the facility's performance matrix showing the performance gaps they had identified. Following the presentations, common performance gaps across all of the clinics were identified and posted on the wall for reference. During the course, content and examples were continually compared to the most common gaps. Participants were then given opportunities to identify potential solutions and plan implementation strategies for the IP problems being faced at their clinics.

On the last day of the course, the representatives from each site presented their implementation action plans. (An action plan format is shown as Exhibit 8.2.) Key stakeholders from the central management team attended the last day; they participated in discussions about implementation plans and needs to support efforts by reinforcing guidelines and protocols, and by ensuring that required supplies were available. In addition, plans were discussed for follow-up visits by the trainers, and a follow-up meeting of all participants was scheduled within three months of the course.

Exhibit 8.2. JHPIEGO's Action Plan Format

Action Plan				
Name:	**Training Intervention:**			**Date:**
My Support Team/Partners:	Supervisor: Trainer:		Co-worker(s):	
Specific Areas to Improve: (Think about distinct accomplishments and activities to be achieved.) **Problems to Overcome:** (Describe the barriers that must be eliminated or reduced and how this will be done.)				
Detailed Specific Actions (in sequence): Be sure to include regular progress reviews with the support team as a part of the specific actions.	**Responsible Person(s)**	**Resources**	**Date/ Time***	**Changes to Look For**
Step 1				
Step 2				
Step 3				
Step 4				
Step 5				
Step 6				
Step 7				
Step 8				
Step 9				
Step 10				
*Establish set day and time for ongoing activities				
Commitment of Support Team/Partners: *I support the action plan described above and will complete the actions assigned to me. If I am unable to complete an activity, I will help make arrangements to modify the plan accordingly.*	Signature of learner: Date: Signature of supervisor: Signature of trainer: Signatures of co-workers:			

In order to monitor and evaluate performance (Step 7) after training, a questionnaire was sent to supervisors to follow up on their facility-level action plans. The questionnaire asked about improvements, resistant gaps, and their suggestions for the follow-up meeting. Trainers compiled the results of the follow-up questionnaire before the follow-up visits and meetings.

Trainers visited the health facilities to observe and help with implementation and problem solving. Trainers met with participants from all the facilities during the follow-up meeting to review and recognize progress to date, motivate the supervisors and workers, identify persistent gaps, and discuss solutions to performance gaps.

Results of the training and follow-up visits and meeting showed that all health facilities had implemented many of the IP practices. There were improvements in decontamination and sterilization processes, hand washing, disposal of sharps, use of antiseptics, cleaning of reusable containers, housekeeping, and care of linen. In addition, an infection prevention policy manual had been developed and was in use, standards for cleaning and the laundry were established, training for cleaning and laundry personnel was being conducted (based on the new standards), and the chlorine supply problem had been corrected. There were still some gaps in some facilities, mostly related to their physical structure and lack of supplies. These gaps would become the focus of the next round of performance needs assessments.

One of the realities of working as an external consultant organization within a complex system is that often pressures such as changing country situations and shifting funding priorities impact your work. In the case of Ecuador, just as we were seeing some results, the project ended. However, we were very encouraged by the initial positive results. JHPIEGO learned in Ecuador, and in all other locations, that when transfer to performance strategies are integrated into the design and implementation of training, the impact of the training is increased, in improved healthcare worker performance and in results with clients in the community.

Summary and Lessons Learned

Our journey started with training individual healthcare providers by bringing them to the United States. This was a very simple system and one over which we had control. However, to better meet the needs of the countries, we reversed the direction of our strategy and conducted training courses for providers in the field. Suddenly we were working within a much more complex system.

In an effort to make training more sustainable, we moved into strengthening training systems, which put us in the middle of a highly complex system. As we moved from training to performance improvement and started looking more closely at performance, we realized that, to maximize the effect of our training, we needed to integrate strategies for transfer to performance into our approach (JHPIEGO and PRIME II, 2002). These are the lessons we have learned in applying transfer of learning to performance within a complex system:

- Design and implement training interventions only after following the performance improvement process. This allows you to make better decisions about when training really is needed to improve worker performance and when non-training interventions would better address the root causes of poor performance.

- Include transfer to performance strategies in training interventions. From the initial design stage, transfer of learning should be a major component of the strategy and should be built into the budget. This should be agreed on in advance with the stakeholders involved. This prevents the common situation of "adding" transfer activities to a project and then trying to generate support as well as locate the necessary funds.

- Orient key stakeholders to transfer of learning to performance early in the planning stages so that they understand the importance of their support for the process and how this process will be applied within the system.

- Plan and budget for communications and collaboration with the supervisors of those being trained. They are very important stakeholders who must be involved before, during, and after training activities.

- Include transfer to performance approaches, activities, and tools in training materials, in guidance communications sent to participating agencies and trainees' supervisors, and in the design of training interventions.

- Orient trainers to transfer to performance strategies. Ensure that train-the-trainer courses include an orientation to the trainer's role in supporting transfer to performance and in coaching other stakeholders on their roles.

- Orient supervisors of those attending training to transfer to performance strategies and gain their agreement to use appropriate strategies with their subordinate trainees.

- Plan and budget for trainer follow-up visits as soon after training as possible, to reinforce transfer-to-performance principles and to coach participants and their supervisors in on-the-job applications.

The primary challenge of working within a highly complex international healthcare system is the possibility of getting lost. There are numerous pressures on labor markets, constant changes within health system leadership, political considerations, and tremendous social and community pressures. As we work with national stakeholders to strengthen their ability to manage human resources for health, we recognize that a component of our strategy will almost always include training to improve the performance of healthcare providers. Based on our experience, transfer of learning to performance will always play a major role in our approach to training.

Suggestions for Further Reading

Several of the references in this chapter may be of particular interest to readers of this book. Widely known professional resources (Broad & Newstrom, Stolovitch & Keeps, and Van Tiem, Moseley, & Dessinger) led to some of the key changes that JHPIEGO has made to strengthen the transfer of learning to performance. Other references listed below document those changes in greater detail.

Broad, M.L., & Newstrom, J.W. (1992). *Transfer of training: Action-packed strategies to ensure high payoff from training investments*. Reading, MA: Perseus Books. This ground-breaking book opened the way for JHPIEGO to widen its focus by involving important stakeholders in the entire performance improvement process.

JHPIEGO and PRIME II. (2002). *Transfer of learning: A guide for strengthening the performance of healthcare workers.* Chapel Hill, NC: Intrah. Available: http://reproline.jhu.edu/english/6read/6training/tol/index.htm. This thirty-three-page pamphlet describes in considerable detail the new approaches that JHPIEGO, and its sister consulting organization PRIME II, have followed to improve services and outcomes for their clients. These include strategies and techniques that support the transfer of knowledge and skills to the workplace: types of interventions, specific strategies for key stakeholders, and an action plan format.

Stolovitch, H.D., & Keeps, E. (1999). *Handbook of human performance technology: Improving individual and organizational performance worldwide* (2nd ed.). San Francisco: Pfeiffer. This comprehensive volume provides information on every important aspect of human performance technology.

Sullivan, R.L. (1995). Training across international borders. *Training & Development, 49*(6), 55–57. This article describes the challenges faced when training is being implemented internationally and concurrently in a number of countries.

Sullivan, R.L. (1998, April). The transfer of skills training. *InfoLine.* Alexandria, VA: American Society for Training and Development. This publication outlines the process used by JHPIEGO to improve the performance of healthcare provider skills. The process describes how to demonstrate a skill, coach skill performance, and evaluate skill competence.

Van Tiem, D.M., Moseley, J.L., & Dessinger, J.C. (2000). *Fundamentals of human performance technology: A guide to improving people, process, and performance.* Washington, DC: International Society for Performance Improvement. Besides a helpful review of key performance technology principles and practices, this book provides very useful performance tools that are adaptable to many work settings and case studies illustrating applications of principles and tools.

9

e-Learning and Support for Performance

Kenneth W. Finley, Jr.

THIS CHAPTER is focused not on e-learning's technology, but on what this new approach to organizational learning is (and what it is not). Transfer of e-learning to performance is greatly enhanced by the workplace setting, and the support of online communities of practice. Electronically networked learning's ease of updating and distributing ever-changing content yields tremendous support for timely transfer of vital skills in the workplace. We explore what e-learning is, its state of the art, and its enablers and disablers. Finally, we look at what stakeholders can do to support the transfer of e-learning to performance.

The major topics for this chapter are

- What constitutes e-learning
- Current e-learning state of the art
- e-Learning enablers and disablers
- Stakeholder support for transfer of e-learning to performance

What Constitutes e-Learning

e-Learning is one of the latest "new things" to sweep through organizations worldwide. (Notice the trendy fashion with which the word is capitalized.) With widespread and rapidly increasing access to the World Wide Web around the globe, the potential of this relatively new technology for supporting organizational learning has become obvious. The basic attributes of this approach must be carefully thought through as its adoption or expansion is considered as a means to improve performance.

What e-Learning Is

The primary feature of e-learning is *the electronic linking of an instructor, remote in distance and/or time, and a performer and other stakeholders.* There are many different names for e-learning: web-based learning, online learning, distance learning, networked learning, or web-enabled learning. e-Learning extends the learning environment beyond the individual learning experience. It incorporates the larger community of performers and other diverse stakeholders, often including a live instructor, participating in real time from a distance.

Within this larger learning environment, a consistent set of features for e-learning emerges:

- Facilitating learning and performance using electronic communications technology;

- Developing and delivering well-designed learning experiences, just in time and place for the performer's need or application to the work;

- Forming communities of practice (networks of performers with common interests and expertise) to contribute to and reinforce individualized, comprehensive, dynamic learning content that is available when and where needed; and

- Establishing accountability for performers to maintain the correct skill sets and implied performance goals.

With good design and delivery, e-learning does all these things. But at its heart it is, simply, learning. From an organizational point of view, learning is about one thing: transforming time-critical information of value into performance. The most obvious flaw of the evolving technology is the focus on the technology (the "e") and not on the learning. It is this same misdirected focus that causes organizations to fail to capitalize on e-learning's strengths to support transfer of learning to performance. The case studies described in this chapter demonstrate how organizations can leverage e-learning's advantages and how some have missed the mark.

What Is Not e-Learning

Two well-known learning media may be confused with e-learning, since both use computer technologies. However, each has one or more clear distinctions from e-learning.

Computer-based training (CBT) is certainly a parent technology of e-learning, and sometimes the distinctions between the two blur. The primary focus of CBT is on the individual learning activity using a computer (in any location) with built-in, structured learning exercises. The instructor is designed into the system, and the learner is required to interact solely with the CBT. However, CBT is not connected to the Internet and provides no interactivity with the instructional source or other learners or stakeholders.

An electronic performance support system (EPSS) is another parent technology that uses computers but is necessarily located in the workplace where the work is performed. EPSSs are usually network-based and may be Internet-based. They contain an information tutorial, an expert advisor to support the user in making decisions, and sometimes a learning component. These components work together with the primary goal of supporting performance directly, and not with a goal of helping the performer learn (Rossett & Gautier-Downes, 1991). Cole, Fischer, and Saltzman (1997) emphasize that an EPSS exhibits "a change in focus from knowing to performing."

In many cases, an EPSS bypasses learning altogether. In an environment where processes change rapidly, such as in custom mass production, it is pointless for the learner to invest in learning a process that will be obsolete for the next production run. The performer follows the guidance of the EPSS to perform the work, not to gain knowledge or skills.

Current e-Learning State of the Art

The rapid growth of the Web suggests that organizations believe leveraging the intranet and Internet can improve organizational productivity. The adoption of universal conferencing standards using standard software or platform-independent applications has brought people, worlds apart, face-to-face. Advanced digital compression allows us to send audio and digital files over traditional phone lines that used to require specialized, dedicated fiber-optic networks. More powerful personal computers, laptops, and PDAs, the World Wide Web, Internet, and intranets have become the tools of choice for direct, synchronous, and asynchronous audio and video communication.

e-Learning Investments and Use

It should come as no surprise that learning strategies follow business strategies. The ASTD *2004 State of the Industry Report* showed that the learning hours provided by technology-based methods had increased from 15.4 percent in 2002 to 23.6 percent in 2003. The same report projected that technology-based methods would increase to 29.4 percent in 2004 (Sugrue & Kyung-Hyun, 2004).

This suggests that John Chambers, president and CEO of Cisco Systems, only slightly exaggerated when he predicted, "The next big killer application for the Internet is going to be education. Education over the Internet is going to be so big it is going to make e-mail usage look like a rounding error" (Muoio, 2000).

CASE STUDY: SUCCESSFUL E-LEARNING: RETAIL POINT OF SALE CASHIER TRAINING

Do e-learning efforts actually transfer to the workplace and provide bottom-line benefits? According to the ASTD *2004 State of the Industry Report* (Sugrue & Kyung-Hyun, 2004), only 14 percent of the companies surveyed measured transfer of learning to performance, and only 8 percent reported impact on organizational results. In short, there aren't many organizations reporting results for e-learning.

One major retail organization (name omitted by request) found that an e-learning implementation yielded significant transfer to performance and impact on the organization's bottom line (Gordon, 2004). The retailer's corporate training department was responsible for 76,000 associates in the United States and Canada. Keeping trained cashiers in the stores was a challenge, with a high turnover rate, huge demand on senior cashiers to provide on-the-job coaching, and generally low job satisfaction and morale. Root cause deficiencies identified were diverse range of reading and comprehension levels, inconsistent training methods, no documentation, insufficient hours scheduled for training, and a push to get the new hires on the front line as soon as possible. The environment set up new hires for failure.

Since the training had to duplicate the work environment, the designers used an online system enabling a point-of-sale keyboard on a personal computer linked to a learning management database. Senior cashiers and front-line managers analyzed and identified performance gaps. They conducted focus groups via teleconference and followed up with e-mail recaps to confirm consensus. Cashiers were trained on existing equipment available to all stores. Connection through a web-based learning management system enabled trainers to update training, track learner progress, and reinforce with face-to-face coaching using on-site senior cashiers.

The retailer reports the following results:

- Daily ring-rate errors were reduced from 25 percent to 20 percent. This resulted in savings of $6,250 to $22,500 per week per store.

- Order rate per hour of new hires increased to the maximum within three days of starting, instead of the usual ten days.

- New hire retraining was reduced from two to four sessions per new hire to one or two sessions.

- On-the-job training time was reduced from five days to two. Senior cashier time savings realized a bottom-line improvement of $10,800 per store per year.

- Cashier job satisfaction and morale (as measured through reductions in absenteeism, tardiness, and errors) was improved 25 percent.

- Improved employee retention resulted in a $122,285 per store reduction, per month, in hiring costs.

The designers involved key stakeholders (senior cashiers and front-line managers) in the design process and involved them in implementation while reducing their workload. New hires were adopted as full performers quickly, with provisions for retraining if needed. Using existing systems reduced the cost of implementation and the stress of adding new systems to the information systems (IS) department workload.

e-Learning Within a Workplace Context

Embedding learning in the workplace has made a significant impact on educational thinking since its early description by Brown, Collins, and Duguid (1989). Learning at the site where the new knowledge is to be used and realistic work-related activities strengthen learning and support transfer to performance.

Learning within the work environment improves transfer because it is right there when the performer needs it, if the system is properly designed. Building in a requirement that the performer go to another machine or have specialized equipment not required for the job defeats the purpose of e-learning.

e-Learning as Just-in-Time Work and Performance Support

With an intranet (a network within an organization), learning providers (performance consultants, instructional technologists, trainers, managers, technology providers, co-workers, and coaches) can give employees just-in-time access to current training materials and job aids. These materials can incorporate text, graphics, video, and audio, available in a self-directed mode at the desktop, the laptop, and even the personal data assistant (PDA). This could include reading the text online or downloading a .pdf document. A centrally stored audio file in MP3 format can be downloaded for listening while driving or as an aid for the visually impaired.

In a rapidly changing environment, web-based training development provides the fastest route to updates and delivery. With proper preparation, performers can use the central organization resources to access learning from any location, based on need. Anyone wishing to use the resources off-line can store them on any of the memory devices available or burn a CD-ROM. This eliminates the labor cost of distribution and collection of outdated materials. Printing and pressing costs are borne by those who choose a permanent medium.

The training function can promote widespread learning while managing instruction conveniently from a central location. With the increased flexibility and bandwidth of the Internet and intranet, blended or mixed media strategies can be employed that are more adaptable to the diverse population of performers. Training via a corporate intranet has the added advantage of offering the ability to customize and control the content of any training intervention.

CASE STUDY: CISCO: STRUCTURING E-LEARNING CONTENT ON AN INTRANET

The Cisco Corporation found itself with an extreme case of rapidly changing documentation and significant challenges in maintaining the information's relevance. With ten million Web pages on its corporate intranet, performers couldn't find what they needed and contributors couldn't keep information up-to-date. Creating a viable e-learning strategy to support access was paramount.

To bolster usability for performance support, the training operation developed a field-employee-oriented infrastructure for the e-learning website. Content on the site was arranged by audience and organized in user-friendly curriculum maps based on job titles, work theatres, specific technologies, and products. Becoming smarter about content meant letting stakeholders outside the training operation create it. This aided the transfer of learning to performance because the stakeholder network had greater ownership in the solution. The training department's motto became: "Content is King, Infrastructure is God" (Muoio, 2000).

e-Learning as Community of Practice

A *community of practice* is a stable group of individuals (performers, co-workers, and other stakeholders) who form a set of habits and conventions and share a consensual goal to support each other in learning. Everybody expects to learn and is prepared to engage in activities at least partly for that reason (Wilson & Ryder, 1999).

In the context of e-learning and transfer of learning to performance, stakeholders provide the community of practice. Communities of practice redefine competence, not as an individual characteristic but in the context of performance as a group to produce accomplishments valued by the organization and the customer, thus keeping the business going (Beer, 2000). Cognitive apprenticeship is one way to initiate performers into authentic practices through activity and social interaction—in this instance, interaction via the Web—and is an important part of workplace learning within a community of practice. In this context employees are not motivated to learn just to have new skills, but to learn "how we do things here" to be able to participate in the community (Henschel, 1996). With wireless communication and virtual protected networks (VPNs), corporate intranet learning extends participation in the corporate community regardless of geographic location or the lack of dedicated lines.

Authors such as Palloff and Pratt (1999) detail how to build learning communities in cyberspace, permitting an unprecedented degree of interactivity via list servers, e-mail, bulletin boards, chat rooms, instant messaging, and other methods. For example, team members can increase their ability to perform various team functions by accessing online training with co-worker coaching. Or, at the click of a hypertext link whenever convenient, the team member can download PDA-friendly documentation, the latest version, without having to rummage through reams of print materials.

Another e-learning community of practice advantage is team building. Corporations do not want to expend training dollars on temporary hires. This automatically detracts from performance because it produces populations of have's and have not's. With e-learning, temporary employees can receive training important for team knowledge and performance at opportune times without major cost to the organization. Also, if a temporary hire is made permanent, prior e-learning experiences reduce the "ramp-up" time for orientation and essential skills training.

Design Elements for e-Learning

The following elements are necessary for effective adult learning for performance (Knowles, 1990; Wlodkowski, 1985):

- Performance objectives mapped directly to the work environment;
- Content focused to the specific valued accomplishment;

- Options to use a flexible learning path;
- Meaningful, relevant learning activities; and
- Useful feedback on performance using measures related to the workplace.

These are the same requirements for effective e-learning (Beer, 2000). Thus, learning is learning, and getting that learning reflected in workplace performance is a function of effective planning and design. Poorly designed e-learning will fail just like any other type of learning intervention. Proponents of e-learning must remember to keep the people it is designed for in mind. How do we learn? How do we acquire and retain skills and information to help us develop? How does the workplace support and reinforce that learning as performance? Only when we address individual learning styles and opportunities for specialized delivery can the "e" in e-learning factor in. Then the technical side—the electronic delivery—can be adapted to the performer.

e-Learning Enablers and Disablers

A 2002 report, "Pillars of e-Learning Success" (Corporate University Xchange), describes an in-depth study of 4,100 e-learners in sixty-five organizations that had implemented successful e-learning initiatives. The study found completion rates to be quite high, about 82 percent. But what is most important for transfer of learning to performance are the top three reasons e-performers cite for dropping out:

1. That managers are not involved in employees' learning and development plans;

2. That managers do not provide the needed time off for learning; and

3. That managers do not publicly reward and/or acknowledge employees for successfully completing programs.

As with any other learning approach, e-learning can be actively supported or unintentionally sabotaged. If e-learning is to thrive as a learning and transfer strategy, senior management must create a supportive learning environment that encourages employees to take time out for learning and reinforces the application of that learning to performance in the workplace. As stake-holders become wiser in the ways of technology and how it supports today's performers, they can be more proactive in taking advantage of the key enablers and minimizing the primary disablers.

Enablers of e-Learning

Significant annual growth rates of e-learning mean increasing numbers of stakeholders who support e-learning and become involved with its adoption in the work environment. Exhibit 9.1 presents the primary enablers that support their efforts:

Exhibit 9.1. Enablers of e-Learning

- Employee-centered learning, independent of time or place
- Upgraded e-learning through technological advances
- Centralized updates, assessment, feedback, and record-keeping
- Relatively platform-independent delivery through uniform standards
- Workforce currency maintained

Employee-Centered Learning Independent of Time or Place

When students access learning to answer questions relevant to them, those students are motivated performers (Wlodkowski, 1985). They are free to choose their best learning approach and seek members of the community of practice who can explain concepts and performance expectations. e-Learning's independence of geography, walls, or time (Driscoll, 2002) meets the organizational need for timely learning and performance.

e-Learning emphasizes job relevance. Providing the learning as a link to the job *embeds learning in the workplace* and greatly improves transfer of learning to performance.

e-Learning, especially well-designed web-based instances, can provide an individual just the amount of training, practice, and review needed rather than a one-size-fits-all delivery. To capitalize on this advantage, instructional designers and managers must take time to thoroughly define the job requirement to ensure that what is created is relevant.

Upgraded e-Learning Through Technological Advances

Since e-learning is technology-driven, universal access to usable and compatible technology makes this approach very attractive. Memory, storage, processor speed and capability, and increasingly user-friendly software make it easier to enable stakeholder participation in the creation and distribution of online learning. Cisco's ten million Web pages are an example of the many corporations already using the intranet and Internet to provide communications and information storage (see Cisco Case Study earlier). The resources used to provide a structure for communication and information to support productivity contain the essential elements to support learning as well. When e-learning is designed to use the same standards as the corporate network, the organization reinforces the impression that the learning is relevant, while realizing the huge cost savings of not replicating expensive equipment.

Centralized Updates, Assessment, Feedback, and Record-Keeping

Maintaining courseware on the Internet or intranet enables rapid updates. With all courses hosted at a single point on the Web, course managers can update one set of files and propagate them throughout the organization. Tools available for the Web can strengthen the involvement of co-workers and other stakeholders by having them supply content within a simple template. A backend database facilitates storing records on versions, responses, times of response, frequency of access, and depth of access. Such data give the designer and analyst a wealth of information that is often lost. Designers and managers can more accurately define the criteria for transfer of learning to performance and measure the result to provide a wealth of useful feedback to the learner as well.

With one entry point for content, consistent standards can be maintained for interfaces, presentations, feedback, and evaluation. e-Learners benefit from a consistent interface and set of resources.

Relatively Platform-Independent Delivery Through Uniform Standards

No other delivery method provides the freedom of delivery available through web-based learning. Unlike videotapes or early CBT systems limited to specific machines and operating systems, web-based training is nearly machine-independent and totally free of the clock. There certainly may be platform and bandwidth issues for some systems; however, the designer has more latitude with this platform than any other. e-Learning materials are available anywhere at any time. Management already funds computer system and networking costs as a part of the organization infrastructure. Better still, the performers already know how to use the equipment in place. e-Learning becomes a natural outgrowth of the information systems managers and stakeholders build for their internal and external customers.

Workforce Currency Maintained

A competent individual focused on one project may experience skills obsolescence by the time that project is completed. With access to online training in new skills and knowledge, that individual has a cost-effective and time-effective way to maintain currency.

There are few high-tech companies that truly respect how much learning has to happen to allow them and their people to stay current. Almost every company talks about "knowledge workers," "the information economy," or even "the learning organization." But few companies act as if they believe what they are saying. There is too much work to do, too many deadlines to meet, too many quarterly results to deliver. Learning time is not a respected part of the work environment. But workers must not be so busy that they allow themselves to "get stupid." People find the time to do whatever it is that they have to do. Staying current is an increasingly important part of everyone's job; everyone must spend time learning. e-Learning communities facilitate the sharing of information and help performers and managers reinforce each other in the creation of an adaptive, flexible organization.

CASE STUDY: KEEPING ENGINEERS CURRENT

One e-learning project involved satellite programs that could be viewed in real time or stored and viewed in off-hours. The corporation involved advocated continuous learning and encouraged engineers to take advantage of these programs. In fact, the corporation provided a special labor account so that any time used to attend these programs would not be charged to any department or project.

After six months, corporate officers were concerned that the account was not being used. Investigation showed that the real-time downloads were not popular, even with company payment, but that off-line materials were employed at close to maximum delivery capacity. Busy engineers accessed the media from home on their own time because they felt that the home environment was far more conducive to learning. The corporation was concerned that there was considerable loss of learning opportunity by missing the real-time question-and-answer sessions, but the engineers were forming their own special interest groups involving peers and other stakeholders to discuss and review the material.

An interesting postscript to this case speaks highly of autonomous learning. The corporation decided to develop some post-tests to determine the effectiveness of this informal learning network. Program usage dropped to nearly zero as a result. Engineers who were learning on their own time, with their own networks, made it quite clear that if they didn't know how they were going to use the information except to stay current, there was no way the organization could develop a fair or valid test to measure what they learned. The organization canceled the testing program and decided to trust the employees. For the organization, this was a very mature decision. It also shows a relatively undocumented stratagem for enabling transfer after any training intervention: trust. Managers and other stakeholders will find that encouraging the community of practice and trusting performers is much more effective than oversight. This is especially true for populations that have the internal discipline and motivation to employ e-learning (Finley 1999).

Disablers of e-Learning

Some difficulties remain to be overcome in the e-learning arena in complex organizational systems. Exhibit 9.2 presents several factors that serve as disablers for effective use of e-learning.

Exhibit 9.2. Disablers of e-Learning

- Investments required in e-learning structure and methods
- Myopic management decisions
- Redefinitions required for reliable information and evaluation
- Cross-functional team required to design, develop, and deploy

---

Investment Required in e-Learning Structure and Methods

For any learning to be successful, it must be a product of the proper instructional method (Clark, 1983). Learning requires interaction, practice, and review. With e-learning, there is no physical instructor to direct learner focus. Just putting up a website with information is not workable. As the Cisco learning team found, there must be a well-thought-out structure. If the access to learning is confused or complicated, learners will not see the value. Information must be clear on two levels: (1) how to access it and (2) how it fits into performance requirements. Just telling learners what you want them to know is not sufficient to the task (Stolovitch & Keeps, 2002).

Learners can feel alone in the world of online learning. Organizations must prepare the learner with focused objectives and a clear idea of successful performance. Also, the Internet is an open architecture. Motivated individuals can easily find themselves following promising leads but losing the original objective. Organizations must develop ways to help the learner to stay on track. Again, communities of practice can support and reinforce the learner regarding objectives and success.

Myopic Management Decisions

e-Learning is by far one of the easiest victims of poor management decisions. When subunits within an organization minimize their cost by not funding key components to the detriment of the organization as a whole, performance suffers. e-Learning must be a collaborative effort focused on the greater benefit to the organization. As long as training and information systems principals do not see performance as a joint mandate, there will be difficulties implementing e-learning as a viable strategy.

Two common disconnects occur when there is no joint mandate: (1) often, network and security functions will not allow online delivery of training content and (2) when the training function does not include the IS department in requirements definition, planning, and evaluation, then e-learning strategies will be incomplete.

For example, in another organization, the IS department had set up access to Internet and intranet as an optional feature for which there was a price. Managers often refused to pay that price and thus invalidated the entire e-learning approach.

Managers often choose not to include temporary hires in learning activities because of expense and loss of that ROI when the "temp" moves on. The cost that is not counted is reduced motivation of trained performers when they find that some individuals don't need the training to perform. The temporary employees who are disenfranchised remain as part of the co-worker network.

Redefinitions Required for Reliable Information and Evaluation

e-Learning requires rethinking the quality of information and how training is evaluated. Users are often unfamiliar with how they need to think differently.

Reliable Information. The Internet is an open forum. There is no gate-keeping function that keeps false or erroneous information from being placed in cyberspace. Users are as likely to access poor information as good. This requires training the users how to be (1) good consumers of large amounts of information and (2) effective judges of what is reliable and what is not. All individuals should use caution in accepting net-based information as factual. Stakeholders must be involved in helping the learner to assess what are gems of wisdom and what is cut glass.

Evaluation. As e-learning takes its rightful place in the organization infrastructure, traditional training evaluation models that focus on trailing-edge metrics (such as numbers of students, test scores, trainee satisfaction, or completion rates) must fall by the wayside. Instructional designers must return their focus to accomplishments and the behavior that produces them. Cisco's Tom Kelly tries to measure success by how well employees do their jobs or by how satisfied customers are with the work of employees who have been through e-learning programs (Muoio, 2000). Measures such as resource investments, "butts in seats," and scores on comprehensive tests are not good measures of learning from a transfer to performance point of view, and they suffer even more from e-learning's exaggeration of their faults.

Cross-Functional Team Required to Design, Develop, and Deploy

The training designer/developer must solicit the involvement of other groups within the organization to move learning from the classroom to the workplace. For example, a database might require IS personnel to provide a server and database hardware. Performers might require new software or accessories to take advantage of multimedia aspects of e-learning. Managers might have to reconsider what constitutes work. There might have to be changes to the actual workplace to accommodate the new learning strategies. Certainly, new learning methods will impact work flow. All appropriate functions must be involved in the project from the beginning.

CASE STUDY: CALL CENTER: EXAMPLE OF DYSFUNCTIONAL COMMUNICATION

An organization can be enamored of the "e" in e-learning without fully considering the impact on the organization. A loan qualifying call center implemented a new assessor tracking system to enable a centrally located call center operator to match and schedule assessors for a national financial company. The division manager was very interested in the potential of multimedia learning, driven off a central server that each operator could access from the workstation computer. The design called for full-screen video of the required steps to use each portion of the system, along with audio and text-based narratives.

When the developer prepared to test the system with volunteers from the call center, he discovered that none of the operator computers had an audio card, let alone speakers or headsets. The IS department was never consulted about the feasibility of the project. The design and development team did not have cross-functional representation.

During the following discussions, the developer learned that corporate management had decided to pull all audio cards for two reasons:

1. Audio headsets were impractical since operators already had a hands-free headset for the phones, and

2. Speakers were banned because the operators preferred not to have any background noise when on the phone with financial centers, customers, or assessors.

This hindered the effectiveness of the solution and sent a negative message about the importance of the whole approach to the operators. The company finally decided to record the audio for specially equipped learning centers and rely on the text-based narrative for the workstations. During follow-up, the developer learned that the learning centers were never used and the machines were eventually distributed to operators, with the sound cards removed. A careful consideration of all the stakeholders would have greatly enhanced the success of this e-learning project. Some transfer to performance was achieved, but the approach never reached its full potential (Finley, 1999).

Stakeholder Support for Transfer of e-Learning to Performance

What actions do various stakeholders need to take to ensure that e-learning interventions and systems pay off in transfer of learning to job performance? The Matrix for Transfer of e-Learning to Performance (Table 9.1) indicates many useful actions, based on research and best practice experience of many performance consultants. Co-workers and other stakeholders, when participating as part of the community of practice, have several crucial roles:

- Developing design requirements and setting expectations;

- Anticipating many performer questions and planning responses;

- Supporting the virtual instructor inherent in well-designed e-learning by providing guidance to learners with unanticipated questions; and

- Recommending and helping to implement the changes to the intervention that are so much a part of an adaptive organization.

The matrix in Table 9.1 presents stakeholder actions to support transfer of e-learning to performance. Remember, even with an innovative technology, learning is still learning and most conventional stakeholder strategies (such as those in Table 4.4) apply. Most of those are omitted here (such as evaluator strategies), except for guidelines and strategies that require special emphasis.

Table 9.1. Matrix for Transfer of e-Learning to Performance

	Before Learning	*During Learning*	*After Learning*
Executives, Managers, and Supervisors	Help to identify the performance need Determine the technology component available to support performance need Establish standards for e-learning delivery components Provide integrated resources to develop and implement e-learning and support performance Encourage co-worker and community of practice evolution Provide content to the network Support and encourage performers Include supervisor and manager participation in their job responsibilities Include co-worker and teammate participation in job performance evaluation	Assure e-learning resources are available Develop cyberspace presence to participate in e-learning activities Serve as online proctor or information provider Encourage community of practice participation Provide interim feedback on progress Provide content to the network Assist in evaluation of learning Moderate Web discussions to keep on track and model collaborative behaviors Suggest resources that might assist in collaborations or discussions Make managers and supervisors accountable for learning Provide distraction-free time for e-learning	Establish recognition for community of practice participation Maintain cyberspace presence Continue participation in community of practice interactions around desired performance Encourage regular update of online material Evaluate performers' performance and provide structured feedback Moderate Web discussions to keep on track and model collaborative behaviors Suggest resources that might assist in collaborations or discussions Hold managers and supervisors accountable for learning
Performance Consultants	Develop cyberspace presence Coach supervision and management	Provide work-related exercises and appropriate job aids Develop community	Maintain community of practice discussion after training event

Table 9.1. Matrix for Transfer of e-Learning to Performance, Cont'd

	Before Learning	During Learning	After Learning
	on how to partici-pate in cyberspace community of practice activities (stealth training) Coach community of practice members on interaction guidelines Validate technical and skills com-ponents perfor-mance needs assessment Use instructional design and learn-ing principles to create appropriate objectives, con-tent, and inter-action for the online delivery Test and verify that online delivery functions correctly in the work environment	of practice re-sources to provide clear and relevant feedback Help performers develop realistic action plans using online resources Give feedback on performance Clarify community of practice norms and standards Clarify role as moderator Identify those in-cluded in commu-nity of practice Consider partici-pation in public discussion group	Monitor community of practice com-munications to learn what ad-ditional support is needed and revise instruction and communica-tion channels accordingly Help strengthen supervisors' skills Encourage super-visors and man-agers to continue participation in community of practice Coach supervisors and managers on participation as part of their job responsibilities Maintain commu-nication with supervisors and performers
Performers	Provide accurate input on skills and knowledge Provide preferences for learning methods Begin establishing a support network	Participate actively in performance intervention Use communication network Develop cyberspace presence Join e-learning com-munity of practice Provide feedback on what works and what inhibits	Continue to use community of practice to support performance Openly accept feedback and community of practice guidance Use online tools and job aids Monitor own perfor-mance and seek

(Continued)

Table 9.1. Matrix for Transfer of e-Learning to Performance, Cont'd

	Before Learning	*During Learning*	*After Learning*
			validation through the e-learning community of practice When in doubt seek input from e-learning community of practice
Co-workers	Participate in needs assessments and discussions of the training's intended impact Ask performers to share learning via community of practice network	Complete performers' reassigned work duties Participate in learning exercises at the request of performers and trainers	Be supportive of performers' accomplishments Participate in e-learning community of practice
Other Stakeholders	Contribute to the needs assessment Contribute to the skills assessment Provide online resources to support e-learning and transfer to performance	Provide systems-level input during performer's information acquisition phase Introduce links from performers' deliverables to both process inputs and outputs Participate in community of practice discussions Assist in evaluating learning and performance Suggest resources that might assist in collaborations or discussions	Provide feedback of systems-level outcomes Support the continued existence of the performance community of practice Provide access to related information Suggest resources that might assist in collaborations or discussions

Table 9.1. Matrix for Transfer of e-Learning to Performance, Cont'd

	Before Learning	During Learning	After Learning
Communities of Practice	Identify key network components	Provide safe forum for offering ideas and testing concepts Provide value-added shortcuts and lessons learned	Support expected performance Provide both positive and constructive feedback on progress Provide timely input on changing requirements

The matrix illustrates how stakeholder support for e-learning simplifies the instructional designer's and manager's tasks of keeping learning current and relevant. Since the job context defines the need for the learning, it also defines the content and encourages stakeholders to actively participate in its maintenance. The experience of the community of practice reinforces stakeholder involvement and ownership. The strategies in this matrix reflect the many points and concerns discussed in this chapter.

Please note that Table 9.1 focuses specifically on strategies to support e-learning. It does not duplicate many generally supportive strategies by primary and other stakeholders (such as evaluators), which are shown in Chapter 4, Table 4.4. So it is important for e-learning performance consultants and other stakeholders to use both tables to develop a complete set of strategies for each e-learning project.

Summary of This Chapter

In this chapter we have reviewed the basics of e-learning with particular emphasis on how it supports transfer of learning to job performance. In terms of analysis and design, e-learning is no different from conventional training. Because e-learning does not involve an instructor who might compensate for design flaws, it simply highlights the risks of ignoring any portion of the rigorous analysis and design process.

Where e-learning and transfer of learning to performance really develop their greatest synergy is in the wealth of support inherent in online communities of practice. The freedom of communication across boundaries of time, space, and position encourages performance and generates nearly instant feedback. Performers can begin their apprenticeship in the community of practice while they are still absorbing key concepts and skills. The apprenticeship evolves into competence as they move their skills into a workplace ready and willing to receive them.

As shown in the Corporate University Xchange (2002) research quoted earlier, the key to successful implementation of e-learning, and therefore transfer to performance, is enthusiastic involvement in employees' learning and development plans by managers and other stakeholders. This involvement supports the needed time off and resources for learning as well as public rewards and acknowledgement for employees who successfully improve performance.

The final caveat regarding e-learning is that people tend to get so wrapped up in the technology that they forget that e-learning is still learning. As a medium for delivery and a process facilitator, electronically networked learning has tremendous potential to support transfer of vital skills in the workplace. There is tremendous appeal in its ease of updating and distributing ever-changing content.

However, if we treat the Web as the latest educational medium rather than just the media container that it is, we will end up repeating the history of unfulfilled expectations that we had with television or computers in the classroom (Clark, 1983). Ultimately e-learning will be most effective when it no longer feels like a novelty, when it doesn't have its own name; it will simply be a natural part of how people work within their community.

Suggestions for Further Reading

Learning communities are an essential component of transfer of e-learning to performance because of the necessary involvement of stakeholders. You will find excellent examples of stakeholder participation in the following books.

Abbey, Beverly. (2000). *Instructional and cognitive impacts of web-based education.* Hershey, PA: Idea Group Publishing. A collection of international authors write about web-based education and how it has changed our understanding of how to design instruction and how the Web influences cognition. This is an excellent background source for web-based learning concepts.

Driscoll, Margaret. (2002). *Web-based training: Creating e-learning experiences.* San Francisco: Jossey-Bass. The author blends adult learning, business, and technical issues into a whole fabric focused on developing training for the Web. She draws a clear distinction among information, presentations, and learning. These distinctions strip away much of the confusion about what is learning, and what isn't, on the Web.

Garrett, Jesse James. (2003). *The elements of user experience: User-centered design for the Web.* New York: American Institute of Graphic Arts. Garrett clarifies many of the concepts of user-centered design from graphic presentation to information architecture and visual design.

Palloff, Rena, & Pratt, Keith. (1999). *Learning communities in cyberspace: Effective strategies for the online classroom.* San Francisco: Jossey-Bass. Palloff and Pratt bring their considerable experience in teaching online to demonstrate how to move learning from the classroom to what they call "cyberspace," the world of the Internet. The authors redefine communities in terms of online support for learning and show how to deliberately create communities of practice online.

GLOSSARY

Action plan

(Chapters 5 and 8) A written document that describes the steps that supervisors, trainers, learners, and co-workers will complete to help maximize the transfer of learning to performance.

Autonomous performers

(Chapter 2) Those who are not required to follow set procedures; are not held accountable for structured supervision; decide for themselves how to operate for some or all tasks; and decide if and when to apply new knowledge and skills to their performance (from Yelon, Sheppard, Sleight, & Ford, 2004).

Community of practice

(Chapters 4 and 9) A network of performers, within or across organizations, that coalesce around common interests and expertise. These communities offer long-range development opportunities through sharing information and ideas. Online communities of practice offer immediate just-in-time assistance to those who seek answers to challenges on a 24/7 basis (adapted from Wenger, McDermott, & Snyder, 2002).

Complex systems

(Chapter 1) A *moderately* complex system has a single organization as its major component; usually (but not always) a traditional hierarchical authority structure, with power transmitted from the executive level through successive levels of the organization's internal stakeholder components (chain of command); and other groups or organizational components outside the boundaries of the organization that also are stakeholders with an interest in the organization's goals and operations.

A *highly* complex system has several relatively independent organizations as its primary components, with other groups or organizations as supportive or opposing components; a common goal shared by the primary components, toward which they work interdependently; some component organizations linked by fully accepted lines of *authority,* and other components linked by lines of *influence* (not authority); and no fully accepted chain of command throughout the system.

Consulting

(Chapters 3 and 6) Coaching and guiding a client through a process of decisions and actions to meet a goal or objective. For the performance consultant, the process is human performance technology (HPT) for a performance improvement intervention.

e-Learning

(Chapter 9) The electronic linking of an instructor, remote in distance and/or time, and a learner or community of learners.

Human performance technology (HPT)

(Chapters 3 and 6) A systematic, systemic, and scientific approach to attaining desired accomplishment from human performers by determining gaps in performance and designing cost-effective and efficient interventions (adapted from Harless, 1995, p. 75).

Partnering	(Chapters 3 and 6) Building a close working relationship with a stakeholder (usually a high-level manager) over time, focused on the partner's business (products and services, desired results, workforce performance concerns, competitors, and other issues) and not based on specific projects.
Performance	(Chapter 2) At the individual, group, and team performer levels: A combination of behaviors by individuals, groups, and teams and the results or accomplishments that they produce (adapted from Dean, 1999, & Gilbert, 1978).
Performance consultant	(Chapters 2, 3, and 6) A change agent who focuses primarily on what people *do,* their performance, and then considers what it takes (in skills, knowledge, and a range of workplace resources) to do that well (adapted from Robinson & Robinson, 1995). *Partnering* and *consulting* are two important aspects of the performance consultant's responsibilities.
Performer	(Chapter 2) The individual, working alone or in groups and teams, who performs some work.
Return on investment (ROI)	(Chapter 5) In training, ROI is the monetary value of organizational results due to training compared with costs.
Stakeholder	(Chapters 1, 2, 3, and 4) An individual, group, organizational component, or organization with a share or interest— a "stake"—in the goals or outcomes of an activity, process, project, organization, or intervention in a complex system.
Transfer matrix	(Chapter 4) A tool to organize stakeholder strategies to support transfer of learning to performance (examples in Chapters 4, 7, 8, and 9). The strategies are organized by stakeholder groups and by time frames—before, during, and after a performance improvement intervention. (In Chapter 7, Julie Hile refers to an adapted matrix as a "scaffold.")
Transfer of learning to performance	(Chapter 4) The full application of new knowledge and skills to improve individual and group performance in an organization or community (adapted from Broad, 2003, p. 98).

REFERENCES

Abbey, B. (2000). *Instructional and cognitive impacts of web-based education.* Hershey, PA: Idea Group Publishing.

Avalon Theatre (2003). History. Available: www.theavalon.org/history.cfm.

ASTD & MASIE Center. (2001). *e-Learning: If we build it, will they come?* Available: http://astd.org/research.

Baldwin, T.T., & Ford, J.K. (1988). Transfer of training: A review and directions for further research. *Personnel Psychology, 41,* 63–105.

Baldwin, T.T., & Magjuka, R. (1991, Spring). Organizational training and signals of importance. *Human Resource Development Quarterly,* pp. 25–36.

Bellman, G.M. (1998). Partnership phase: Forming partnerships. In D.G. Robinson & J.C. Robinson (Eds.), *Moving from training to performance: A practical guidebook.* San Francisco: Berrett-Koehler.

Bellman, G.M. (2002). *The consultant's calling: Bringing who you are to what you do* (rev. ed.). San Francisco: Jossey-Bass.

Beer, V. (2000). *The Web learning fieldbook: Using the world wide web to build workplace learning environments.* San Francisco: Pfeiffer.

Bethune, G., & Huler, S. (1998). *From worst to first: Behind the scenes of Continental's remarkable comeback.* Hoboken, NJ: John Wiley & Sons.

Biech, E. (1999). *The business of consulting: The basics and beyond.* San Francisco: Pfeiffer.

Block, P. (2000). *Flawless consulting: A guide to getting your expertise used* (2nd ed.). San Francisco: Pfeiffer.

Brinkerhoff, R.O., & Montesino, M.U. (1995). Partnerships for training transfer. *Human Resource Development Quarterly,* pp. 263–274.

Broad, M.L. (Ed.) (1997a). *Transferring learning to the workplace.* Alexandria, VA: American Society for Training and Development.

Broad, M.L. (1997b). Overview of transfer of training: From learning to performance. *Performance Improvement Quarterly. 10*(2), 7–21.

Broad, M.L. (2001). Transfer of learning to performance. In L.L. Ukens (Ed.), *What smart trainers know: The secrets of success from the world's foremost experts.* San Francisco: Pfeiffer.

Broad, M.L. (2002). The research is in: Stakeholder involvement is critical. In G.M. Piskurich (Ed.), *HPI essentials: A just-the-facts, bottom-line primer on human performance improvement.* Alexandria, VA: ASTD.

Broad, M.L. (2003). Managing the organizational learning transfer system: A model and case study. In E.F. Holton III & T.T. Baldwin (Eds.), *Improving learning transfer in organizations.* San Francisco: Pfeiffer.

Broad, M.L., & Newstrom, J.W. (1992). *Transfer of training: Action-packed strategies to ensure high payoff from training investments.* Reading, MA: Perseus Books.

Brown, J.S., Collins, A., & Duguid, P. (1989). Situated cognition and the culture of learning. *Educational Researcher, 18*(1), 32–42.

Chevalier, R. (2003). Updating the behavior engineering model. *Performance Improvement, 42*(5), 8–14.

Clark, R.E. (1983). Reconsidering research on learning from media. *Review of Educational Research,* (4), 445–459.

Cole, K., Fischer, O., & Saltzman, P. (1997). Just-in-time knowledge delivery. *Communications of the ACM (Association for Computing Machinery), 40*(7), 49–53.

Corporate University Xchange. (2002). *Pillars of e-learning success.* Available: www.corpu.com.

Csoka, L.S. (1994). *Closing the human performance gap.* New York: The Conference Board, Report No. 1065–04-RR.

Dean, P.J. (1999). Performance engineering. In P. Dean (Ed.), *Performance engineering at work* (2nd ed.). Washington, DC: International Society for Performance Improvement and International Board of Standards for Training, Performance and Instruction.

Driscoll, M. (2002). *Web-based training: Creating e-learning experiences* (2nd ed.). San Francisco: Pfeiffer.

Federal Aviation Administration. (2004). Press release on report of plans to cut O'Hare delays, August 18, 2004. Available: www.dot.gov/affairs/dot13804.hfm.

Feldstein, H.D., & Boothman, T. (1997). Success factors in technology training. In M. Broad (Ed), *Transferring learning to the workplace.* Alexandria, VA: American Society for Training and Development.

Finley, K.W., Jr. (1999*). Solving performance improvement puzzles: Case studies.* Unpublished manuscript.

Fleishman, E.A., Harris, E.F., & Burtt, H.E. (1955). *Leadership and supervision in industry.* Monograph No. 33. Columbus, OH: Personnel Research Board, Ohio State University.

Friedman, T.L. (1999). *The lexus and the olive tree.* New York: Farrar, Straus and Giroux.

Fuller, J. (1997). *Managing performance improvement projects: Preparing, planning, implementing.* San Francisco: Pfeiffer.

Garrett, J.J. (2003). *The elements of user experience: User-centered design for the web.* New York: American Institute of Graphic Arts, Pearson Education.

Gilbert, T.F. (1978). *Human competence: Engineering worthy performance.* New York: McGraw-Hill. Reprint (1996): Washington, DC: ISPI and Amherst, MA: HRD Press.

Gordon, S. (2004). *Point of sale interactive cashier training.* Unpublished paper. Recipient of ISPI award as "2005 Outstanding Product or Intervention."

Greer, M. (1999). Planning and managing human performance technology projects. In H.D. Stolovitch and E.J. Keeps (Eds.), *Handbook of human performance technology* (2nd ed.). San Francisco: Pfeiffer.

Hale, J. (1998). *The performance consultant's fieldbook: Tools and techniques for improving organizations and people.* San Francisco: Pfeiffer.

Hale, J. (2002). *Performance-based evaluation: Tools and techniques to measure the impact of training.* San Francisco: Pfeiffer.

Hale, J. (2003). *Performance-based management: What every manager should do to get results.* San Francisco: Pfeiffer.

Harless, J.H. (1970). *An ounce of analysis (is worth a pound of objectives).* Falls Church, VA: Harless Educational Technologists.

Harless, J. (1995). Performance technology skills in business: Implications for preparation. *Performance Improvement Quarterly, 8*(4), 75–88.

Henschel, P. (1996). Embedded in community. *Wingspread Journal,* p. 12.

Hodges, T.K. (2002). *Linking learning and performance: A practical guide to measuring learning and on-the-job application.* Boston: Butterworth-Heinemann.

Holton, E.F. (1996). The flawed four-level evaluation model. *Human Resource Development Quarterly, 7*(1), 5–21.

International Society for Performance Improvement. (2005). *What is human performance technology?* Available: www.ispi.org.

JHPIEGO & PRIME II. (2002). *Transfer of learning: A guide for strengthening the performance of health care workers.* Chapel Hill, NC: Intrah. Available: http://reproline.jhu.edu/english/6read/6training/tol/index.htm.

Kirkpatrick, D.L. (1959–60). Techniques for evaluating training programs, Parts 1–4. *Training Directors' Journal, 13*(11), 3–9; *13*(12); *14*(1); and *14*(2).

Kirkpatrick, D.L. (1998). *Evaluating training programs: The four levels* (2nd ed.). San Francisco: Berrett-Koehler.

Knowles, M. (1990). *The adult learner: A neglected species* (4th ed.). Houston, TX: Gulf.

Kotter, J.P. (1988). *The leadership factor.* New York: The Free Press.

Langdon, D.G. (2000). *Aligning performance: Improving people, systems, and organizations.* San Francisco: Jossey-Bass.

Langewiesche, W. (2002). *American ground: Unbuilding the World Trade Center.* New York: North Point Press.

Lanigan, M.L. (2001). *Creating evaluation instruments to predict behavior transfer: A new theory and measures in training evaluation.* Tinley Park, IL: Third House.

Long Term Care Innovation and Leadership Institute, Southwestern Ontario. (2000, March 22). Draft Operation Plan. The Institute's URL: http://ltc-innovation.medix.ca

Mager, R., & Pipe, P. (1999). *Analyzing performance problems or "you really oughta wanna"* (3rd rev. ed.). Atlanta, GA: The Center for Effective Performance.

Marquardt, M.J. (2004). *Organizing the power of action learning: Solving problems and building leaders in real time.* Palo Alto, CA: Davies-Black.

Mosel, J.N. (1957). Why training programs fail to carry over. *Personnel, 34*(3), 56–64.

Muir, J. (1911). *My first summer in the Sierra.* San Francisco: Sierra Club.

Muoio, A. (2000). *Cisco's quick study.* Available: http://pf.fastcompany.com/online/39/quickstudy.html.

Oshry, B. (1996). *Seeing systems: Unlocking the mysteries of organizational life.* San Francisco: Berrett-Koehler.

Palloff, R., & Pratt, K. (1999). *Building learning communities in cyberspace: Effective strategies for the online classroom.* San Francisco: Jossey-Bass.

Peterson, D. (1975). *Safety management: A human approach.* Goshen, NY: Aloray.

Phillips, J.J., & Stone, R.D. (2002). *How to measure training results: A practical guide to tracking the six key indicators.* New York: McGraw-Hill.

Pucel, D.J., & Cerrito, J.C. (2001). Perceptions as measures of training transfer. *Performance Improvement Quarterly, 14*(4), 88–96.

Raybould, B. (1990). *Special reports: Performance support systems technologies.* Northboro, MA: Barry Raybould & Associates.

Rein, L., & de Tantillo, L. (2004, December 27). For travelers, bagfuls of sorrows. *Washington Post,* p. B1.

Robb, J. (1998). The job of a performance consultant. In D.G. Robinson & J.C. Robinson (Eds.), *Moving from training to performance: A practical guidebook.* San Francisco: Berrett-Koehler, and Alexandria, VA: ASTD.

Robinson, D.G., & Robinson, J.C. (1995). *Performance consulting: Moving beyond training.* San Francisco: Berrett-Koehler.

Robinson, D.G., & Robinson, J.C. (Eds.) (1998). *Moving from training to performance: A practical guidebook.* San Francisco: Berrett-Koehler, and Alexandria, VA: ASTD.

Robinson, D.G., & Robinson, J.C. (1999). Performance consultant: The job. In H.L. Stolovitch & E.J. Keeps (Eds.), *Handbook of human performance technology: Improving individual and organizational performance worldwide.* San Francisco: Pfeiffer.

Rossett, A. (1998). *First things fast: A handbook for performance analysis.* San Francisco: Pfeiffer.

Rossett, A., & Gautier-Downes, J. (1991). *A handbook of job aids.* San Francisco: Pfeiffer.

Rummler, G.A. (2004). *Serious performance consulting according to Rummler.* Silver Spring, MD: International Society for Performance Improvement.

Rummler, G.A., & Brache, A.P. (1995). *Improving performance: How to manage the white space on the organization chart* (2nd ed.). San Francisco: Jossey-Bass.

Saturn Corporation. (2005). *Guide to Saturn: Student guide.* Available: www.saturn.com/aboutus2/student/guide.jsp.

Senge, P.M. (1990). *The fifth discipline: The art and practice of the learning organization.* New York: Doubleday Currency.

Senge, P.M. (2003). *Creating desired futures in a global economy.* Available: www.reflections.solonline.org/repository/download/Reflections5–1.pdf? item_id=481839

Senge, P.M., Kleiner, A., Roberts, C., Ross, R.B., & Smith, B.J. (1994). *The fifth discipline fieldbook: Strategies and tools for building a learning organization.* New York: Doubleday Currency.

Sierra Club. (2004*). Majority opinion of the U.S. Supreme Court, June 24, 2004.* Available: www.sierraclub.org/environmentallaw/cheney_case/ opinions2004june24/03–475o.pdf.

Stolovitch, H.D. (2000). *Learning and performance support: Best practices and lessons learned.* Available: www.hsa-lps.com/Performance_SF_2000.htm.

Stolovitch, H.D., & Keeps, E. (1999). *Handbook of human performance technology: Improving individual and organizational performance world-wide* (2nd ed.). San Francisco: Pfeiffer.

Stolovitch, H.D., & Keeps, E. (2002). *Telling ain't training.* Alexandria, VA: American Society for Training and Development.

Stolovitch, H.D., & Keeps, E. (2004). *Training ain't performance.* Alexandria, VA: American Society for Training and Development.

Sullivan, R.L. (1995). Training across international borders. *Training & Development, 49*(6), 55–57.

Sullivan, R.L. (1998, April). *The transfer of skills training. InfoLine.* Alexandria, VA: American Society for Training and Development.

Sullivan, R.L. (2002). The PIE factory. *T&D, 56*(11), 18–20.

Sugrue, B., & Kyung-Hyun, K. (2004). *2004 ASTD state of the industry report.* Alexandria, VA: ASTD.

Svenson, R. (2004). Learning systems for the new millennium. *Performance Xpress.* Available: www.performancexpress.org/0402/.

Tannenbaum, S.I., & Yukl, G. (1992). Training and development in work organizations. *Annual Review of Psychology,* pp. 399–441.

Tyson, A. (2004). Personal interview by author with her sister, longtime employee at Nordstrom.

Ulrich, D. (1997). *Human resource champions: The next agenda for adding value and delivering results.* Boston: Harvard Business School Press.

Van Tiem, D.M., Moseley, J.L., & Dessinger, J.C. (2004). *Fundamentals of human performance technology: A guide to improving people, process, and performance* (2nd ed.). Silver Spring, MD: International Society for Performance Improvement.

Waldrop, M.M. (1992). *Complexity: The emerging science at the edge of order and chaos.* New York: Simon & Schuster.

Weisbord, M.R. (2004). *Productive workplaces revisited: Dignity, meaning, and community in the 21st century* (2nd ed.). Hoboken, NJ: John Wiley & Sons.

Weisbord, M., & Janoff, S. (2000). *Future search: An action guide to finding common ground in organizations and communities* (2nd ed.). San Francisco: Berrett-Koehler.

Wenger, E., McDermott, R., & Snyder, W.M. (2002). *Cultivating communities of practice.* Boston: Harvard Business School Press.

Wheatley, M.J. (2001). *Leadership and the new science: Discovering order in a chaotic world* (rev. ed.). San Francisco: Berrett-Koehler.

Wheatley, M.J., & Kellner-Rogers, M. (1996). *A simpler way.* San Francisco: Berrett-Koehler.

Wilson, B., & Ryder, M.(1999). *Dynamic learning communities: An alternative to designed instructional systems.* Available: www.ai.dynamiclearning-communities.htm.

Wlodkowski, R.J. (1985). *Enhancing adult motivation to learn.* San Francisco: Jossey-Bass.

Xiao, J. (1996). Relationship between organizational factors and the transfer of training in the electronics industry in Shenzhen, China. *Human Resource Development Quarterly, 7*(1), 55–73.

Yelon, S., Sheppard, L., Sleight, D., & Ford, J.K. (2004). Intention to transfer: How do autonomous professionals become motivated to use new ideas? *Performance Improvement Quarterly, 17*(2), 82–103.

INDEX

ABOUT THE AUTHORS

Dr. Mary L. Broad, with *Performance Excellence,* helps organizations improve human performance systems through strategic planning, performance technology, and transfer of learning. For high-priority performance improvement interventions, she helps clients identify performance requirements and results and develop stakeholder support to ensure improved workforce performance. She designs evaluation methods and materials to assess improved job performance and organizational results. Clients include the National Weather Service, Centers for Disease Control and Prevention of the National Institutes of Health, Georgia Department of Human Resources, Pfizer Pharmaceuticals Group, Long Term Care Institute (Ontario), and CyberMBA (South Korea). A widely published writer, she is co-author of *Transfer of Training: Action-Packed Strategies to Ensure High Payoff from Training Investments* (Addison-Wesley, 1992) and editor of *In Action: Transferring Learning to the Workplace* (ASTD, 1997). Dr. Broad served on ASTD's Board of Directors (1993–1995) and has consulted and presented in Canada, El Salvador, Hong

Kong, Ireland, Indonesia, Kuwait, Mexico, Panama, Singapore, South Korea, and throughout the United States. She is also an experienced Future Search facilitator for public and private sector clients. She can be reached at 301-657-8638 and marybroad@earthlink.net.

Kenneth W. Finley, Jr., is Performance Measurement Specialist at Check Point Software Technologies Limited, a software security company specializing in firewalls and virtual private network technologies. Finley is responsible for the psychometric analysis and exam performance for Check Point's worldwide set of certification exams. He is also adjunct faculty at Collin County Community College, teaching computer science and instructional design for web-based applications, and is Frisco High School Academic Decathlon coach in the topics of speech, interview, science, and statistics. He is past president of the DFW Chapter of the International Society for Performance Improvement and has written articles for ISPI's *Performance Improvement* journal. He is author of a variety of papers on tools for front-end analysis, performance improvement, and performance measurement and book reviews for the *ASTD Perspectives* newsletter. Finley also wrote a case study, "Accelerating Cultural Change for an Engineering Process," for *In Action: Transferring Learning to the Workplace* (ASTD, 1997). He is a skilled facilitator for Joint Application Design (JAD) activities and is currently working on his doctoral dissertation on the importance of structured interactivity in e-learning. He can be reached at 972-712-1474 and kwfinley@ev1.net.

Julie Hile, principal of the *Hile Group*, applies her consultative and facilitation skills to the clarification and transformation of organization cultures. An experienced performance partner in the freight rail and maritime transportation industries, she supports safety, health, environmental, and operations functions with performance management, collaborative safety rulebook revision, transformational management and team development, and other human factors-based services. Recent customers include the Alaska Railroad, Canadian National-Illinois Central Railroad, Canadian Pacific Railroad, Kansas City Southern, Burlington Northern Santa Fe Railroad, SeaRiver Maritime, and Crounse Corporation. Hile has written *Five Minutes or Five Days: Strategies for Leading, Learning, and Collaboration* (Hile Group). A detailed case study of her application of transfer of learning to performance is featured in Broad's Chapter 14 in Ukens' *What Smart Trainers Know* (Pfeiffer, 2001.) Her current research centers around the extension of transfer of learning theory into nontraining performance improvement strategies, with a particular focus on its application in five- to ten-minute peer-to-peer interventions. She can be reached at 309–829–7800 and hile@hilegroup.com.

Dr. Richard L. Sullivan is the former Director of Learning and Performance Support for JHPIEGO Corporation, a nonprofit organization affiliated with Johns Hopkins University. Dr. Sullivan is now a senior training advisor for the Ironworker Management Progressive Action Cooperative Trust (IMPACT), where he works to strengthen apprenticeship training. At JHPIEGO, he was involved in training healthcare professionals internationally. He and his team guided the organization's innovative performance improvement efforts to support the U.S. Agency for International Development in family and health-related projects in developing countries. They pioneered involving host-country stakeholders, including families, community members, healthcare workers, and policy-makers and officials at local, regional, and national levels. They followed systematic performance technology approaches in the planning, design, delivery, and evaluation of interventions to improve the performance of healthcare workers. Dr. Sullivan has published several books, over sixty articles, and three ASTD InfoLines (*Effective Classroom Training Techniques, Make Every Presentation a Winner,* and *Transfer of Skills Training*). He can be reached at rsullivan@impact-net.org.

Pfeiffer Publications Guide

This guide is designed to familiarize you with the various types of Pfeiffer publications. The formats section describes the various types of products that we publish; the methodologies section describes the many different ways that content might be provided within a product. We also provide a list of the topic areas in which we publish.

FORMATS

In addition to its extensive book-publishing program, Pfeiffer offers content in an array of formats, from fieldbooks for the practitioner to complete, ready-to-use training packages that support group learning.

FIELDBOOK Designed to provide information and guidance to practitioners in the midst of action. Most fieldbooks are companions to another, sometimes earlier, work, from which its ideas are derived; the fieldbook makes practical what was theoretical in the original text. Fieldbooks can certainly be read from cover to cover. More likely, though, you'll find yourself bouncing around following a particular theme, or dipping in as the mood, and the situation, dictate.

HANDBOOK A contributed volume of work on a single topic, comprising an eclectic mix of ideas, case studies, and best practices sourced by practitioners and experts in the field.

An editor or team of editors usually is appointed to seek out contributors and to evaluate content for relevance to the topic. Think of a handbook not as a ready-to-eat meal, but as a cookbook of ingredients that enables you to create the most fitting experience for the occasion.

RESOURCE Materials designed to support group learning. They come in many forms: a complete, ready-to-use exercise (such as a game); a comprehensive resource on one topic (such as conflict management) containing a variety of methods and approaches; or a collection of like-minded activities (such as icebreakers) on multiple subjects and situations.

TRAINING PACKAGE An entire, ready-to-use learning program that focuses on a particular topic or skill. All packages comprise a guide for the facilitator/trainer and a workbook for the participants. Some packages are supported with additional media—such as video—or learning aids, instruments, or other devices to help participants understand concepts or practice and develop skills.

- *Facilitator/trainer's guide* Contains an introduction to the program, advice on how to organize and facilitate the learning event, and step-by-step instructor notes. The guide also contains copies of presentation materials—handouts, presentations, and overhead designs, for example—used in the program.

- *Participant's workbook* Contains exercises and reading materials that support the learning goal and serves as a valuable reference and support guide for participants in the weeks and months that follow the learning event. Typically, each participant will require his or her own workbook.

ELECTRONIC CD-ROMs and Web-based products transform static Pfeiffer content into dynamic, interactive experiences. Designed to take advantage of the searchability, automation, and ease-of-use that technology provides, our e-products bring convenience and immediate accessibility to your workspace.

METHODOLOGIES

CASE STUDY A presentation, in narrative form, of an actual event that has occurred inside an organization. Case studies are not prescriptive, nor are they used to prove a point; they are designed to develop critical analysis and decision-making skills. A case study has a specific time frame, specifies a sequence of events, is narrative in structure, and contains a plot structure—an issue (what should be/have been done?). Use case studies when the goal is to enable participants to apply previously learned theories to the circumstances in the case, decide what is pertinent, identify the real issues, decide what should have been done, and develop a plan of action.

ENERGIZER A short activity that develops readiness for the next session or learning event. Energizers are most commonly used after a break or lunch to stimulate or refocus the group. Many involve some form of physical activity, so they are a useful way to counter post-lunch lethargy. Other uses include transitioning from one topic to another, where "mental" distancing is important.

EXPERIENTIAL LEARNING ACTIVITY (ELA) A facilitator-led intervention that moves participants through the learning cycle from experience to application (also known as a Structured Experience). ELAs are carefully thought-out designs in which there is a definite learning purpose and intended outcome. Each step—everything that participants do during the activity—facilitates the accomplishment of the stated goal. Each ELA includes complete instructions for facilitating the intervention and a clear statement of goals, suggested group size and timing, materials required, an explanation of the process, and, where appropriate, possible variations to the activity. (For more detail on Experiential Learning Activities, see the Introduction to the *Reference Guide to Handbooks and Annuals*, 1999 edition, Pfeiffer, San Francisco.)

GAME A group activity that has the purpose of fostering team spirit and togetherness in addition to the achievement of a pre-stated goal. Usually contrived—undertaking a desert expedition, for example—this type of learning method offers an engaging means for participants to demonstrate and practice business and interpersonal skills. Games are effective for team building and personal development mainly because the goal is subordinate to the process—the means through which participants reach decisions, collaborate, communicate, and generate trust and understanding. Games often engage teams in "friendly" competition.

ICEBREAKER A (usually) short activity designed to help participants overcome initial anxiety in a training session and/or to acquaint the participants with one another. An icebreaker can be a fun activity or can be tied to specific topics or training goals. While a useful tool in itself, the icebreaker comes into its own in situations where tension or resistance exists within a group.

INSTRUMENT A device used to assess, appraise, evaluate, describe, classify, and summarize various aspects of human behavior. The term used to describe an instrument depends primarily on its format and purpose. These terms include survey, questionnaire, inventory, diagnostic, survey, and poll. Some uses of instruments include providing instrumental feedback to group members, studying here-and-now processes or functioning within a group, manipulating group composition, and evaluating outcomes of training and other interventions.

Instruments are popular in the training and HR field because, in general, more growth can occur if an individual is provided with a method for focusing specifically on his or her own behavior. Instruments also are used to obtain information that will serve as a basis for change and to assist in workforce planning efforts.

Paper-and-pencil tests still dominate the instrument landscape with a typical package comprising a facilitator's guide, which offers advice on administering the instrument and interpreting the collected data, and an initial set of instruments. Additional instruments are available separately. Pfeiffer, though, is investing heavily in e-instruments. Electronic instrumentation provides effortless distribution and, for larger groups particularly, offers advantages over paper-and-pencil tests in the time it takes to analyze data and provide feedback.

LECTURETTE A short talk that provides an explanation of a principle, model, or process that is pertinent to the participants' current learning needs. A lecturette is intended to establish a common language bond between the trainer and the participants by providing a mutual frame of reference. Use a lecturette as an introduction to a group activity or event, as an interjection during an event, or as a handout.

MODEL A graphic depiction of a system or process and the relationship among its elements. Models provide a frame of reference and something more tangible, and more easily remembered, than a verbal explanation. They also give participants something to "go on," enabling them to track their own progress as they experience the dynamics, processes, and relationships being depicted in the model.

ROLE PLAY A technique in which people assume a role in a situation/scenario: a customer service rep in an angry-customer exchange, for example. The way in which the role is approached is then discussed and feedback is offered. The role play is often repeated using a different approach and/or incorporating changes made based on feedback received. In other words, role playing is a spontaneous interaction involving realistic behavior under artificial (and safe) conditions.

SIMULATION A methodology for understanding the interrelationships among components of a system or process. Simulations differ from games in that they test or use a model that depicts or mirrors some aspect of reality in form, if not necessarily in content. Learning occurs by studying the effects of change on one or more factors of the model. Simulations are commonly used to test hypotheses about what happens in a system—often referred to as "what if?" analysis—or to examine best-case/worst-case scenarios.

THEORY A presentation of an idea from a conjectural perspective. Theories are useful because they encourage us to examine behavior and phenomena through a different lens.

TOPICS

The twin goals of providing effective and practical solutions for workforce training and organization development and meeting the educational needs of training and human resource professionals shape Pfeiffer's publishing program. Core topics include the following:

 Leadership & Management

 Communication & Presentation

 Coaching & Mentoring

 Training & Development

 e-Learning

 Teams & Collaboration

 OD & Strategic Planning

 Human Resources

 Consulting

What will you find on pfeiffer.com?

- The best in workplace performance solutions for training and HR professionals

- Downloadable training tools, exercises, and content

- Web-exclusive offers

- Training tips, articles, and news

- Seamless online ordering

- Author guidelines, information on becoming a Pfeiffer Affiliate, and much more

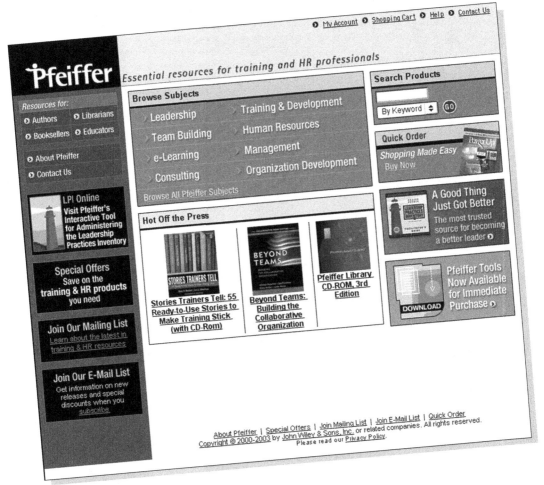

Discover more at www.pfeiffer.com